WEDDED PERFECTION: TWO CENTURIES OF WEDDING GOWNS

Cynthia Amnéus | with contributions by Sara Long Butler & Katherine Jellison | Cincinnati Art Museum 2010

This catalog accompanies the exhibition *Wedded Perfection: Two Centuries of Wedding Gowns* on display at Cincinnati Art Museum from October 9, 2010–January 30, 2011.

First published jointly in 2010 by GILES
An imprint of D Giles Limited
4 Crescent Stables, 139 Upper Richmond Road,
London SW15 2TN, UK
www.gilesltd.com

ISBN (hardcover): 978-1-904832-84-3
ISBN (softcover): 978-0-931537-36-3

The exhibition was curated by Cynthia Amnéus, Curator of Fashion Arts and Textiles, Cincinnati Art Museum

Library of Congress Cataloging-in-Publication Data

Amneus, Cynthia.
 Wedded perfection : two centuries of wedding gowns / Cynthia Amneus, with
contributions by Sara Long Butler & Katherine Jellison.
    p. cm.
 "This catalog accompanies the exhibition Wedded Perfection: Two Centuries
of Wedding Gowns on display at Cincinnati Art Museum from October 9th,
2010 -January 30, 2011."
 Includes bibliographical references and index.
 ISBN 978-0-931537-36-3 (softcover : alk. paper)
1. Wedding costume--United States--History--Exhibitions. 2. Costume
design--United States--History--Exhibitions. I. Butler, Sara Long. II.
Jellison, Katherine, 1960- III. Cincinnati Art Museum. IV. Title.

GT1753.U6A56 2010
392.5'4--dc22

For the Cincinnati Art Museum:
Stephen Jaycox, Deputy Director, Presentation
Cynthia Amnéus, Curator of Fashion Arts and Textiles
Scott Hisey, Photographic Services
Lynda C. Lucas, Assistant Director of Graphic Design
Connie Newman, Retail Coordinator

Photographs are by Tony Walsh
Edited by Anita Buck
Designed by Lynda C. Lucas

For D Giles Limited:
Proof-read by Sarah L. Kane
Produced by GILES, an imprint of D Giles Limited, London
Printed and bound in China

All measurements are in inches and centimeters;
Height precedes width precedes depth.

Front cover: United States, *Wedding Dress*, 1915; silk, beads, faux pearls; Gift of Mr. and Mrs. Robert W. Wenning, 2000.220

Photo credits: The Cincinnati Art Museum and contributing authors thank institutions, galleries, and collectors for permission to publish comparative photographs of the work in their collections and archives as cited in the figure captions.

The Cincinnati Art Museum wishes to offer sincere gratitude to the exhibition media sponsor WLWT.

The Cincinnati Art Museum gratefully acknowledges the generous operating support provided by the Fine Arts Fund, Ohio Arts Council, City of Cincinnati and Carol Ann and Ralph V. Haile, Jr./U.S. Bank Foundation, Western & Southern Financial Group, and Cincinnati Bell, and our members.

cincinnati ✳ art museum

g

CONTENTS

United States, *Wedding Dress*, 1840; silk (detail)
Gift of Jane R. Faran, 1986.220a-b

DIRECTOR'S FOREWORD: A PERFECT PIECE OF DESIGN

There are few objects in our lives on which we lavish more attention than the wedding dress. It is not surprising that this garment has become more than just a dress for a special occasion. It is the site for incredible craft and design, displaying a wealth of fabric and decoration in celebration not only of the event for which it is made, but also of the woman who wears it and the values for which she then stands. Though all in attendance at a wedding will admire the bride's dress, few ask what ideas guide its appearance, where its essential elements come from, or what they mean. This exhibition and catalog, the result of insightful collecting and research by our Curator of Fashion Arts and Textiles, Cynthia Amnéus, answers those questions.

The wedding dress we know today dazzles us with white. We associate our nuptial rituals almost exclusively with that color which, from antiquity, we in Western cultures think of as standing for virginity and purity. That color also removes the dress from the everyday, turning it into a seemingly abstract point in the middle of the many colors that surround us before, during, and after the ceremony. We can thus concentrate on the masterful ornamentation and the finesses of the dress's form, while all that art serves to frame the woman to perfection.

The historical survey this volume presents reveals that the ideas surrounding this ritual garment were not always so refined or simple. Not only were purpose-made wedding dresses once the province only of those who could afford them, but the form and even the color of the garment has fluctuated continually over the ages. It was not until the middle of the nineteenth century that the white wedding dress with the accoutrements we now take for granted—the train, the veil, the fitted bodice—was popularized, and even then, the wedding dress continued to evolve. It was the formation of the bridal industry in the first half of the twentieth century that resulted in the standardization of the wedding gown as we know it. Against the conventions dictated by the marketplace stand the strong individuals who choose alternative forms and colors, and those designers who create such beautiful exceptions to the status quo.

The collection of wedding dresses assembled in this volume and exhibition are a perfect illustration of how we can understand much about our society and its history by looking carefully at the objects on which it lavishes its art. It is what we believe we make possible at the Cincinnati Art Museum. Ms. Amnéus traces the relationship between this ritual dress, the terms of marriage, and the fluctuating social and economic status of women. The emergence of the wedding dress stands as a stellar example of middle-class self-definition through the acquisition of objects—even those that are meant to be used only once. Through her efforts, we come to admire the wedding dress not only as the site for elaborate decoration, a form-fitting piece of clothing that elongates and extends the woman's body to fulfill a role on a larger stage, but also as a symbol of what we hold dear in our society.

This exhibition would not have been possible without the dedication and acumen of Ms. Amnéus, and we are grateful for her work. The Cincinnati Art Museum gratefully acknowledges the generous operating support provided by the Fine Arts Fund, Ohio Arts Council, City of Cincinnati and Carol Ann and Ralph V. Haile, Jr./U.S. Bank Foundation, and our members for making this exhibition possible. In addition, we would like to thank our Fine Arts Fund Partners Western & Southern Financial Group and Cincinnati Bell, and the exhibition media sponsor, WLWT Channel 5.

Aaron Betsky
Director
Cincinnati Art Museum

ACKNOWLEDGMENTS

At the completion of a manuscript, it is always a revelation to realize how many contributed to its creation and a pleasure to recognize them. First and foremost, I must acknowledge the support of the staff of the Cincinnati Art Museum without whom this project would not have come to fruition, particularly director Aaron Betsky. I am also sincerely grateful to Anita Ellis, deputy director of curatorial affairs, who was always encouraging, enthusiastic, and interested in the project's progression. Jade Sams, administrative assistant, provided a daily dose of good humor and moral support. This project could not have been completed without her attention to detail, assistance in acquiring images, managing the budget, and taking other tasks off my plate, which enabled me to give my full attention to this project.

Similarly, two invaluable assistants in the Fashion Arts and Textiles Department, Margie Rothermich and Marla Miles, spent endless hours restoring the gowns illustrated in this volume. From the simple task of securing a button to painstakingly pleating yards and yards of silk net, these two women made the gowns both photo- and exhibition-ready. Harold Mailand of Textile Conservation Services succeeded in making even the most fragile of garments look beautiful. None of this work would be visible were it not for the expert photography of Tony Walsh. Both Scott Hisey, photo services coordinator, and Rob Deslongchamp, photo services technician, insured that all images were publication-ready. This volume would not be what it is without the outstanding skills of copyeditor Anita Buck, to whom I owe great thanks. I am grateful also to Lynda C. Lucas who executed the beautiful design of the book.

I offer my deep gratitude to Maggie Briedenthal, Sara Long Butler, Courtney Mitchell, Deanne Thompson, and Marlise Vance, who assisted me with research. My dear friend, Gail Connell, created many of the mannequins' hairstyles and provided me with gentle, and much needed, moral support. Librarians Môna Chapin and Galina Lewandowicz in the Mary R. Schiff Library at the Cincinnati Art Museum, and librarians and staff at the Public Library of Cincinnati and Hamilton County, Cincinnati Historical Society Library, Mercantile Library, University of Cincinnati Libraries, New York Public Library, and Worcester Historical Society, were exceedingly generous in lending their time and expertise.

I am most appreciative of the many lenders, donors, and brides whose gowns are included in this publication. Their foresight in preserving their wedding gowns and generosity in donating or lending them to the museum made this exhibition possible. Most importantly, I am indebted to my mother, Rosemary S. Hueil (1920–2009), for teaching me the importance of style— and whose wedding gown I wore when I married.

Cynthia Amnéus
Curator, Fashion Arts and Textiles
Cincinnati Art Museum

INTRODUCTION

Who doesn't love a wedding gown? It is clear from the plethora of publications about wedding dresses that they possess both an emotional and a monetary magnetism. Although there are many worthy titles on the shelf, there seemed to be nothing that thoroughly examined the aesthetics of the dress and how this iconic gown became what it is today. Histories in most coffee-table volumes are limited to brief overviews that offer the same information about Queen Victoria's sanctioning of white as *the* bridal color and the romance of the Edwardian-style gown. Others offer up the origins of traditions, an examination of women's rights, and justifications for abolishing marriage altogether. And, of course, there are the ubiquitous guides to choosing the right wedding dress for every body type.

I wanted to look deeper. The wedding dress has an almost hypnotic power over women—even those who regularly defy or ignore tradition. There seems to be an internal switch that clicks inside most women when they make the choice to marry—a switch that was planted there at an early age and to which females are socialized to respond. A wedding day is a woman's opportunity to be a princess, live the fairy tale, become Cinderella—in other words, to be transformed into something she has fantasized about all her life. It is *the* day she will be the center of attention and, despite the contemporary groom's increased involvement in wedding planning, that day is still really all about the bride. And that is how it has always been. Even when women had no choice in the matter, when marrying was "a dark leep," [sic] when their chance of enjoying a satisfying relationship and a fair division of labor within the bond was completely improbable, the wedding day was a more significant moment of transition for the bride than the groom.

Through the centuries, wives have been bought and sold, chosen for their social standing, political alliances, wealth, and reproductive capabilities and regarded as chattel, domestic servants, junior partners, and childcare workers. This is not to say that many women did not experience authentic love and caring within marriage, but they were not valued as equal partners until well into the twentieth century—and some may still question the equality of their standing.

Historically, the step into marriage for a woman meant leaving her family of origin—a move she was less likely to have made than her male counterpart prior to marrying. It meant binding herself to someone who had legal rights over her and her children, experiencing sexual intercourse for the first time, bearing and rearing children, and taking on the management of a household with little or no opportunity for disengagement from the bond. Unlike her spouse's, her virginity and subsequent fidelity was of the utmost importance. Revered for her ability to bear children, the woman as bride was costumed angelically with a mantle of modesty and subservience.

Today, brides step of their own free will into what most consider an equal bond. Most have been sexually active, have lived independently, have at least begun a career, and make their own decisions. Yet, the conventions of bridal dress and wedding ceremony that most women embrace remain the same. There seems to be a need to engage in a ritual that deeply embodies cultural values, and contemporary bridal attire expresses those concepts.

The main essay of this volume examines the role of women within the institution of marriage and parallels it with the evolving aesthetics of wedding gowns. It attempts to understand the ideas that have influenced styles of bridal attire over time and equalize some of the more egregious assumptions that color our beliefs about all things bridal. It is supplemented with an essay by Katherine Jellison that discusses the establishment of the bridal industry in the post-World War II era, providing perspective on invented traditions and excessive commercialization. In addition, Sara Long Butler's essay presents a fascinating and detailed look into the democratization of the white wedding gown for working-class brides.

It cannot be refuted that cultural values are manifested in dress. Within the framework of fashion, wedding gowns may seem a rather banal subject—a throwback, a costume that is not worthy of study. My hope is that this publication establishes the opposite—that bridal attire has been, and continues to be, a compelling signifier of the cultural values surrounding one of society's most deeply rooted rituals. Over time, bridal dress has charted the evolution of women's status in the Western world— and in many ways, the changing face of the institution itself.

Cynthia Amnéus

WEDDED PERFECTION

*THE EVOLUTION
AND AESTHETICS
OF THE WEDDING GOWN
IN WESTERN CULTURE*

CYNTHIA AMNÉUS

In 2009, columnist Manohla Dargis of the *New York Times* reviewed *Bride Wars*, a feature film in which the plot revolves around a wedding—in this case, two weddings. Best friends are driven to the brink of destroying their lifelong relationship in a spat over conflicting wedding preparations. Predictably, they end up in a physical fight in their wedding gowns. Dargis opens her review, "Do Hollywood studio executives think that women have a gene for tulle?"[1] As much as I would hate to think that Hollywood producers might actually have any valid insight into what women care most about, the characters in the film exhibit the manic behavior that overtakes many women when they are planning their wedding.

Looking at the average cost for a wedding in twenty-first-century America—between $20,000 and $30,000—in addition to the time, and physical and emotional energy spent on finding *the* dress, it seems somehow plausible that biology does figure into women's seeming obsession with tulle—or at least, with their fixation on the formal white wedding dress.[2]

Even the most successful and independent women often succumb to the allure of a fairy-tale-style dress that is the culmination of girlhood fantasies. This is not to say that there are not many exceptions; numerous contemporary publications, articles, and websites encourage or provide ideas and guidance for couples who wish to create an individualistic alternative to the traditional wedding ceremony. Nonetheless, the majority of women, regardless of age, economic status, religious affiliation, or sexual orientation, choose to participate in a white wedding. This tradition is the norm in Western societies, and in recent decades has been popularly incorporated into wedding celebrations in other cultures, particularly in Asia.

What is this fixation on the white single-use wedding dress? When did it begin? How has it so thoroughly permeated Western culture? What does it say about our society, about women, and their perceived roles? (fig. 1) A number of authors have addressed these questions. Chrys Ingraham in her book *White Weddings: Romancing Heterosexuality in Popular Culture*, discusses the role the white wedding plays in reinforcing the dominance of heterosexual unions and the consumer capitalism integral to the bridal industry. In *Brides, Inc.: American Weddings and the Business of Tradition* and *One Perfect Day: The Selling of the American Wedding*, Vicki Howard and Rebecca Mead, respectively, analyze the exponential expansion of the bridal industry since the mid-twentieth century, its invention of traditions, and its encouragement of the excessive consumerism that permeates modern weddings. Jaclyn Geller, author of *Here Comes the Bride: Women, Weddings, and the Marriage Mystique*, exposes the persistence of nineteenth-century expectations of contemporary women in marriage, their assumed domestic role, and the continuing social inequalities based on marital status in Western culture. Nancy F. Cott has produced several important works that thoroughly examine women's evolving roles and rights. These and many other scholars have contributed significantly to our understanding of the white wedding.

Numerous publications relate a brief history of wedding traditions combined with a photographic presentation of gowns, from the most traditional to the outrageously avant-garde. This volume will take a further step by examining the relationships between Western socio-cultural concepts of marriage, the act of being wed, and bridal gown aesthetics from antiquity to the present. It will discuss not only the reasons why women wear what they wear for their wedding, but how wedding gown styles have been, and continue to be, influenced by historical and contemporary wedding customs, evolving attitudes toward women and marriage, and consumeristic tendencies.

THE NATURE OF RITUAL

Rituals mark the passage of individual members of society through significant life transitions—birth, initiation, engagement, marriage, healing, and death. In 1908, the ethnographer and folklorist Arnold van Gennep published his influential work *Les rites de passage*. Van Gennep discerned the yin/yang of ritual transitions as a constant that relentlessly spurs progression. "For groups, as well as for individuals, life itself means to separate and to be reunited, to change form and condition, to die and to be reborn. It is to act and to cease, to wait and rest, and then to begin acting again, but in a different way."[3]

Van Gennep identified three distinct foci of a ritual: separation, transition, and incorporation, each ceremony addressing each of these but with varying emphasis. In doing so, he recognized that there is an overall pattern or schema to rites of passage across cultures. Van Gennep believed that an individual's transition must be "regulated and guarded so that society as a whole will suffer no discomfort or injury."[4] In other words, rites of passage affect both the individual and society at large and should benefit both.

Rituals may act upon specific individuals, but they are communal in nature. While those who assemble to participate in a ritual may be diverse and not even hold the same beliefs, they do constitute a group with common goals. Ritualized practices require the external consent of the participants, but in the modern world often tolerate a high degree of individuality.[5]

Although rituals vary widely across cultures, they all incorporate signifiers that differentiate them from everyday behavior and communicate that the activities being performed are distinctive. These signifiers include a designated structure or space to which access may be restricted; a particular time frame in which the ritual takes place; traditional combinations of formalized gestures and verbiage; specialized personnel; artifacts, texts, and dress that are used only for the ritual; mental and/or physical preparation; and the gathering of a particular audience that does not congregate for other reasons. While these indicators are not universal, those that are traditional within a particular society are employed to create a sense of authority and power. Ultimately, rituals are constructed to address the concerns and needs of a particular culture in a particular era and, while they may evolve over time, are relatively invulnerable to casual change.[6]

THE MARRIAGE RITUAL

A rite of passage from youth to adulthood, marriage is both a social and private, sacred and secular institution.[7] It represents one of the most important life transitions, involving separation from family of origin in conjunction with sub-rituals of fertility and protection with an emphasis on incorporation. One of the most prolonged rituals, marriage as a rite of passage is not confined merely to the wedding ceremony. The process begins with the betrothal or engagement in which the individuals are promised to one another, initiating a defined period of mental and physical preparation for the individuals and their families.[8]

In the past, betrothal and marriage were often based on economics—the joining of two powerful monarchies, land-holding aristocracies, or families of great wealth. Even betrothals in low socio-economic groups involved the transference of money, goods, a shared meal, or even a single coin that recompensed, if only symbolically, the bride's family for the loss of a productive member. Marriage also creates a new family unit from which it is expected offspring—productive members of the community—will arise. Historically this outcome was so important that infertility, impotence, or an unconsummated marriage were recognized by many cultures as legitimate grounds for annulment.[9]

The wedding ceremony itself serves as both ritual and performance, marking passage to the married state. Although

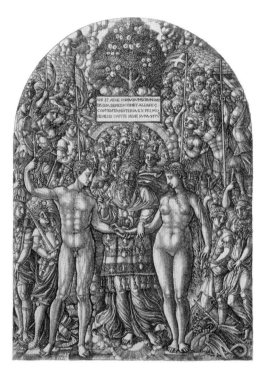

Figure 2
Jean Duvet. *The Marriage of Adam and Eve*, 1540–55, engraving, 11 ¾ x 8 ¾ in. (29.8 x 21.3 cm). Cincinnati Art Museum, Bequest of Herbert Greer French (1943.173).

it has transmogrified over time, some if not all of the common signifiers have been part of wedding rites. It is generally assumed that one of these aspects—distinctive dress—has always been employed. The elements of bridal attire that are considered traditional include a head covering or veil, a formal or full-length dress, a train, a white hue, the use of flowers as an adornment or accessory, and elaborate embellishments such as embroidery or beading. When assembled, these components immediately suggest a bride to the modern eye. The use of these

elements, however, has been discontinuous, and using these attributes as identifiers excludes brides of diverse social and economic standing and particular time periods.

A judicious understanding of the origins, use, form, and aesthetics of female wedding clothing requires an examination of the history of marriage, wedding ritual, and the role and rights of women in that bond. This essay will focus on European and American customs, interwoven with a discussion of bridal attire. The relationship between women's fashionable clothing, in general, and bridal clothing specifically, to society's evolving attitudes toward women, and therefore women's view of themselves, is telling. The embodiment of cultural values is nowhere more evident in dress than in the marriage rite.

Marriage in Western civilization is an institution that has been shaped by a patriarchal society. Its rituals and codes of behavior have been dictated by moral and legal principles. These rules define the status of males and females, distribute power and duties between the sexes, determine which pairings are legitimate, and define who has the power to sanction or terminate such a union. In past centuries, marriage was used to control bloodlines, dynastic structures, and kinship.[10] It has also been the arena in which women's destinies were played out.

MARRIAGE AND THE FEMALE SEX IN ANTIQUITY

In the Book of Genesis, the creation of woman was prompted by God's feeling that "it is not good for the human [Adam] to be alone. I shall make him a helpmate" (fig. 2).[11] The concept of woman as helper or partner to man is fundamental in the Christian and Jewish faiths. The last words of Genesis, often incorporated into the Christian wedding rite, state that man and woman must cling to each other and become one flesh when they are wed.[12] This presupposes an equal partnership in which each helps the other. Early Christian teachers promoted this idea, describing marriage as a yoke that joined husband and wife, suggesting working in tandem toward a common goal.[13]

However, subsequent biblical texts show us clearly that women were not considered equal partners. In fact, they became the property of their husbands. In the earliest Hebrew communities the bridegroom paid a *mohar,* a prescribed sum of money, to the father-in-law who in turn provided his daughter with a *chiluhim,* or dowry of household goods and, if he were wealthy enough, servants, livestock, and land. Wives were bound to obey their husbands, who alone had the power to dissolve the union at will.[14] Little is known about these early marriage rites, although some clues about special bridal attire can be gleaned from the Old Testament. Brides are described as adorned in jewels or ornaments and wearing a veil.[15] Passages recount banquets and lengthy feasts as part of the wedding celebration.[16]

In ancient Greek society, marriage was also a matter of exchanging property. The betrothal or promise was an oral agreement between a woman's family and the bridegroom or his guardian. A brideprice or dowry exchanged hands. Often a child when her marriage was arranged, the bride-to-be was not consulted and it was not uncommon for her husband to be ten to twenty years her senior. Betrothal was a binding commitment with legal and financial consequences if not actuated.[17] The contemporary practice of a father giving away the bride is a vestige of this ancient transaction in which a woman was passed from the legal authority of one male to another.

The ancient Greek marriage rite included festivities, music, and dancing. The two- to three-day celebration ended in the consummation of the union in which the husband took possession, both literally and figuratively, of his wife. At this point, he became her *kyrios,* or master and guardian, a position previously held by her father. A wife's role was to produce offspring and maintain the home. While marriage arrangements in ancient Greece were generally not a matter of the heart, it did not preclude the growth of love and affection between the partners over time.[18]

Marriage by purchase was also practiced in the early Roman republic (510–130 BC). In the late republic (123–23 BC), however, laws were revised to require both the bride's and groom's consent, as well as that of the bride's father. Many wedding traditions still practiced today originated in the Roman Empire in this period. Once betrothed, the man gave a ring to the woman to be worn on the third finger of her left hand. June was the preferred month for weddings, which generally took place in the bride's home.[19] A friend or priest (*auspex*) presided over the ceremony, which was witnessed by friends and family members, and a matron of honor was present. The couple kissed when the ceremony was complete and received gifts from the guests. The bride's parents hosted a wedding banquet, after which the couple was escorted to the bridegroom's home, where it was expected the marriage would be consummated that night.[20] The similarities between this latter version of the Roman marriage rite and Western practices today are remarkable.

The concept of mutual consent, while seemingly a radical change from earlier law, was more theoretical than practical. In this period, marriages were not a product of falling in love and marrying at will. Parents chose suitable mates for their children and the participants' agreement was assumed.

In reality, marriages were generally arranged for financial, political, and social reasons and it was understood that love would follow. If not, household harmony or simple tolerance was adequate. Marriages maintained social stability. They were too important a cultural institution to be undermined by fickle love.[21]

Dress played a highly symbolic role in the ancient marriage rite. Prior to her wedding day, the bride would have woven by hand both her tunic (*tunica recta*) and her hairnet (*reticulum*). The manual production of these pieces of dress signified that she had mastered her weaving skills and could provide cloth, and therefore clothing, for her husband. Both articles were woven of wool—the fiber used for religious ritual garments. The tunic was white—the color associated with the gods, consecration, and purity. It represented the woman's role as custodian of her chastity before marriage. The hairnet signified the confinement of her sexuality to her husband. Around her waist was a belt (*cingulum*) that was made from the fleece of a ewe, the female sheep—a symbol of fertility. The fibers, twisted into a cord, represented the binding of the woman to her husband and the belt was tied in the knot of Hercules. Considered difficult to untie, it would be loosened by her husband only when the new couple lay in the marriage bed. The knot represented the bride's fidelity, with the understanding that no other man should untie the belt through the act of adultery.

The bride's hair and face were covered by the yellow-red bridal mantle or veil (*flammeum*). The ritual color served as protection as the woman passed from the guardianship of her family to that of her husband's. The veiling also hid the bride's face from evil spirits and obscured from her vision any bad omens she might see in the procession to her new home. Once married, she would continue to wear a veil for modesty whenever she was in public.[22]

In early Christian and Jewish marriage rites, the custom of wearing a veil was attributed to the biblical story of Rebecca, who hid her face from Isaac before they married. Although clearly adopted from the pagan practice, the veil was endorsed as a symbol of modesty and the woman's change of state.[23] The use of the veil was continued in Jewish tradition but largely abandoned for centuries in Christian rites until the nineteenth century. Even in this period, its use was sporadic, gaining greater popularity in the early twentieth century.

THE MIDDLE AGES AND RENAISSANCE

Marriage rites in the Middle Ages (fifth–fifteenth centuries) evolved from a mixture of customs derived from the ancient world, Judaism, the early Christian church, and barbarian tribes, particularly Germanic groups, who began to make contact with the Roman Empire in the middle of the third century. In general, women continued under the control of men—either father or husband—until reaching the age of maturity or widowhood. Females generally married at a young age, often between twelve and fifteen.[24]

In this period, the alternative to an arranged union was marriage by capture, in which the bride may or may not have willingly complied. If the abduction were consensual, the captor-turned-bridegroom could make verbal and monetary recompense and the couple was lawfully wed. It is clear, however, that the crime was committed against the woman's family and the community at large, not against the woman herself, as compensating her kin was of the utmost importance.[25] Obviously, bridal attire was not an issue in this situation.

By the end of the fifth century, a new custom called the bridegift evolved, providing women with a modicum of financial security. These funds, provided by the bride's guardian, were received in part or whole after the wedding and remained in her control. In addition, women could inherit and retain property from their parents and female relatives. They also received a trousseau consisting of household and personal goods. These modifications signified that the bride was no longer merely purchased, but brought something of value to the union over which she retained power. Nevertheless, women had few, if any, legal rights. Husbands could easily initiate divorce, while wives were required to remain faithful to their mates despite offenses such as drunkenness, gambling, abuse, or infidelity.[26] Marriages of the upper class continued to be arranged with concern for dynastic continuance, political alliances, and the apportionment of property and wealth. In these transactions, the woman was valued primarily for her reproductive potential. Love, affection, or sexual attraction might be present, but more often than not had little or nothing to do with determining a match.[27]

As in Greek and Roman society, females of the medieval age occupied a subservient role. Women were reduced to a creature ruled by her sexual organs—"a body undisciplined by mind." Much mystery surrounded female anatomy with regard to sexual pleasure, childbearing, and disease, and this ambiguity was feared by men. The uterus was described as a distinct living organism that strayed about the body. It had a strong desire to bear children, could cause physical pain when distressed, and provoke disease. Menstrual blood was considered a foul substance that could kill plants, rust iron, transmit leprosy, and give dogs rabies. The gaze of a menstruating woman was believed to darken mirrors. Women were believed to be the purveyors of sin, which in turn fostered abuse and persecution toward them. [28]

In the eighth and ninth centuries, the Christian church began to exert more power over the marriage rite by vigorously promoting the ideas of monogamy and indissolubility. Legitimate marriage was defined by four conditions: Both parties must be free and consenting; the bride must be given by her father along with an appropriate dowry; the wedding must be celebrated publicly; and the marriage must be consummated. Adherence to these principles made the union legal in the eyes of the Church. These attitudinal changes attempted to shift the focus of marriage from a contractual and economic event toward one of personal choice and consent.[29]

By the eleventh century, the Church claimed full jurisdiction over the rite, elevating it to sacramental status. The Church delineated for its followers not only a specific liturgy, but the requirements that constituted a valid union. Commonly, weddings had been celebrated in a domestic setting, officiated over by a family member, or perhaps a notary, as master of the feast. The Church, however, exhorted Christian couples to be wed before a priest or cleric "at the church door"—the most public place in the village—in the presence of witnesses. The rite was performed and the wedding ring blessed and placed on the bride's hand with the priest's assistance. The gathering was then invited inside to celebrate the liturgy, but this was voluntary and many chose not to even enter the building, as the ceremony outside the church was complete and binding.[30]

Despite its attempts, the Church's control over marriage was not absolute by any means, and local customs and variations persisted. For instance, self-weddings and clandestine unions in which the couple essentially married themselves, or professed their vows in secret with a cleric officiating, were common, although much controversy surrounded such marriages. The Church, of course, asserted that such unions were not only invalid but sinful, and severe penalties were enacted upon offenders. Nevertheless, young men and women who wished to escape parental marriage arrangements sometimes resorted to self-weddings, as did those in which one party wished to marry well below his or her social rank—a match that would never be approved by guardians. The marriage of Shakespeare's Romeo and Juliet, performed by Friar Laurence, is perhaps the most notorious clandestine union.

Sources disagree, but there is evidence to suggest that in the eyes of the community the validity of such a marriage depended more on how the rite was performed rather than where or before whom. In an age when there were neither ecclesiastical nor civil marriage registers, making the promise, consummating the union, and cohabiting constituted a marriage, particularly in rural areas and among the poor, who simply had neither easy access to clergy nor the funds to pay them for their services.[31]

Detailed records describing bridal attire in this period are scarce. Needless to say, clandestine marriages were performed in whatever the participants happened to be wearing; ostentatious or special dress would have compromised the secrecy of the event. Some inferences about traditional wedding attire can be made from the Venetian sumptuary laws of 1299, which allowed otherwise forbidden ornamentation on wedding gowns, suggesting that this was a desired enhancement on the costume. Brides were permitted to embellish their dress with borders of pearls and to decorate their headpiece—though for their first marriage only. A bride was also permitted to wear a train that was as long as she wished, differentiating her from other women, whose trains were limited to one arm's length.[32]

Most information must be gleaned from artists' renderings. Although these images are subject to artistic license, they do provide clues to wedding dress styles. A miniature by Nicolò da Bologna, ca. 1350, illustrates a wedding ceremony taking place in public, perhaps outside the bride's home (fig. 3). The presence of the cleric, the falcon held by the gentleman to the groom's left, and the presence of bridesmaids indicate this Italian couple is of high social rank.

The bride wears a light pink gown trimmed with gold-colored braid, not unlike those around her. The dress puddles on the ground in the fashionable style of the day and not necessarily in adherence to bridal convention. It is possible that the bride's family decided that the indulgence of additional yards of fabric was a justifiable expense for this particular, highly visible dress. The bride and her attendants wear crowns—a symbol of virginity.[33] The bride also wears a translucent veil, which differentiates her in this illustration, but such veils were not

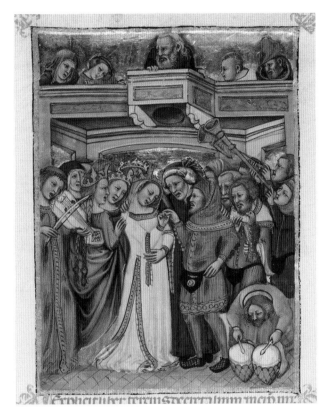

Figure 3
Nicolò da Bologna. *The Marriage; the Kiss of the Bride (initial P); the Bride Abandoned (initial D)*, ca. 1350, miniature on vellum, page dimension 44.5 x 27.3 cm (17 ½ x 10 ¾ in.). Rosenwald Collection, Image courtesy of the Board of Trustees, National Gallery of Art, Washington.

an uncommon accessory during this period. It is interesting to note that the groom and his companions are depicted wearing pouches at their waists, perhaps to collect the dowry promised at the couple's betrothal.

The primary action taking place in this miniature—a ring being passed from a man to a woman—provides the viewer with all the visual cues needed to understand this as a wedding ceremony. Significantly, there is nothing of note in the bride's dress itself that would suggest a wedding. Remove her virginal crown and take her out of this particular setting and she is no longer a bride, but a fashionably dressed woman. The full-length dress, train, and veil—elements of her dress that are associated today specifically with wedding attire—are simply *au courant*. While brides of high social standing would have had a new gown made for the occasion, it is unlikely the dress would have been worn only once, or that the costly fabric would not later have been appropriated for another use. In other words, there was no acknowledged concept of single-use bridal attire. Certainly, the arranged marriages common in this period did not elicit the same level of sentimentality that is associated with weddings today. In this period, wedding gowns were more often a vehicle for publicly displaying the bride's family wealth.

The specific employment of bridal clothing to this end is exemplified in an elaborate gown intended for the wedding of Lena Alamanni, daughter of a wealthy Florentine, who married in 1448. The dress was a matter of lengthy family discussion and fervent price negotiations, as it was purposefully intended for public exhibition. It was constructed of the highest-quality figured silk velvet and designed to be elaborately embellished with silver, gold, and pearl embroidery. Such costly ornaments were frequently removed from dresses at a later date to embellish another gown, or simply sold because of their intrinsic value. Such was the case with a belt that was part of Caterina del Bene's wedding ensemble. The silver metalwork was removed from the article and sold by her husband in 1458, eleven years after their wedding.[34] There was no sentimental reticence toward disassembling and profiting from the extravagant trims that decorated wedding clothes; trims and textiles were investments to be bought and sold.

A lack of distinctive bridal clothing is also illustrated in *"The Sacrament of Marriage"* from *Livre de bien vivre* dated 1492 (fig. 4). Here, the bride's gown is indistinguishable from the other women's dresses, except that she holds a long train over her arm. It is not clear if her skirt is especially elongated, as the image truncates her attendants' gowns and, again, a train was merely a feature of fashionable dress. The only observable difference in the bride's appearance is her circlet of flowers in contrast to the typical headdress seen on those behind her. It is the action of joining right hands, the presence of the cleric, and the cathedral-like framing of the image that defines the ceremony as a wedding, not mere distinctive dress. A bride of low social rank would most likely have worn a best (or only) dress and singled herself out by decorating her hair as in this illustration, if at all. Flowers have long been a symbol of fertility and are easily annexed to bridal costume, whether carried by the bride or adorning the dress itself. This floral element of wedding attire is perhaps the single most universal tradition, as it was readily available to women of every economic status.

In this image, a ruddy hue is used for the wedding clothes of the bride and groom, as well as elements in the background. The color serves the artist's purpose of unifying the composition. Contemporary readers of this manuscript, however, would not have balked at this coloration of the bride's gown. Although white signified purity even in antiquity, it was not necessarily the bridal color of choice in the fifteenth century. White fabric was difficult to keep clean in an era when laundering clothing was an inconvenient and thus infrequent undertaking. A survey of images of brides printed or painted during this period suggests that colorful gowns were favored.

Figure 4
The Sacrament of Marriage, from *Livre de bien vivre,* Paris:
[Gillet Couteau and Jean Ménard] for Antoine Verard, 1492.
This item is reproduced by permission of The Huntington Library, San Marino, California.

The miniature that records the late-fifteenth-century marriage of Philippa of Lancaster to King John I of Portugal naturally illustrates much more opulent clothing, as it is a royal marriage (fig. 5). The artist has rendered the bride's gown in pale blue with a woven pattern in gold. The sleeve ends and hem of the dress are trimmed with brown fur, while the gold-colored petticoat has a deep border of ermine. The bride wears a fashionable veiled steeple hat, as does the attendant who holds her lavish train. While the painter might have exercised artistic license to create an enticing visual, it is clear he felt entirely at ease portraying a colorful bridal gown. This suggests that even for royalty, who could afford to wear any color, wedding dresses were not necessarily white, and the symbolic nature of the color did not override other aesthetic choices. A colored gown indicated the luxury of having the fabric woven with colored silk threads, and expensive trims such as the fur were not dismissed in deference to wearing only white to convey purity.

Between 1500 and 1700, political and religious changes resulted in the reshaping of marriage through a new emphasis on the nuclear family. Previously, loyalty to an extended family or kinship was uppermost, and arranged marriages served this system by sheltering wealth and controlling lineage. In the sixteenth century, however, the guarantees of the state for individual rights inculcated new loyalties. The protections of a centralized government provided individuals with a new sense of security. The subjugation by and dependence on kin was lessened, thereby fostering a stronger nuclear family.[35]

This new emphasis was strongly supported by the theology of the Protestant Reformation and emerging Calvinist and Puritan sects. In the seventeenth century, marriage was likened by reformers to "an earthly paradise of happiness"[36] and husbands and wives were encouraged to "be as two sweet friends" by laity and theologians alike.[37] English clergyman and author William Gouge insisted that reciprocal affection was

Figure 5
Marriage of Philippa of Lancaster, late 15th c., miniature taken from
Chronique d'Angleterre (vol.3), author Jean de Wavrin. Detail.
© The British Library Board. Royal 14e. IV, f.284

the foundation of marriage. He allowed that parents should advise couples on a wise choice, but maintained that "good liking of each other is as glue." Likewise, Robert Cleaver, a Puritan minister, encouraged "knitting of hearts before striking of hands." What these domestic advice authors encouraged was not sexual attraction, but a mutual liking from which love would grow, resulting in a solid companionate marriage.[38] In England, the marriage of Charles I and Henrietta Maria of France was glorified. Although theirs was an arranged match that had begun rather contentiously, Charles and Henrietta Maria were devoted to each other, and their union exemplified the idealization of love and harmony between husband and wife.[39]

Authors, preachers, and church leaders walked a fine line in promoting both "joint governorship" in a marriage and what Gouge called "that small inequality which is betwixt the husband and the wife." Men were decidedly the dominant figure in the relationship and the ideal woman was obedient and submissive. Her duty before God was to love, cherish, and serve her husband. Perhaps the fact that this role was a prerequisite for salvation made it more palatable to women.[40] As a matter of course, however, a woman simply had no choice. Living outside the matrimonial bond was almost unthinkable. How would she live? How could she support herself? Who would care for her when she was ill or old? Marriage was a woman's natural destiny, the desirable goal that assured a respectable place in society or, at the very least, survival.

Although love and compatibility were emphasized, it was during the sixteenth and seventeenth centuries that the dowry became increasingly formalized. For the aristocrat, this meant strategic planning and placement of some but probably not all of one's children in advantageous unions. A generous dowry was a marker of social status, not only for the bride, but for her family as well. Young women were groomed in social and aesthetic skills that would make them worthy of a good match. The "knitting of hearts" would come after the wedding. Strong-spirited girls who defied parental authority risked disinheritance and might even be imprisoned at home, creating significant disadvantages for marrying anyone, much less the suitor the girl preferred.[41]

For women born into a farming or laboring family, having a dowry was equally important, even if it consisted of nothing more than a bed, a cow, and some household utensils. If a lower-class bride's family could provide nothing in the way of a marriage portion, there were charities that dowered girls, or couples might be aided by relatives and the community through traditional giving of both household items and funds at the wedding feast. In many such families, however, both sons and daughters left home at an early age—eleven or twelve—to find employment and accumulate their own assets. In this case, parents generally relinquished any control over spousal choices. These were the matches most likely based on "good liking."[42]

Diaries, autobiographies, and court records from the sixteenth and seventeenth centuries reveal that young men and women from financially stable laboring or trade families seem to have had the proper calculating approach to choosing a mate. Most men marrying for the first time were in their mid-twenties, having completed an apprenticeship and accrued sufficient resources to establish an independent household. A particular person was seldom specified when they decided to marry. Men were free to seek a partner who caught their eye and had an adequate dowry; women were passive participants. They were able to reject or accept suitors' advances but not initiate a courtship—a situation they seem to have found exceedingly frustrating. For both parties, the ability to know each other more than superficially was thwarted by social convention, which prevented spending extended time alone. Courtship was generally limited to polite conversation in the presence of others.[43] The young merchant Ralph Thoresby of Yorkshire decided he was ready to be married at the age of twenty-six or, as he put it, "I was solicited to change my position." His marital priorities were to find a wife of appropriate social standing who would also bring a suitable dowry to the match. Recommended by an acquaintance, he first "made his application" to Mary Cholmley, finding her "lovely, pious and prudent, and withal a considerable fortune." A date was set but, unfortunately, Cholmley—or more likely her father—was approached by a member of Parliament whose estate exceeded Thoresby's, and the match was broken off. Cholmley's parents then tried to persuade Thoresby to marry their second daughter, but he refused and, after praying for guidance, in 1684 married Anna Sykes, "the comely and virtuous daughter" of a senior lord of the manor of Leeds.[44]

Figure 6
Pieter Brueghel the Younger (ca. 1564–1638). *A Wedding Procession*.
Christie's Images / The Bridgeman Art Library

Samuel Woodforde, a seventeenth-century poet and cleric, met Alice Beale, the youngest daughter of Theodore Beale of Buckinghamshire, in London and fell in love. Finding that Beale too "had an inclination," he promised to marry her without first consulting friends or family. Although Woodforde's impetuosity resulted in strained relations with his family, Samuel and Alice, whom he subsequently referred to as "his dear and loving wife," finally married in 1662.[45]

As evidenced by these accounts and others, some young couples actually fell in love, others acquiesced to their parents' wishes, and still others sought not a soulmate but a suitable partner. It was important for men and women alike not merely to marry, but to make the right marriage. An appropriate choice weighed wealth, status, religious affiliation, age, temperament, and moral qualities. Destined to be legally dependent on their husbands, women needed assurances that their mate could support them financially, was sober, and of good character. Likewise, suitors carefully weighed the resources potential spouses brought to the marriage, as these additional funds often meant the difference between poverty and success.[46] Just as matches of the period were as individual as the couples themselves, the same was true for a woman's choice of wedding attire. The new emphasis on reciprocal affection in marriage did not alter or lend a noticeably refined sentimentality to bridal dress. Its ostentation and style were entirely dependent on social class, wealth, and fashion trends.

Alice Wandesford's widowed mother provided the initiative for her daughter's marriage at the age of twenty-five. Several suitors were considered, but Alice had the final say in choosing William Thornton. In her diary, she recounts that she had no real desire to alter her situation as a single woman. Wandesford probably could have refused Thornton's offer, but was willing to do what seemed pleasing to God and her family, and agreed to the match once she had satisfied herself that Thornton was godly, sober, and of adequate estate. They were married in December of 1651.

The paintings of Pieter Brueghel the Younger (ca. 1564–1638) are perhaps the best visual documentation of wedding clothing in the mid-sixteenth century. A prolific master, Brueghel's caricature-like peasants are illustrated participating in a variety of activities, including weddings. His painting *Wedding Procession* depicts a Flemish bride and bridegroom, accompanied by villagers, parading to the church (fig. 6). The bride, at center, is flanked by two boys or pages holding her skirt, symbolically keeping it from touching the ground, although it is actually too short to do so. Her black dress is not unlike those worn by the other women in the procession. Her folded hands, held at waist height, accentuate what appear to be fur cuffs. While this may seem to be a special embellishment, another woman in the group wears a similar trim on her sleeve. The two elements that distinguish the bride from the others are the bridal crown or headdress and her uncovered hair flowing down her back. This display of the bride's hair was a symbol of virginity—a custom that was common to peasants and royalty alike and served as a substitute veil in this period.[47]

It is obvious that this peasant bride did not have a special dress in which to be wed, although she is clearly pleased with her traditional ceremonial escort. The seventeenth-century novelist Thomas Deloney describes a comparable procession, and bride, in *The Pleasant History of John Winchcomb* (1672). Winchcomb's bride, a woman of middle rank, was dressed in a gown of sheep's russet—a coarse homespun fabric usually of a reddish-brown hue—and a kirtle of fine worsted wool. She wore a head ornament of gold with her long hair loose down her back and was escorted to the church between "two sweet boyes."[48]

In contrast to the common black dress worn by the bride depicted in Brueghel's painting, Princess Elizabeth, daughter of James I, was married to Frederick the Elector Palatine in Westminster Abbey in 1613 in white, "the emblem of Innocency." However, Elizabeth too wore her "amber-coloured haire dependantly hanging, playted down over her shoulders to her waiste" rather than tied up. Similarly, when Anne of Cleves was wed to Henry VIII she was "attired in cloth of gold, embroidered with flowers in pearl. . . . Her long yellow hair, no longer confined by a caul, hung over her shoulders."[49]

Certainly the most extreme bridal attire in this period was worn by women who married *en chemisette*, that is, bareheaded and

in only a shift or slip. By law, if a woman married *en chemisette*, thereby presenting herself as owning no worldly goods, the groom was not legally responsible for her debts. It is unknown how often such marriages occurred, as it was assuredly an embarrassment for the bride, but there were documented instances.[50]

THE AGE OF ENLIGHTENMENT

The emphasis on the nuclear family, individual choice, mutual affection, and more equality between spouses was strengthened by far-reaching economic, political, and philosophical changes in the late seventeenth and eighteenth centuries. As early as the mid-seventeenth century, philosophers of the Age of Enlightenment (ca. 1650–1790) championed the ideas of autonomy, individual rights, reason, and the pursuit of happiness. Scientific discoveries that increased the perception of man's control over certain aspects of nature weakened religious fervor and created indifference to the authority of the Church. The disallowance of divine right and the decline of absolute monarchy began to erode patriarchal authority within the nuclear family. Economically, cooperative farming was being abandoned, artisanal guilds and the apprentice system were weakening, an entrepreneurial middle class began to emerge, and the expansive spread of wage labor resulted in a more mobile population. Delaying marriage to assume responsibility for the family business, acquire an inheritance, or complete an apprenticeship was no longer a necessity. Like the farmers and laborers of the previous century, wage-earning parents who had no accumulated wealth to pass on propelled their children into the workforce, hoping they would find their own means of securing a livelihood and a spouse. By the second half of the eighteenth century, young men and women enjoyed far more freedom in choosing a partner than had their predecessors.[51]

These alterations in thought and circumstance set the stage for the modern marriage. Enlightenment philosophies furthered marital union as a relationship born of sentiment—a means to personal satisfaction for both husband and wife, rather than economic and social convenience. Such a marriage was considered more stable, therefore contributing to the greater good. However, even though now defined as a contract between two consenting parties with reciprocal rights and obligations, the woman's role remained subordinate.[52] Even the great philosophers, including Rousseau, Diderot, and Voltaire, were unwilling to incorporate woman equally into their concept of the species of man. Despite the fact that women hosted the salons that helped engender Enlightenment ideas, they were viewed as a different kind of being. Like the theologians, moralists, and physicians of previous centuries, these thinkers maintained that women's ability to reason was inferior to men's. Woman was a creature of passion and child-like imagination governed by her sexual parts, particularly the uterus, and therefore incapable of forming or understanding abstract thoughts.

Rousseau's writings indicate that he believed the female's limited powers of reasoning need only be cultivated to the extent required to accomplish her natural duties—obeying her husband, managing the home, and caring for their children. This opinion was shared by most philosophers. Nicolas de Caritat, marquis de Condorcet (1743–94), was one of the few who applied Enlightenment concepts to women. In his article "On Granting Civil Rights to Women" (1790) in the *Journal de la Société de '89*, de Caritat disputes prejudices against women and promotes equal education and civil rights. Like Rousseau, the majority of men believed women capable of partnering in a loving relationship, but expected they would be satisfied performing the duties appropriate to them, and no more.[53]

As in the Middle Ages and Renaissance, the concept of a distinct style of dress in which to be wed had not yet been formed. During the Enlightenment women wore their best dress, augmented with as extravagant trims as they could afford. If the family were aristocratic, a new dress was custom made but it was apt to be worn again. The formal full-length cut, a train, or ostentatious trimmings were merely indicators of favored styles. The expanse of the fashionable paniered skirt in the eighteenth century might require up to twenty yards of fabric—a luxury not to be wasted on a single occasion, even by the wealthy. The style is recorded in *Les Quatre Ages: La Promenade (The Four Ages: The Marriage of Antoinette de Bertier de Sauvigny to the Marquis de la Bourdonnaye)*—a tapestry commissioned by the bride's father at the Manufacture Royale de Beauvais between 1788 and 1790 (fig. 7).[54] This aristocratic bride processing out of the church on the arm of her husband has chosen to wear white—a choice probably based more on conspicuous display than purity. Her gown follows the fashionable style of the period—a low décolleté or neckline, three-quarter-length sleeves, *paniers* that hold the skirt out from the hips, and colorful ribbon trims. This bride had no concerns about keeping her gown clean, as she could easily have another.

Mary Waters, however, made a different choice. Wed in Boston in 1740, she chose a much more serviceable color than Antoinette de Bertier de Sauvigny, though it is luxurious nonetheless (see cat. 1). The dark green silk with a colorfully brocaded pattern of flowers and fruit was in vogue and not an inexpensive choice, as it was woven at Spitalfields.[55] Waters seems to have decided to expend a sizeable amount on the fabric specifically for her wedding gown, but she could easily have worn this dress on subsequent formal occasions, thereby justifying the cost. The fact that the gown was remodeled in 1763 and worn by Waters's daughter for her wedding is an indication of the longevity expected of such a costly textile.

The depiction of the de Sauvigny wedding party also exemplifies the private celebrations usually preferred by the aristocracy. While Brueghel's rural bride is processed to church with the entire community in tow, the bridal couple in the tapestry is surrounded only by close family members. Weddings among the lower classes often served as an opportunity for rowdy communal gatherings. In contrast, the upper class maintained a reserved decorum and avoided the vulgarity of display before a curious wider public—much like celebrities today who marry in secret.

REVOLUTION

The end of the eighteenth century brought revolution in America and France. Both conflicts reinforced the ideal of the companionate marriage and exalted women's position. Prior to the American Revolution, it was not considered appropriate for women in the colonies to participate in political discussions. Public affairs fell outside the feminine sphere. But women could hardly have remained detached as they watched the escalating violence, read accounts of skirmishes in newspapers and pamphlets, prepared food for the militia, marched in protest, and harassed their loyalist neighbors. They were particularly affected by the call to boycott household commodities such as tea, fabrics, and other luxury goods imported from England. Men realized they needed women's support to force the repeal of British taxes on these items, and women made significant sacrifices to further the effort. It must have been empowering for these women to be relied upon and acknowledged for their contribution. As the war continued, women became increasingly vocal in their political discussions, some in public, but more often among friends and family. Their reticence in breaking the social code is evidenced in their frequent apologies for speaking about politics in the pre- and early war years. These regrets faded, however, as they gained a new confidence, not only in their ability to discourse on public affairs, but as productive members of society.[56]

In France, women traditionally were more politically active than their American counterparts. They were not permitted to take part in political deliberations, but they frequented the assembly galleries to monitor debates and influence

Figure 7
Manufacture Royale de Beauvais. *Les Quatre Ages: La Promenade (The Four Ages: The Marriage of Antoinette de Bertier de Sauvigny to the Marquis de la Bourdonnaye)*, 1778–80, linen, wool, silk, 122 ½ x 83 ½ in. (311.2 x 212.1 cm)(detail). Cincinnati Art Museum, Gift of John J. Emery (1960.558).

officials. It was not uncommon for working-class women to instigate riots when they felt their rights were being violated or they recognized a social injustice. While women did not initiate the French Revolution, their public speeches, printed petitions, riots, and street demonstrations incited the populace and sparked the first rebellions. Once the revolution began, however, French women were not accorded equal roles. They might have been useful in activating the citizens, but they were then relegated to the sidelines.[57]

The delegates to the National Constituent Assembly penned the Declaration of the Rights of Man (1789) and subsequent revolutionary laws that dispensed civil status to women in France. Likewise, the Constitution of 1791 defined civil majority identically for both sexes. It was recognized that women possessed sufficient intellect to serve as witnesses to public documents, enter into contracts, and wield equal parental authority. Most importantly, marriage became a civil contract giving women equal rights within that relationship. Marriage was defined as a means to personal happiness. Once it failed to serve that purpose, either party could terminate it. For the first time, women were looked upon as rational creatures—rationality being a characteristic with which they had never been credited.[58]

Ultimately, however, the new governments in both France and America were organized by and for men. *"Liberté! Égalité! Fraternité!"* might have been the rallying cry of the French Revolution, but this did not include the female sex. The United States Constitution did not equally protect women's rights either. In both nations, the citizenry discovered that women could play a civic role, but this did not award them one. Wives still belonged at home, instilling in their offspring the love of freedoms and equalities in which they themselves could not fully participate. American women remained as oppressed after the revolution as they had been before. Once married, an American woman was "feme covert"—one whose legal rights were subsumed or "covered" by her husband's. A married woman could not legally sue or be sued, draft wills, make contracts, or buy or sell property—including property that she had inherited or brought to the marriage. Neither did she have any rights to her children if she separated or divorced.[59]

In France, uncompromising supporters of the status quo, and even most revolutionaries, decried women's new freedoms, declaring they destroyed the very boundaries of civilization itself. They believed that the natural order had been destabilized and found it intolerable that women might have

an equal footing with men. Those who had fought for equal rights for the humblest peasants rejected the idea that women warranted the same respect. The revolutionary Pierre Gaspard Chaumette (1763–94) complained, "Since when is it considered normal for a woman to abandon the pious care of her home, the cradle of her children, to listen to speeches in the public forum?"[60] At the end of the day, men returning from work wanted their wives at home. According to the laws of nature, they believed this was where women belonged.

Spurred by revolution, the late eighteenth and early nineteenth centuries brought deep social changes, including intensified economic growth, social stratification based on wealth, expansion of educational opportunities, political democratization, and—most important in this context—the emergence of a defined social ethic of domesticity.[61] In Europe and America, this transitional period resulted in the rise of a middle class that formulated its own values, material culture, and domestic structures—a reshaping that laid the foundation for the twentieth-century family.

In America, the marital bond was used as a metaphor for political union and the social contract of the new democracy. In 1776, politicians, clerics, and authors idealized marriage as a symmetrical partnership, comparing it to the new nation, the sum parts of which voluntarily chose union. As in a marriage, loyalty and allegiance between the states and to the federal government would insure a successful coalition. This comparison threw a spotlight on marriage itself and the institution was re-envisioned, once again, as a reciprocal relationship of mutual love and friendship.[62]

In the post-revolutionary years, political rhetoric and beliefs regarding correct social order became more conservative, focusing on the element of consent. Wives were compared to citizens who rightly acquiesced to the authority of the federal government. A husband, the wiser and more judicious of the pair, made the decisions, much as elected representatives made choices for their constituents. One essayist wrote in the *Weekly Museum* in 1793 that once married, a woman gained the "right to be protected by the man of her own choice," just as "men, living under a free constitution of their own framing, are entitled to the protection of the laws."[63] Submission was cast in an agreeable light. This comparison to the married state quickly became more than an analogy. Proper marriages in which loving partnership was practiced were believed to produce the type of citizen who would insure the success of the new republic. The perceived differences between the sexes made marriage the perfect environment in which to nourish the desired social virtues of a good citizenry. Men had superior powers of judgment and reasoning, while women's strength lay in the virtues of the heart. Their sensitivity and refinement were attributes that could temper the roughness of men and be taught to the next generation of republican citizens.[64]

In comparison to men, the female sex continued to be characterized as physically and intellectually inferior. Up to this point, they had also been considered morally inferior. The recognition, however, that personal virtue was the foundation of an enduring republic focused attention on child rearing and early education—a task that fell primarily to mothers. The future of the nation was seen as resting with women, thereby elevating their moral stature. Education, including religious instruction, was required for raising upstanding, intelligent children, particularly boys. In service of this need, educational standards for females were advanced and tailored to their societal duties. They were trained to excel as daughters, sisters, wives, and mothers—to the exclusion of any other role.[65]

Just as revolution transformed social and political beliefs, it also metamorphosed fashion within a brief time span. In fact, fashion served ideological purposes during the French Revolution. Luxurious silks were seen as the emblem of the enemies of *liberté*, and therefore cotton fabrics gained new prominence. As each successive change in the French political milieu occurred, a new style of clothing was required to divide followers from non-followers. By the late 1790s, the Empire gown of embroidered white cotton or linen had become the predominant mode. Influenced by mid-eighteenth-century excavations of Roman ruins and the emphasis on naturalness and simplicity advocated by philosopher Jean-Jacques Rousseau, the artificiality of eighteenth-century dress was abandoned. The idealization of classical aesthetics resulted in soft gowns with a waistline just beneath the bust and slim skirts that clung to the body. In pronounced contrast to previous styles, these dresses revealed the natural female form. White, a favored color, was erroneously believed to mimic classical dress.[66] Although wedding gowns followed this trend in fashion, they were merely that—fashionable (see cat. 2). The fact that the gowns women married in were white did not signify a trend toward the ubiquitous white wedding dress.

The nineteenth-century marital relationship also differed from that of the previous century in its rejection of the strict hierarchy of husband as sole authority over wife and children. Wives were now considered junior partners, although husband and wife each had separate spheres of control. Men dominated the public realm of business, politics, and finance. They were the movers, the doers, and the actors in the public world. Women, the weaker vessels, were submissive, meek, pure, and, most importantly, domestic. They were responsible for home management and child rearing. This division of responsibilities constituted the ideology of the separate spheres that stratified male/female relationships for most of the nineteenth century. Woman's role included creating an oasis where her husband could be rejuvenated and her children nourished, spiritually as well as physically. While glorified as an "angel in the house," a woman was securely bound within the narrow confines of the home (fig. 8).[67]

Figure 8
The idealized nineteenth-century woman. *Godey's Lady's Book,* November 1849.

Although women gained rhetorical stature, they were still effectually dependent. At the age of eighteen, when a woman came of legal age, she was able to marry without parental consent. As long as she was single, she could retain any and all earnings. However, she had no rights as a citizen. She could not vote, sign legal documents, initiate lawsuits, execute a will, or serve on a jury. Once a woman married, her husband gained legal control of his wife's earnings and any property she brought to the marriage. It was much more difficult for a woman to divorce her husband than vice versa, and if a woman managed

to be granted a divorce she had no rights to her children. This was true in the United States, France, and England. According to Sir William Blackstone in his *Commentaries on the Laws of England* (1765–69), "By marriage, the husband and wife are one person in the law: that is, the very being or legal existence of the woman is suspended during the marriage."[68]

Both the legal and ideological inequalities made marriage a much more momentous life change for a woman. The new ennoblement of woman's role and the emphasis on a loving partnership, however, heightened expectations for a young girl. A true love match was what they sought. Eliza Chaplin, a single working-class woman in Salem, Massachusetts, imagined her ideal mate as possessing "every quality I could desire," rejecting the possibility that she would marry for economic rather than emotional motives. Similarly, author Elizabeth Prentiss, daughter of Congregationalist cleric Edward Payson, anticipated falling in love "madly and absorbingly."[69]

The idea of marriage based on a heady romance was encouraged by the proliferation of sentimental fiction that had flourished since the eighteenth century. In Catherine Sedgwick's 1830 novel *Clarence* a woman contemplating marriage pronounced, "I have always said I would never marry any man that I was not willing to die for." Critics complained that girls who read these stories were subject to overpowering sentiment and "exaggerated strain." It robbed them of the "seductive innocence which is the most charming ornament of a young girl."[70]

Similarly, fictional romances featured in weekly women's magazines such as *Godey's Lady's Book* and the *Ladies' Monthly Magazine* encouraged fantasies of idealized relationships. Many such narratives centered on finding true love. Often the heroine was a poor working girl who was pure of heart, but had fallen into dire circumstances through no fault of her own. Inevitably, her savior was an honorable gentleman of higher economic and social rank who was astute enough to see through her unfortunate circumstances, fall in love, and marry her. Such stories were inspirational to young women who worked twelve-hour days in factories for poor pay.[71]

With expectations raised so high, reports of marital unhappiness created intense distress. In their diaries and letters, women often expressed more grief than joy when considering marriage. While some girls spoke elatedly of their upcoming wedding, many experienced an almost paralyzing fear as "the fatal day" drew near. Women used words like anxious, mortified, fretful, fearful, and depressed to describe the prospect of marriage. In contrast to their suitors, who were anxious to marry, women often tried to prolong the betrothal period. One New Englander in 1824 did not think she would be happier once married, "but as the die is cast, and there is nothing but death to separate us, I may as well look upon the bright side of the question." Another characterized marriage as "a sad, sour, sober beverage." Blanche Butler, who married in 1870, resigned herself to the possibility of a less than satisfying marriage: "If worse comes to worse, I will just . . . screw up the corners of my mouth, devote myself to household duties, and vanish."[72]

There were many reasons why women may have feared marriage. They knew that this step would bind them to a partner with little chance for release if the pairing were unsuccessful. Socialite Caroline Drayton—a lifelong friend of Eleanor Roosevelt— lamented, "I know I could be blissfully happy with the right man, and so frightfully miserable with the wrong one and I have so little confidence in my own judgment of men, that I don't know what to do." Another woman longed for the subjugation of earlier centuries. "I almost wish I were not so free, that I were restrained or controlled, so that I would not have the responsibility for my future unhappiness or happiness. . . . This is not child's play, this is a matter of my whole life. . . . It's all so chancy."[73]

Women also knew that once they wed, pregnancy would soon follow. The chance of dying in childbirth was high: In mid-nineteenth-century England, six in every thousand women died. If she were sufficiently fertile, a woman could expect to give birth to her first child nine months to one year after her wedding, and every eighteen months to two years thereafter. Women were often pregnant for the majority of their married life—a condition that frequently took a serious toll on their health. Ambitious women realized that marriage required them to abandon dreams of independence, education, or a career. They feared the inevitable isolation and aimlessness of a life spent doing housework and caring for children.[74]

Despite their trepidations, during the nineteenth century ninety percent of American women married. Marriage was their destiny. Offered limited means of earning a respectable income, women generally saw no other choice. Financially, they needed a husband to support them. Nineteenth-century feminist Charlotte Perkins Gilman described women's lot most accurately: "Wealth, power, social distinction, fame . . . home and happiness, reputation, ease and pleasure, her bread and butter—all must come to her thro' a small gold ring." French politician and historian Alexis de Tocqueville (1805–59) traveled throughout America in the early nineteenth century to observe the workings of democracy. In his subsequent book, *Democracy in America* (1835), he marveled at the acquiescence of American women in contrast to those in Europe. "In the United States the inexorable opinion of the public carefully circumscribes woman within the narrow circle of domestic interests and duties and forbids her to step beyond it. She has learned by the use of her independence to surrender it without a struggle and without a murmur when the time comes for making the sacrifice."[75]

Perhaps the greatest pressures to marry, however, were emotional and psychological. Marriage and home were synonymous, and home was the woman's sphere. The dual roles of wife and mother were glorified as the only true fulfillment for a woman. In popular fiction, novelists including Fanny Burney and Jane Austen asserted that marriage was the only proper condition for a well-bred woman. In William Makepeace Thackeray's *Vanity Fair* (1847–48), the ambitious Becky Sharp unabashedly engages in the marital quest: "Of what else have young ladies to think, but husbands?"[76] Marriage was the yardstick of success for women in the nineteenth century. It was only within marriage that woman could truly be feminine and fulfill her role of self-abnegation for the redemption of others. Many happily accepted the role and were successful in devoting their lives to home, husband, and offspring. Some acknowledged, as Caroline Drayton did, that what she wanted and needed was a kind but firm master. In a husband, acquiescent women sought a mentor who would guide, teach, mold, and even speak for them.[77]

As in previous centuries, fashionable bridal gowns, both white and colorful, continued to be worn throughout the nineteenth century. Women of lesser means, probably those who were not particularly enthusiastic about being wed, and those who simply took the ritual in stride often chose a best dress or acquired a new colorful gown that was worn on numerous occasions after its initial use.

It has been widely held that Queen Victoria, wed in 1840, instituted the exclusive tradition of wearing white. A young woman of twenty, Victoria broke with royal convention by choosing not to wear her coronation robes. Instead, she chose a gown in exact accordance with the fashion of the day—white satin trimmed with lace, a low wide neckline, and puff sleeves. She wore a court train attached at the waist, and her veil was held in place by a coronet of orange blossoms (fig. 9).[78] The wedding ceremony of Victoria and Prince Albert of Saxe-Coburg-Gotha was described in detail in newspapers and periodicals across Britain and America, and no small attention was given to the bride's dress.

Victoria was a powerful icon whose image and activities were a constant presence in the news in England and America alike. Her ascension to the throne in 1837 coincided with, perhaps codified, the emerging ideal of woman as a moral, domestic angel. When Victoria married, she personified all the characteristics of the ideal woman. As literary historian Elizabeth Langland writes, Victoria took on a "signal role in the construction of a new feminine ideal that endorsed active public management behind a façade of private retirement."[79]

Victoria's gender instigated a much greater attentiveness to the domestic or feminine aspects of the royal family, such as her relationship with Prince Albert, the birth of their nine children, and their family life in general. In 1867, the journalist Walter Bagehot commented that this focus on the monarchical family brought "the pride of sovereignty to the level of petty life." The young monarch embodied beauty, morality, romance, motherhood, and both power over and reliance upon men. She was an icon to whom women, in particular, could relate.[80]

Despite the young queen's widespread celebrity and influence, it is a long-held misconception that she single-handedly brought about the exclusivity of white wedding dresses. While the simple styling of Victoria's gown was well within the reach of women of almost every social class, it did not preclude the wearing of colored dresses, which were far more practical a choice for most. As evidenced in museum collections, both white and colorful wedding gowns were worn by brides before and long after Victoria's ceremony. At the same time, illustrations and descriptions of bridal dresses in women's magazines post-1840

Figure 9
Franz Xaver Winterhalter. *Queen Victoria (1819–1901)*, 1842, oil on canvas, 52.5 x 38.5 in. (133.4 x 97.8 cm)
The Royal Collection © Her Majesty Queen Elizabeth II, RCIN 401413

were predominantly white, suggesting that Queen Victoria's choice may have popularized the hue, although it remained simply too impractical for many women. Unquestionably, both the style and color of her gown were emulated just as gowns of royalty and celebrities are today, creating a preference for white gowns in the following decades.

Two other factors may have contributed to the attribution of the white wedding dress to Victoria's example. Based on a contemporary bias, it is likely that the dresses that were most recognizable as wedding gowns—those that were white—were preserved by descendants, creating the impression of a preponderance of white wedding attire in the period. In addition, the bridal dresses that most frequently make their way into museum collections are those of the elite, who were more likely to wear white.

However, in August 1849, the discussion of bridal dress in the fashion section of *Godey's Lady's Book* begins, "Custom has decided, from the earliest ages, that white is the fitting hue, whatever may be the material. It is an emblem of innocence and purity of girlhood and the unsullied heart which she now yields to the keeping of the chosen one."[81] Clearly, the periodical's fashion editor was aware, or at least assumed the presence of, a precedent of wearing white bridal attire since antiquity, and does not attribute its popularity to Queen Victoria. Instead, white was defined as most appropriate because it symbolized innocence and purity—the same qualities that made white the choice for early Greek and Roman brides. It might be suggested that in the mid-nineteenth century, white became the color of choice for those brides who were affluent enough to indulge in such a dress.

The aspiration to be dressed like a youthful, attractive queen was coupled with the rise of the middle class in the second half of the nineteenth century. The expansion of mass manufacturing, improved transportation systems, technological advances in the printing industry, and the expansion of commerce contributed to capital accumulation for this new class, creating both a demand for and an abundance of goods and services to purchase. By mid-century, Western cultures had broken with their agrarian past and embraced urbanization. Early department stores such as Wanamaker's and Stewart's in America, Le Bon Marché in Paris, and later, Harrods in London were massive purveyors of consumer goods that were attractively displayed in palatial establishments. Desire seemed to consume the middle class and the democratization of luxury enticed women, in particular, to create the visual appearance of greater wealth both in their homes and dress.[82] In Émile Zola's novel *Au bonheur des dames,* the female desire for goods is described as a religion that "awakened new desires in her flesh; they were an immense temptation, before which she succumbed fatally, yielding at first to reasonable purchases of useful articles for the household, then tempted by their coquetry, then devoured."[83]

Much of the middle class's wealth was focused on imitating social superiors and "aspiring to gentility by copying the education, manners, and behaviour of the gentry." Gentility became a purchasable commodity through the mass-produced imitation luxuries that soon filled middle-class homes. Afternoon teas evolved as an affordable substitute for the elaborate dinners and soirées of the wealthy, and mimicked the intricate reparation of social obligations. The rules of respectability were studied in etiquette manuals that were widely available beginning in the 1830s. These books precisely defined every aspect of conduct from artful letter writing to table manners and appropriate dress.[84]

Etiquette manuals targeted both specific and general audiences, but it was women who were responsible for the management of the home and moral upkeep of the family. They were particularly motivated to adopt identifiable class signifiers that defined their family as respectable and upwardly mobile,

Figure 10
Fashion illustrations in popular periodicals regularly featured bridal gowns.
Godey's Lady's Book, November 1858.

differentiating them from the unrefined working class. Dress played a prominent role in these aspirations as a standardized outward display of one's social status and virtue. Women's magazines and etiquette manuals instructed the female sex, in detail, in the art of dressing correctly for every social situation imaginable.[85]

Wedding dresses were, perhaps, the article of clothing in which this aspiration reached its height. Many manuals included a separate section on weddings that described appropriate dress for everyone in attendance and extensive directions for each aspect of the event. Overall, simplicity in bridal dress was considered most tasteful; the excessive embellishment that had been regulated in thirteenth-century Venice was considered vulgar in the nineteenth century. Some advice books went so far as to stipulate what type of silk should be utilized based on the age of the bride. Moiré, for instance, was considered suitable for an older bride, but too heavy for a young one. The bride wore white unless she was older or a widow, in which case pearl-grey or lavender was more appropriate as "the significance of the emblem is lost on such an occasion."[86]

It was women's magazines, however, featuring the latest fashions, that most brides-to-be would have consulted when determining their wedding gown design. Despite the admonitions in etiquette manuals to dress simply, fashion plates in these periodicals illustrated endless variations of elaborately trimmed white gowns (fig. 10). Not wishing to deny any bride the privilege of a white wedding dress, the December 1868 issue of *Harper's Bazar* listed prices per yard of different silks in an article written specifically for brides whose budget was limited. Rather than satin, the preferred choice that season, economical fabrics such as *poult-de-soie*, taffeta, and faille were suggested. If these were still too expensive, Irish poplin was recommended as a better choice than "a flimsy, cheaper silk." Choosing not to mince words, the writer discouraged wool fabrics, stating that they "are better suited for shrouds than wedding dresses."[87]

The widespread consumption of these magazines, even among the working classes, created a common desire. What woman would not want to be attired like the beautiful and youthful English queen? Which young lady would not want to be dressed sumptuously on this important day? Just as nineteenth-century women fantasized about a romantic, loving relationship in marriage, they desired to be conspicuously and beautifully attired on the one day of their entire life that they would capture the sole attention of their friends and family. For a middle- or working-class woman, choosing a white gown equated her with a higher social and economic status—the expense of which could only be justified for this particular significant life event.

Figure 11
Frank Duveneck. *Elizabeth Boott Duveneck*, 1888, oil on canvas, 65 ⅛ x 34 ¾ in. (164.4 x 88.3 cm).
Cincinnati Art Museum, Gift of the Artist (1915.78).
Although Elizabeth Boott was quite wealthy, she wed Frank Duveneck, a painter whose economic status was well below hers, and her father did not approve of the match. Perhaps this explains why she married in a colored gown so typical of middle- and working-class women in the nineteenth century.

For some brides, a white gown even of a cheaper fabric was simply not practical. In 1870, *Godey's Lady's Book* suggested that "brides of small means who can have but one silk dress should choose a black one, as it is stylish, serviceable, and suitable for all occasions and should be married in a travelling dress and hat" (fig. 11 and see cat. 15). And, in many cases, as in previous centuries, what one had was good enough. The wedding attire of a young Lawrenceburg, Indiana, couple was described in an 1851 issue of the *National Era*. The young man "was barefooted, and wore a coarse but clean tow linen shirt and pants, and rough straw hat of home manufacture. His fair companion was dressed in a blue cotton frock, pink cotton apron, fine bonnet, and coarse brogan shoes without stockings." This couple arrived in town unceremoniously on foot to be wed.[88] Their relaxed attitude toward wedding attire is similar to that illustrated in Brueghel's paintings, or that of a seventeenth-century couple who self-wed.

In her diary, Mollie Dorsey Sanford recounts her 1860 wedding day and the ceremony in detail but fails to describe what she was wearing, perhaps an indication of how insignificant the dress itself was even in her own mind. She and Byron Sanford were married in the kitchen of her family's farmhouse. Her small wedding in the family home was typical of nineteenth-century celebrations, which tended to be private. Displaying oneself in public, even in church, was considered vulgar and in direct opposition to the ideal of womanly reserve and modesty. The ceremony was often followed by a meal or simple refreshments provided by family and friends, rather than the elaborate festivities accorded modern newlyweds.[89]

Sanford also records her sister Dora's wedding a few months later. Dora wore a blue wool gown, which Mollie made for her.[90] The Dorseys were a middle-class family who moved from Indiana to the Nebraska Territory, looking for better opportunities. Dry goods stores and dressmakers were many days' journey away. The girls were content with what was at hand and practical to boot. A blue gown would serve well as a best dress for church or for special occasions on the Nebraska prairie. Both Mollie and Dora married for love and not even wishful thinking about a white wedding gown was recorded, although presumably both had new dresses made specifically for the occasion.

It was at this same time in the second half of the nineteenth century that the first steps were taken away from homemade weddings, like Mollie and Dora Dorsey's, toward more commercialized events. Merchants and service providers including jewelers, florists, confectioners, caterers, engravers, and photographers saw opportunities for profit in the weddings of the consumeristic middle class. These vendors, along with popular women's magazines, raised the expectations of brides for more opulent weddings. Consequently, it was during this period that "traditional" signifiers of bridal attire were more frequently employed— although they were not yet pervasive. Trains, when they were in fashion, were prevalent. Orange blossoms, an ancient symbol of fertility, decorated almost every bride; the fragility of the bloom and its unavailability in all seasons, however, prompted the production of wax facsimiles that embellished bodices, skirts, and headdresses. Veils fell in and out of favor, although wearing a white veil was not precluded by a colored dress, as many period photographs confirm.

Social commentators of the time criticized the trend toward conspicuous consumption as a corruption of a sacred rite. In *Whisper to a Bride,* Lydia Sigourney advised brides that the trappings offered by merchants were debasing. "Be not studious to deck thyself in costly array. Trouble not thine heart about the silks of the merchant, or the gems of the lapidary. . . . For it is a sacred festival, and around the pure bride, there is ever a mantle of dignity"—a dignity many felt was sullied by crass commercialism.[91]

Relatives and acquaintances of an engaged couple, particularly those of the bride, were also caught in the consumerism of weddings by being obligated to purchase gifts. The display of wedding presents for guests was condemned for mimicking commercial displays that spurred competitive gift-giving, especially among the wealthy. Most gifts, including both household and personal items, were chosen specifically for the bride. Ada M. Davis, married in 1874, meticulously recorded the wedding gifts she received, ranging from the practical—a valise, silverware, and towels—to the personal—garnet and pearl jewelry and a perfumery stand (see cat. 10).[92]

Wedding-related vendors of the nineteenth century garnered importance and additional business through their connection with high-profile personages. For instance, the nuptial arrangements, and especially the purchases, of Señor Don Esteban Santa Cruz de Oviedo and Frances Amelia Bartlett, who married in New York in 1859, were widely publicized. The bride's trousseau, purchased from New York department stores A. T. Stewart's and Genin's Bazar, was estimated to be worth $28,000 at the time. Two jewelry houses, Ball, Black & Co. and Tiffany & Co., published images of a selection of the jewelry they had designed for the bride. Similarly, *Harper's Weekly* ran an extensive article on the 1863 wedding of the Princess of Wales, as did *Harper's Bazar* on the occasion of the Queen of Spain's marriage in 1880.[93] This lust for the eminence of royalty caused more than 450 American heiresses to marry into the European aristocracy between 1870 and 1914. Most of these marriages proved to be unhappy unions, but the sensationalized weddings were meticulously detailed in newspapers and ladies' magazines. Perhaps the best-known transatlantic marriage was that of Consuelo Vanderbilt and Charles Richard John Spencer Churchill, the ninth Duke of Marlborough, in 1895. Although the recently divorced Alva Vanderbilt forced her daughter into this arranged marriage, the wedding was described as "the most magnificent ever celebrated in this country," as befitted

Figure 12
Consuelo Vanderbilt's wedding gown. *Harper's Bazar*, November 9, 1895.

a bride of her station and the title she was to assume. Four thousand invitations were issued for the wedding.[94]

The public devoured widespread newspaper coverage leading up to the wedding on November 6, as well as of the event itself. On October 27 the *New York Times* published a detailed account of the contents of Consuelo Vanderbilt's trousseau, down to the gold filigree clasps on the Fasso brand corset she would wear under her wedding dress. *Harper's Bazar* provided an exacting description of the gown chosen for the bride by her mother. Designed by

Parisian couturier Jacques Doucet, it was of ivory satin with tiered lace flounces, fashionable leg-of-mutton sleeves, a wide belt, a court train four yards long, and decorated with orange blossoms (fig. 12). It was certainly not an example of the tasteful simplicity promoted in etiquette manuals.[95]

The event was described the following day in the newspaper in painstaking detail. The church setting was described as a "scene like one in fairyland." The "magnificent spectacle" included floral arrangements that had been labored over for days by the florist and multiple assistants, who succeeded in decorating the ninety-five-foot-high dome of St. Thomas Episcopal Church. The church organist was joined by the New York Symphony Orchestra and a choir of sixty.

So intense was the desire to see the bride that some female guests refused to be seated in their assigned pews and insisted on a better vantage point in the center of the church; others indecorously climbed onto their seats when the bride entered. The streets between the Vanderbilt townhouse at Seventy-second and Madison and the church at Fifty-third and Fifth were packed with onlookers. Fifty patrolmen and twelve detectives were required to keep the sidewalks and street in front of the house partially clear; a total of three hundred policemen was assigned to the event. Every window and doorway along the route was crowded with people hoping to catch a glimpse of the bride or, for that matter, anyone associated with the wedding. It was reported that "small but lively battles were waged between the police and over-curious women" at the street corner nearest the Vanderbilt home.

After the wedding, 115 guests were invited to a celebratory breakfast at the Vanderbilt townhouse. Guests were awed by ceiling-high floral arrangements of tall palms, imported tree ferns, chrysanthemums, roses, and orchids. The company was entertained by the forty-member Royal Hungarian Band, "especially brought from Buda Pesth," wearing their colorful national garb. Each of the guests received a boxed piece of wedding cake and floral favors. A description of the gifts indicates many were specifically for the bride. Candlesticks, an inkstand, and a silver box were the few utilitarian objects mentioned among the sea of gem-encrusted jewelry, fans, and hair combs meant for Consuelo alone.[96]

It is obvious from the crowds of onlookers and street-corner skirmishes that day that there was massive interest in how the elite lived. Weddings were occasions that conspicuously displayed wealth on any social level, even if among a small group of acquaintances. This wedding was exceptional in that regard. Like the wedding of Diana Spencer and Prince Charles in 1981, the Vanderbilt wedding served to feed the fantasies of women who aspired to a fairyland wedding of their own. Obviously, virtually no one could match this spectacle, but a young woman might choose one element of such a high-profile wedding—the gown design, the bouquet, the floral decor, the breakfast menu, or the wedding cake— and orchestrate a modest version for her own nuptials. This allowed her to participate in the celebrity-elite lifestyle, thereby intensifying the emotional power—and expense—of this long-anticipated event.

Just six months prior to the Vanderbilt wedding, Blanche Richardson and Franklin Loveland were united in Glendale, Ohio (see cat. 22). In like manner, the setting, floral arrangements, wedding gown, and attire of the bridesmaids and female guests were all described in the local newspaper. The wedding supper following the evening ceremony was catered by Wilson and Reeder, a local confectioner. While the Loveland-Richardson wedding bore only a cursory resemblance to the extravagance of the Vanderbilt spectacle, the couple did participate in a growing trend toward publicizing their wedding in the media and purchasing services from a caterer and probably a florist.[97]

In the late nineteenth and early twentieth centuries, brides like Blanche Richardson made increasing use of commercial services. In 1906, guests attending the Ryan-Williams wedding breakfast were serenaded by an orchestra and impressed by the elaborate table decorations, as reported in the *Cincinnati Enquirer* (see cat. 24). Miss Ryan was married in church, with the reception following at her parents' home. Miss Ethel Page, married in 1910, had her photo published in the newspaper announcing her upcoming nuptials (cat. 25). This was a bold departure from past generations. Previously, most women pictured in newspapers had been foreign dignitaries or morally suspect actresses. The newspaper article recording the event described a quiet wedding at the Page home, followed by a twelve-course dinner—presumably catered—for two hundred guests. A description of some of the wedding gifts, including decorative household items and artwork, was also relayed to the reader.[98]

In the early years of the twentieth century, women's magazines began to participate in the commercialization of weddings. These publications had long been financed in part by advertisers of everything from medicinals to corsets. By 1910, advertisements for bridal services began to appear regularly in *Vogue*. In May 1914, *Harper's Bazar* itself proffered a personal shopping service. Addressing either the bride or her mother, the magazine suggested its staff might alleviate the burden of the many details associated with a wedding. It offered to prepare the trousseau, provide the presents, engrave the invitations, and arrange for flowers, decorations, catering, and the cake: "The comfort and convenience of placing all those things in experienced hands are beyond measure, and obviates the possibility of some embarrassing oversight." It is doubtful a bride would turn the entire planning of her wedding and trousseau over to such a provider, but she might engage the magazine's Personal Shopping Service to order the invitations, for instance, or to identify a worthy caterer. Similarly, Dean's of New York offered to assist with various aspects of wedding arrangements. A bride could receive the company's "Wedding Suggestions"—presumably a booklet—free upon request. Although purveyors of wedding goods and services profited from both high-profile and typical weddings of the late nineteenth and early twentieth centuries, their influence in no way matched that of the organized bridal industry that established itself after World War II.[99]

THE TWENTIETH CENTURY

The cultural relegation of women to caretaking roles did not change significantly between 1900 and the middle of the twentieth century. Despite admirable strides in political, educational, and economic opportunities, most women continued to fulfill the domestic ideal. In 1920, more than seventy-five percent of American women functioned exclusively as wives, mothers, and housekeepers. The 1940 United States Department of Commerce census summary stated that women began to leave the workforce at an accelerated rate at the age of twenty, generally when they married. Few remained once they started to raise a family, and only twenty-three percent of women aged forty-five to fifty-four continued to work outside the home.[100]

As in the nineteenth century, occupations available to women were largely those compatible with traditional notions of proper female tasks such as needlework, food preparation, or positions that resembled or related to housework or childcare. As types of employment expanded, jobs were often redefined, reducing the responsibility and modifying them into more subservient roles. Clerical positions previously held by men on the rise were filled by women, who were unlikely ever to be promoted. These women were paid lower wages, partly as a discriminatory tactic, but also because they were expected to resign once they married; they were viewed as temporary workers. The question whether married women should be employed at all continued to be debated, and some companies actually required a woman to have her husband's permission to work.[101]

The exceptions to this rule were the war years. During both world wars, women performed masculine jobs in place of men on the front. War work was a patriotic duty. It was clearly understood, however, that women were in the workplace "for the duration" only and were expected to return to their appropriate roles after the war. In England after World War I, a marriage bar was instituted for women pursuing professional careers.[102]

Expanding occupational prospects between 1920 and 1945 reduced the need for women to marry solely for financial security. This, in turn, increased the importance of a companionate marriage. The ideal marriage was evolving, in actuality, into a state of mutual satisfaction for both parties. It was no longer a relationship in which a wife merely served her husband.[103]

In the decades between the two world wars, brides were able to choose from a wider variety of fashionable dress styles. Brides of the 1920s embraced the androgynous straight-cut designs as well as more feminine alternatives, or modes that referenced historical dress (see cats. 27 and 29, respectively). Fashion magazines reported on the latest couture collections and illustrated and described the toilettes of royal brides and prominent socialites on both sides of the Atlantic.

The April 1922 issue of *Vogue* included a number of articles that discussed an attitudinal shift toward weddings and brides in the new "free-and-easy age." There was reportedly less pageantry, a trend toward simplicity, and informality. One wedding toilette was described as carrying modes "further and further from the traditional virginal wedding." Another article addressed "The Bride of All Ages," suggesting her wedding dress should be suited to her "April freshness" or "the riper grace of her September maturity. . . . Brides who have never been brides before. Brides who have been brides more than once and are still annexing new husbands with the entire good-will of their discarded ones. Brides who have been widows many years." These articles reflected a more independent, individualized woman who did not marry to please her parents or for economic security. This was a woman who had more sexual freedom in a society where divorce and less adherence to tradition was increasingly accepted. Brides might be eighteen or thirty, slim or stout, single, divorced, or widowed. Such diversity in brides fostered variety in bridal attire and in the wedding event itself.[104]

In the fall of 1934, Brides House, Inc., launched *So You're Going to Be Married: A Magazine for Brides*, the first periodical dedicated solely to this audience. The magazine originally targeted affluent brides and was available only in New York, New Jersey, and Connecticut. After a few years, it was offered nationally and renamed *Bride's Magazine*. A regular feature article titled "What Shall I Wear for My Wedding?" highlighted the newest in wedding gowns and headpieces. In the Autumn 1935 issue, staff writer Gladys Tilden discussed dolman sleeves, Renaissance-style dresses, the *robe de style*, fabrics ranging from velvet to gold lamé, detachable trains, and halo headdresses—all in a single article. The magazine offered interviews with couturiers and suggestions for correct trousseau items, going-away outfits, and lingerie. A recurring feature was a full-page chart detailing what type of attire was appropriate for every individual in the wedding party based on the time of day and formality of the wedding, much like the directives in nineteenth-century etiquette manuals. *Bride's* was also filled with advertisements that targeted not only the bride-to-be but the homemaker-to-be. The growing wedding service industry and retailers' advertisements used bridal images as a selling point for everything from refrigerators to chewing gum.[105]

One of the major changes in bridal attire, beginning in the 1930s, was the widespread introduction of synthetics such as rayon and nylon. Gowns made of Duplon's Satin Ultra, for instance, were touted as "liquid, shimmering beauty, its exquisite texture

and pearly whiteness, will live glamorously through many an anniversary." In contrast to wedding gowns of the previous century, these dresses were optical white rather than shades of cream or ivory. Gowns made of synthetics were alternatives for brides who wanted a white wedding dress, but struggled with limited budgets as the country strained to pull out of the Great Depression. In the Winter 1936/37 issue, Lord & Taylor offered dresses constructed of synthetic fabrics ranging in price from thirty to one hundred dollars. Higher-priced gowns made of silk were still the choice of those who could afford them, but the basic designs, regardless of the fabric, were the same. Consequently, even those of lesser means could participate in high style. [106]

Significantly, it was in the 1930s that wedding dresses began to retain characteristic elements that are ubiquitous even today. In the 1920s, the hemlines of wedding dresses fluctuated with fashion trends, and most were tea length or shorter. The majority of bridal gowns of the 1930s, however, were full length, suggesting the formality of evening wear in contrast to shorter daytime attire. The dresses were generally trained and worn with a veil—an accessory that had become increasingly popular at the turn of the twentieth century. Brides depicted in advertisements bore all the typical trappings. They wore white, formal, full-length, trained gowns with veils, flowery embellishments often decorated their dresses and headpieces, and they carried bouquets. As bridal retailers promoted their goods, they democratized the white wedding dress and all its "traditional" accoutrements.

The popularity of designs that referenced historical styles of previous centuries also increased during the decade. While fashion designers often reinvented earlier modes in fashionable dress, these modified designs now appeared in wedding dresses, but not in everyday attire. Beginning in 1936, several *Bride's Magazine* cover images depicted nineteenth-century brides drawn by the French illustrator Pierre Brissaud (1885–1964).

The key article of the Spring 1936 issue declared that wedding dresses had "gone back a generation—to the sentimental decade of our mothers." The 1937 season alone featured two gowns inspired by Margaret Mitchell's novel *Gone with the Wind* (1936), as well as a Grecian tunic and several gowns with a decidedly medieval look. In 1940 Lord & Taylor offered a custom-made replica, or adaptation, of a gown worn by a bride's mother or grandmother; the accompanying illustration showed a modernized version of an 1870s dress.[107] This trend toward the sentimentalization of historic styles is something that has never faded from the bridal market.

During World War II, options for wedding attire expanded further. While one might expect that marriage rates would have declined during wartime, the opposite is true—the number soared. Early in the war, the draft deferment for married men hastened weddings, as did imminent departure for foreign fronts. Many women simply purchased a ready-made evening dress or wore a tailored suit (see cats. 34 and 37). Wartime fabric restrictions hampered the production of wedding gowns. However, this problem was soon rectified when the fledgling bridal industry established the Association of Bridal Manufacturers. The Association successfully persuaded Congress to ease fabric limitations for wedding gowns. The traditional marriage, it argued, was one of the primary reasons for fighting. It was part of the American way of life that gave hope to many soldiers in the trenches.[108]

Women understood the importance of wartime constraints and felt compelled to compromise their dream of a formal wedding gown. *Bride's Magazine* addressed this issue head-on. While it offered plenty of suggestions for "bridesy" suits, women were urged to wear a "real" wedding dress because it was their right and they owed it to the groom.[109] One department store advertisement plainly asserted that "a wedding gown with a train, a veil and a bridal bouquet . . . belong to the American way of life, and they should be yours." The Autumn 1943 issue

of the *Bride's Magazine* featured a full-page ad by the New York Dress Institute headed "Your Right to a Wedding," reminding brides that "your government has recognized the importance of preserving the traditional bridal gown."[110] The wedding industry successfully turned the debate on its head, convincing many women that it was nothing short of patriotic to be wed in a white gown. Manufacturers and department stores increasingly offered ready-made gowns that could be procured for a hastily planned wedding. Dresses had a straighter, "clean-cut silhouette" with shorter trains and veils. After the war, when fabric was still difficult to obtain, some brides had gowns made from parachutes brought home by veterans.[111] Others shared gowns: Cincinnati bride Carol Homan Haile lent the custom-made, full-length, trained gown she had worn to her friend, Mary Louise Hackstedde, when Hackstedde married a few months later (see cat. 36).

Descriptors equating brides and weddings with fairy tales or royalty were introduced in the 1930s, with terms such as "fairy princess," "prince charming," "queen," and "regal." Throughout the nineteenth century, fiction and fashion writing had characterized brides as solemn, innocent, demure, virginal, and heavenly, but did not reference royalty or fairy tales. Perhaps the earliest association of a wedding with "fairyland" was that of Consuelo Vanderbilt in 1895. In the 1930s, however, inspired by current events, these comparisons became common.

The coronation of the new English king and queen, George VI and Elizabeth, took place in May 1937, but anticipation of the event fostered royal references as early as the previous year. Bridal headdresses, in particular, were described using terms such as "tiara," "diadem," and "coronet."[112] A Lord & Taylor advertisement used the tagline "Court Splendor for a Bride" and described a particular gown as "regal" with a "Guinevere basque"—referring to the mythic Queen Guinevere of King Arthur's court.[113] The Spring 1937 issue of the *Bride's Magazine*

Figure 13
Prince Charles (Prince of Wales) and Princess Diana (Diana, Princess of Wales) pictured on their wedding day in July 1981.
© Daily Mail / Solo Syndication.
The wedding of Princess Diana and Prince Charles was not only a highly visible royal wedding but a fairy tale come true for the shy Diana Spencer. Design elements of Diana's wedding dress were incorporated into gowns throughout the 1980s.

clearly acknowledges the influence of the upcoming coronation on bridal designs.[114] *Bride's* continued to use the event as an advertising ploy in the summer issue, illustrating a design

that "embodies all the charm of the English bride and all the glamour of a Coronation Year Wedding."[115]

Similarly, during the following decades, popular films, romantic fiction, new editions of classic fairy tales, and celebrity weddings influenced not just gown design, but the rhetoric accompanying it. Walt Disney's animated feature film *Cinderella* premiered in 1950, resulting in a host of references such as the "culmination of a girl's dream" and "no fairy godmother needed."[116] The musical adaptation *The Glass Slipper* (1955), starring Leslie Caron, was specifically cited in text that urged women to "Be a Cinderella bride and live happily ever after."[117] Women were equally enchanted by the real-life wedding gowns of such celebrities as Jacqueline Bouvier Kennedy (1953) and Grace Kelly (1956), whose lives seemed to imitate a fairytale existence (fig. 13).

These persistent references to and adulation of fairytale lives reflected the aspirations of Americans, in particular. Veterans had emerged from World War II eager to pursue the American Dream for which they had fought: a wife, children, a single-family house, and a car to get them there. The overwhelming majority of women abandoned the workplace to become full-time homemakers and mothers. A renewed emphasis on domesticity permeated society.

This relegation of male and female roles was reminiscent of the nineteenth century. Presidential candidate Adlai Stevenson wished the 1956 Smith College graduating class no better vocation than "the humble role of housewife." Periodicals like the *Ladies' Home Journal* reinforced the domestic ideology with editorial comments such as "Few men . . . ever amount to much as long as their wives work." The *Journal*, in an uncanny echo of the nineteenth century, exhorted women to cater to their husband's needs while performing the vital business of staying at home and raising a family. Advertisements, TV, and films characterized the suburban 1950s housewife as meticulously dressed, perfectly coiffed, placing dinner on the table when her husband arrived home from work.[118] Women's role as "a server of food and putter-on of pants and a bedmaker, somebody who can be called on when you want something" had not changed.[119] Bridal gowns of the decade followed the fashions of the times, featuring restrictive wasp waists, girdled hips, and full skirts supported by nineteenth-century-style hoop skirts (cat. 38). Woman was once again in her place.

The defining change for women in the second half of the twentieth century was the Women's Liberation movement when, during the 1960s and 1970s, women's perceived role was transformed. Reflecting a period of intense cultural change, fashion offered a wide variety of choices for brides, from elegant Empire-waisted gowns to mini dresses to the avant-garde (see cats. 43, 44, and 42).

THE MODERN BRIDE

When we examine the veneer of the contemporary middle- and upper-class bride in Western cultures, we see a different creature from those who preceded her. She is educated, employed, financially independent, and sexually active. She is entering into a loving partnership of her own volition. No payments or goods are being exchanged on her behalf. It is not obligatory for her to relinquish her career and become a full-time homemaker and mother. She is not expected to be meek, subservient, or merely ornamental.

On a deeper level, however, she is participating in a ritual that has not changed significantly for centuries. When she weds, a period of preparation occurs, the ceremony takes place at a specified time in a particular place, formalized words are spoken, and the audience gathered is unique to the event. The modern bride, like those before her, participates in the ritual of the wedding. On that day, she wears a special costume and she is the center of attention.

What the bride wears on this highly ritualized occasion, however, has been consistent only in its ability to continually change. There is a persistent perception that brides always wore white because it was the symbol of purity and virginity. These two attributes were of the utmost importance in the past because they insured purity of bloodline and uncontestable inheritance rights. British designer Vivienne Westwood's introduction of brightly colored and tartan plaid wedding gowns in the 1990s seemed revolutionary, almost sacrilegious at the time. In reality, it was nothing new. There have always been brides who wore non-white attire, whether by choice, for economy, or by tradition. From Brueghel's medieval peasant bride in black to Mary Waters's 1740 floral silk damask to Evelyn Wright's 1935 blue lace to Alexandra Posen's red poppy gown worn in 2004, bridal attire has been colorful through the ages (see fig. 6, and cats. 1, 33, 51, respectively). Even in the 1950s, when every bride seemed to wear white, *Bride's Magazine* promoted pastel gowns of ice blue, pale yellow, and shell pink, as it had periodically since the magazine's inception.[120]

Although it is tempting to disparage the majority of modern bridal gowns as too revealing, the low neckline of Angelina Faran's 1840 dress (see cat. 5) left little to the imagination, nor did the form-fitting gown worn by Ida Peltz Rost in the early 1880s (see cat. 16), or the slip of a dress worn by Catharine Harding in 1921 (see cat. 27). Even historical examples that at first glance appear perfectly modest utilize design elements that draw attention to erotic zones, such as the pleated bow that spans the bust of Blanche Richardson's 1894 gown (see cat. 22). The designer of Katherine Magrish's 1952 wedding dress used a technique common in the nineteenth century—covering the upper chest with sheer fabric.[121] Although Magrish's gown has a high neckline, the transparent netting used to create it suggests a much lower one (fig. 14; see cat. 38). Likewise, twenty-first-century brides do not have a monopoly on the avant-garde. The aesthetic dress worn by Minnie Crosby Emery in 1892 (see cat.

21) was as bold a choice in its time as the gown commissioned from designer Paco Rabanne in the late 1960s (see cat. 42).

Another commonality in wedding culture through history is the focus on the bride. Although the wedding is a rite of passage for both participants, until the second half of the twentieth century the transition for the woman, both physically and psychologically, was far more significant. Therefore, the bridal costume, in contrast to the groom's attire, customarily remains more elaborate and the physical preparation more intense. The ritual importance of the wedding garment could not be more evident than in the fifteenth-century bridal gown of Lena Alamanni, which was discussed and planned by the groom, members and friends of both families, the tailor, the dyer, and the embroiderers over an extended period of time. Although the gown was never completed, Lena would have worn it for the *ductio*, a public event during which the bride, followed by a family entourage, was led through the city on horseback. This presentation of the bride to the public wearing ornate clothing was of vital importance in displaying the Alamanni family wealth and maintaining their honor in their community.

Similarly, despite her significantly lower economic status, Brueghel's peasant bride parades to the church, surrounded by her family, friends, and neighbors, in the finest dress she can muster (see fig. 6). In 1895, Alva Vanderbilt created an unprecedented spectacle for her daughter's wedding, including a lavish gown designed by Jacques Doucet (see fig. 12), one of Paris's most celebrated couturiers. Thousands thronged the streets to catch a glimpse of the bride; even respectable society ladies clambered onto the church pews to be the first to see the bride enter. In *How to Buy Your Perfect Wedding Dress* the experts at Kleinfeld, an upscale bridal gown retailer in New York, urge brides to remember that "this is your opportunity to be the center of the universe."[122]

Figure 14
Kate Magrish with her mother in her wedding gown, June 1952. The dress appears to have a low neckline but the yoke of the bodice is constructed of sheer net, creating an appropriate sense of modesty.

Much has changed for a twenty-first-century woman, but the wedding day retains a ritualistic sense of transfer. It has become for all women, not just the affluent, a moment of presentation and display—a theatrical performance preceded by a rehearsal. For most women, it is a moment that has been fantasized about

Figure 15
George Benjamin Luks, American (1867–1933). *The Wedding Cake*, ca.
1910–1915. Oil on canvas, 30 x 25 in. (76.2 x 63.5 cm).
Gift of Walter P. Chrysler, Jr. © Chrysler Museum of Art, Norfolk, Va., 71.678

since girlhood. Playing with bride dolls, dressing up like a
princess, and watching female family members participate in the
ritual all contribute to the vision of oneself as a future bride (fig. 15).

In March 1959, the Barbie doll was introduced. Barbie's first
wedding gown retailed that same year—one of over thirty
created since that time. Of all the clothing sets produced for

Barbie, the wedding gown continues to be the best seller every
year. A more recent addition to the line is My Size Barbie—a
three-foot-tall doll wearing a wedding dress that fits girls sizes
four to ten.[123] Not only can a girl play with a bride doll to satisfy
the fantasy, she can become the bride. Western cultures socialize
women from an early age to anticipate participating in this
ritual, wearing the customary costume.

Part of bridal display is looking perfect on that day when a
woman presents herself in public. Women, in general, are
continually bombarded with images of perfection that they
feel compelled to measure up to, and this is intensified a
thousandfold for their wedding day. Once engaged, many brides
embark on a concentrated self-improvement course, spending
hours at the gym toning arms that will be bared in their strapless
gowns and trimming their waists to fit into a dress that was
purposefully purchased sizes too small. A 2008 survey by *Fitness*
magazine revealed that eighty percent of brides wanted to shed
weight before their wedding. In her article "Legs, Thighs, and
Butt: Workouts for Buff Brides," author Lexi Walters outlines
the "best moves" for the woman wearing a specific type of dress,
including sheath, trumpet, and mermaid styles.[124] In the film
Bride Wars, the saleswoman at the Vera Wang boutique states
emphatically that a Wang design will not be altered to fit the
bride. The bride must alter herself to fit the dress—a statement
reiterated in the film.

The Wedding Channel website contains an entire section on
health and fitness. Particular topics include "When Should You
Start a Bridal Beauty Routine?" and "My Pre-Wedding Workout
Secrets," the latter written by Jen Schefft of the reality television
series *The Bachelorette*.[125] Many bridal gowns are designed to
create the illusion of a perfectly proportioned body. Puffy sleeves
and full skirts make the waist seem smaller by comparison—as
did styles of the 1890s, for instance (see cat. 22). In 1941, the
Bride's Magazine offered their readers the "waist-diminishing

Figure 16

The Wedding © 1994 Sandy Skoglund. Sandy Skoglund, American, b. 1946. *The Wedding*, 1994. Silver dye bleach (Cibachrome).

© Columbus Museum of Art, Ohio: Museum Purchase, Howald Fund, 1994.003.

Both bride and groom are pictured in Sandy Skoglund's photograph, but the composition draws the eye to the bride. The groom, with his back to the viewer, is of lesser importance. Although the subject depicted is a modern bride, there is a sense of trepidation reminiscent of the nineteenth century as she steps carefully toward the groom in a room covered with jam.

princess line"—a style periodically popular in the nineteenth century (see cats. 7, 14). Similarly, the hours prior to a wedding ceremony are customarily spent having nails done and makeup applied. A bride's hair is often supplemented with extensions and styled in an elaborate coiffure that does not relate in any way to her everyday appearance. The bride is transformed physically and presents herself as "perfect."

Even for modern women, the wedding day takes on great power and significance. In the nineteenth century, the day represented a darker melodrama. It was considered a "dark leep" [sic] and "the important crisis" upon which her fate depended.[126] Today's bride enters into the union happily, willingly, and experienced, without the shadows of fear and trepidation. This is a glory moment. It is the single day when all attention will be focused on her. While the involvement of the groom in planning has grown decidedly in past years, most people will agree that the wedding remains all about the bride. As early as the turn of the twentieth century, it was recognized that the groom was "a mere detail," "an unimportant factor," a "black blotch" who served as a background for the bride (fig. 16).[127] One mid-nineteenth-century French author went so far as to say that the groom "is taken as an accessory, just in the same way as carriages are hired. Many [brides] would very likely prefer to be married without a husband—but that is not the custom."[128]

Nudged by tradition and goaded by the pervasive marketing of the bridal industry, many contemporary women are caught in a tug-of-war between reason and long-held fantasy. Even those who do not routinely participate in such traditionally feminine concerns as trendy clothing or beautifying activities often deviate from that stance when they become a bride. Since the establishment of the Association of Bridal Manufacturers during World War II, the white wedding dress has been elevated to an iconic and irresistible status. Its codified elements—the formal length, train, veil, and floral bouquet— tempt even the

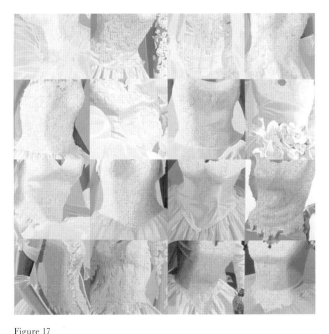

Figure 17
Julia Jacquette. *White on White (Sixteen Wedding Dresses) I*, 2001, oil on linen, 72 x 72 in. (182.9 x 182.9 cm).
From the collection of Lisa and Richard Perry. Photo by Bill Orcutt.
Julia Jacquette's painting illustrates sixteen different wedding dress bodices that, in reality, look much the same. The images call into question the concept of the bride-to-be finding what is perceived of as a unique gown that defines her as an individual.

most independent and nontraditional women. Slogans from *Bride's Magazine* in the 1950s and 1960s crooned, "After years of make-believe, your favorite fantasies grow up and come true" and "Bridal dresses so lovely they can turn your bridal dreams into sweet reality"—not so different from the advertisements in current issues of the many contemporary periodicals specific to brides-to-be. Again, the owners of Kleinfeld sum it all up when

Figure 18
Logan Shannon and Derek Janiak designed custom Converse shoes to wear with their formal wedding clothes. Photo by Erick Straghalis.

they suggest that shopping for this most important garment is a "personal journey into the land of the wedding gown." The dress "defines you as a bride" (fig. 17).[129]

In her book *I Do But I Don't*, author Kamy Wicoff recounts her struggle with the idea of wearing a wedding dress. She describes her first visit to a bridal boutique and trying on what she called "Super Size"—a full-skirted "poufy" model. "It wasn't

me at all [but] I wasn't supposed to be myself in that dress! All that talk about a woman finding a dress . . . that is distinctly 'her' obscures the fact that things like the dress are meant to obscure, to subsume the self into a larger entity, a shared cultural thing. The veil and the majestic dress had distilled my entire person . . . into a feminine ideal . . . that femininity is best expressed by passivity, appearances, and silence. . . . I had not been prepared for the power of the traditional, historical clothing to . . . set me into a continuum that connected me with brides, past and present." With the help of the saleslady, Wicoff saw herself as a presentation piece, "an offering," "a publicly understood expression of consent." Deciding it was too much of a "costume," Wicoff eventually rejected the dress but she discovered what authors Guy, Green, and Banim state in their book about women's relationships with their clothes. "Women shopping for a wedding dress are seeking an image that is distinctive from their 'non-bride' selves, but at the same time conforms to the dominant image of a bride."[130]

For the contemporary woman, the conflict arises from participating in an ancient ritual in which she is eclipsed by centuries of conventions—conventions that define what a woman should be, even though those ideas have changed. Many brides-to-be seek out a way to disengage from these cultural idioms, and are supported by numerous publications and websites that encourage them to individualize their weddings. Diane Meier Delaney's book *The New American Wedding: Ritual and Style in a Changing Culture*, discusses what she calls "no cookie-cutter options." She states that the new American wedding is "a state of being self-aware and self-determining." She points to bridal designers like Maggie Norris, who acknowledge a new kind of bride who refuses to slavishly adopt the traditional bride "costume."[131] Offbeatbride.com offers a host of nontraditional ideas and opportunities to communicate with other couples who are planning or have held unconventional weddings. Some modern brides individualize by choosing a black wedding gown

Figure 19
Ellen De Generes and Portia de Rossi at their wedding in August 2008.
Photo by JLC/Lara Porzak Photography.

or wearing flip-flops with a formal gown. Logan Shannon and her fiancé, Derek Janiak, who married in May 2010, designed matching custom Converse shoes for their ceremony (fig. 18). These novel gestures indicate a need on the part of modern brides to individuate from a custom that retains deferential connotations (see cats. 46, 48).

The "face" of the modern bride is changing in more ways than one. After California's Supreme Court upheld the right of same-sex couples to legally marry in 2008, the state's civil courts were swamped by gay and lesbian couples who wanted to be married. Although the decision was soon reversed by a voter referendum overturning the ruling, the 18,000 same-sex couples wed during that time remain legally married. One of the most famous couples was TV personality Ellen DeGeneres and actress Portia de Rossi, who celebrated their nuptials in ensembles created by American designer Zac Posen. DeGeneres wore a pants suit and de Rossi a halter dress with a pale pink tulle skirt (fig. 19). In many instances, both brides choose to wear long white gowns. This was the case in the first lesbian wedding seen on daytime television, in the soap opera *All My Children* in February 2009. Characters Bianca Montgomery and Reese Williams spoke tearful vows in pure white, classically styled gowns by designers Andrew Gn and Monique Lhuillier (see cat. 55). This was a groundbreaking episode, as the soap opera audience represents mainstream, middle America.[132]

What women have chosen to wear as they wed has always been indicative of their status in Western culture. In the fifteenth century, the bride was an object of display and barter. In the nineteenth century, she was a domestic necessity in containment. Today, she is an individual who struggles with antiquated concepts that continue to limit and confine her.

The democratization of the modern white wedding gown in the post-World War II years offered all women the opportunity to wear "the dress of their dreams," to be a queen, a princess, an angel. On one hand, this iconic piece of clothing grounds brides and contextualizes who they are on a grand scale within their culture. On the other hand, wearing a wedding gown, white or otherwise, is an opportunity for women to express their individual beliefs in changing the face of the institution of marriage and their role within it.

1. Manohla Dargis, "Two Weddings and a Furor," *New York Times*, January 9, 2009.

2. The current average cost of a wedding is reported in various studies such as "The Knot Unveils 2008 Real Wedding Survey Results" (2009), http://www.theknotinc.com/press-releases-home/2009-press-releases/2009-04-08-real-wedding-survey.aspx; also Kelly Nolan, "Wedding Bills," BER Business Times (2008), http://journalism.nyu.edu/pubzone/ber/2008/12/08/wedding-bills/. In England the average cost of a wedding ranges between £15,000 and £25,000, according to http://www.weddingsday.co.uk/average-wedding-cost/.

3. Arnold van Gennep, *The Rites of Passage* (Chicago: University of Chicago Press, 1960), 189.

4. Ibid., 3, 10–11, 191.

5. Catherine M. Bell, *Ritual Theory, Ritual Practice* (Oxford: Oxford University Press, 1992), 221–22.

6. Ibid., 204–22.

7. Georges Duby, *Love and Marriage in the Middle Ages*, trans. Jane Dunnett (Chicago: University of Chicago Press, 1994), 3–5.

8. Van Gennep, The Rites of Passage, 116–17.

9. E. O. James, *Marriage and Society* (London: Hutchinson's University Library, 1952), 58, 114; Olwen H. Hufton, *The Prospect Before Her: A History of Women in Western Europe, 1500–1800* (New York: Alfred A. Knopf, 1996), 262.

10. Duby, *Love and Marriage*, 3–5; Christiane Klapisch-Zuber, ed., *Silences of the Middle Ages*, vol. 2, *A History of Women in the West*, ed. Georges Duby and Michelle Perrot, trans. Arthur Goldhammer (Cambridge, MA: Belknap Press of Harvard University Press, 1992), 161–62.

11. Genesis 2:18–19.

12. Genesis 2:24.

13. Kenneth Stevenson, *Nuptial Blessing: A Study of Christian Marriage Rites* (New York: Oxford University Press, 1983), 26–27.

14. Genesis 34:12; Deuteronomy 24:1–4. For a full discussion of biblical relationships within marriage see Marilyn Yalom, *A History of the Wife* (New York: HarperCollins, 2002), 1–16.

15. For instance, Isaiah 61:10, Isaiah 49:18, 2 Isaiah 61:10, and Jeremiah 2:32 mention jewels or ornaments; Song of Solomon 4:1–3 mentions a veil.

16. Genesis 29:22 and Judges 14:10 mention banquets.

17. Yalom, *History of the Wife*, 12–23; Frances Gies and Joseph Gies, *Marriage and Family in the Middle Ages* (New York: Harper & Row, 1987), 21. The brideprice is money paid by a suitor to the father of the bride to compensate him for surrendering his authority over the bride. A dowry is money or property paid to the groom by the bride's family, sometimes consisting of her inheritance. This money was often meant to support the marriage, and the size of the dowry was a serious consideration for a suitor. The prevailing custom of the payment of a brideprice versus a dowry during a specific period implies a shift in the marriage market from a demand for brides to a demand for husbands. A dower was a portion of the groom's estate set aside to provide for the bride in widowhood, which might also have been negotiated at the time of betrothal.

18. Gies and Gies, *Marriage and Family*, 23; Yalom, *History of the Wife*, 21–23. Yalom discusses the Greek marital relationship on pp. 16–25.

19. Gies and Gies, *Marriage and Family*, 23.

20. Yalom, *History of the Wife*, 28–29.

21. Ibid.; Gies and Gies, *Marriage and Family*, 21.

22. Judith Lynn Sebesta and Larissa Bontante, eds., *The World of Roman Costume* (Madison: University of Wisconsin Press, 1994), 48, 54–57; Maria Wyke, ed., *Gender and the Body in the Ancient Mediterranean* (Oxford: Blackwell Publishers, 1998), 110–11. The term *tunica recta* refers to the bride's tunic or garment being woven on an upright loom. *Flammeum*, from flame, *flamma* in Latin, suggests

the yellow-red color was a reference to the flame of the hearth, which would be tended by the bride in her new home.

23. Genesis 24:64–67; Stevenson, *Nuptial Blessing*, 31.

24. Christopher Brooke, *The Medieval Idea of Marriage* (Oxford: Oxford University Press, 1989), 39; Gies and Gies, *Marriage and Family*, 29–30. In AD 313 the Edict of Milan established religious toleration for Christianity in the Roman Empire and Christianity was widespread by the beginning of the fifth century. Suzanne Fonay Wemple, "Women from the Fifth to the Tenth Century," in Klapisch-Zuber, *Silences of the Middle Ages* (see note 10), 173–74.

25. Gies and Gies, *Marriage and Family*, 54–55. Under some legal codes, even if the woman consented and recompense was made, the couple might be required to pay stiff fines, be exiled, or even sentenced to death.

26. Wemple, "Women from the Fifth to the Tenth Century," 176–77. Trousseau originates from the Old French *trousse*, a bundle or package, and refers to the clothes and household items collected by a bride in preparation for her marriage. Gies and Gies, *Marriage and Family*, 33–34.

27. Claude Thomasset, "The Nature of Women," in Klapisch-Zuber, *Silences of the Middle Ages* (see note 10), 43–44.

28. Thomasset, "The Nature of Women," 43–69; *Isidore of Seville: The Medical Writings* (Philadelphia: American Philosophical Society, 1964), 48–50; Plato and R. D. Archer-Hind, *The Timaeus of Plato* (London: Macmillan, 1888), 341.

29. Gies and Gies, *Marriage and Family*, 39, 83, 96–98.

30. Yalom, *History of the Wife*, 46; Gies and Gies, *Marriage and Family*, 39. The sacramental nature of marriage was generally accepted from the eighth century onward, but only became canon law at the Council of Trent in 1563. Brooke, *Medieval Idea of Marriage*, 56; Emilie Amt, ed., *Women's Lives in Medieval Europe: A Sourcebook* (New York: Routledge, Chapman, and Hall, 1993), 83–89. "The Liturgy for the Marriage Service" transcribed by Amt is very similar to the liturgy used today. Stevenson, *Nuptial Blessing*, 28; Edwin Hall, *The Arnolfini Betrothal: Medieval Marriage and the Enigma of Van Eyck's Double Portrait* (Berkeley: University of California Press, 1994), 24, 43. "At the church door," in Latin, *facie ecclesiae*, is translated literally as "in the face of the church," meaning before the community. John R. Gillis, *For Better, For Worse: British Marriages, 1600 to the Present* (New York: Oxford University Press, 1985), 18.

31. Hall, *The Arnolfini Betrothal*, 24–31; Gies and Gies, *Marriage and Family*, 243–45; Henry Swinburne, *A Treatise of Spousals or Matrimonial Contracts* (London: S. Roycroft for Robert Clavell, 1686), 55–153, 193–202. Christopher Lasch, *Women and the Common Life: Love, Marriage, and Feminism* (New York: W. W. Norton, 1997); Chapter 3 discusses the suppression of clandestine marriages in England.

32. Amt, *Women's Lives*, 74–75. Sumptuary laws were a method of regulating consumption of luxury goods. In the late Middle Ages the nobility used these laws to limit the conspicuous luxuries, such as extravagant clothing, of the prosperous bourgeoisie.

33. Hall, *The Arnolfini Betrothal*, 55–56. Early eastern Christian sources describe crowning the bridal couple at the wedding ceremony, first with plant garlands and later with crowns of precious metals. Crowning symbolized the couple's personal victory over sexuality and lust, assuming they were both virgins upon marriage. Early Church fathers, particularly Tertullian (ca. AD 160–220), criticized crowning as a pagan practice. See Paul F. Bradshaw, "Weddings," in *Encyclopedia of Early Christianity*, ed. Everett Ferguson, 2nd ed. (New York: Garland Publishing, 1997), vol. 2, 1776–77.

34. Carole Collier Frick, *Dressing Renaissance Florence: Families, Fortunes, and Fine Clothing* (Baltimore: Johns Hopkins University Press, 2002), 115–27. The gown described for the marriage of Lena Alamanni was never completed, as the embroiderer, Giovanni Gilberti, died and his firm closed. The garment was not recovered by the family until after the wedding.

35. Lawrence Stone, *The Family, Sex and Marriage in England, 1500–1800* (New York: Harper & Row, 1977), 123–35; Gies and Gies, *Marriage and Family*, 295–96.

36. Robert Crofts, *The Lover: or, Nuptiall Love* (London: B. Alsop and T. F[awcet] for Rich: Meighen, 1638), sec. XI, n.p.

37. Daniel Rogers, *Matrimoniall honovr* (London: Th. Harper for Philip Nevel, 1642), 200.

38. William Gouge, *Of domesticall duties eight treatises* (London: John Haviland for William Bladen, 1622), 197; Robert Cleaver, *A Godly Forme of Houshold Gouernment* (London: Eliot's Court Press for the assignes of Thomas Man, 1630), STC/1542:14, n.p.; Stone, *Family, Sex and Marriage*, 136–37; Gillis, *For Better, For Worse*, 14, cautions that this new idea was not widely accepted; Gillis, 82.

39. See Henrietta Haynes, *Henrietta Maria* (New York: G. P. Putnam's Sons, 1912) regarding the marriage of Charles I and Henrietta Maria.

40. Yalom, *History of the Wife*, 110–11; Gouge, *Of domesticall duties*, 271.

41. Hufton, *The Prospect Before Her*, 62–69; Claudia Opitz, "Life in the Late Middle Ages," in Klapisch-Zuber, *Silences of the Middle Ages* (see note 10), 273–74; Brooke, *Medieval Idea of Marriage*, 144–48; Stone, *Family, Sex and Marriage*, 182–87.

42. Hufton, *The Prospect Before Her*, 69–101.

43. Stone, *Family, Sex and Marriage*, 181; Rosemary O'Day, *The Family and Family Relationships, 1500–1900: England, France and the United States of America* (London: Macmillan Press, 1994), 153–54. The frustration regarding women's inability to choose a spouse was expressed by an English and an American woman, writing a century apart. In 1700 Mary Astell wrote: "A woman indeed can't properly be said to choose, all that is allowed her, is to refuse or accept what is offer'd." *Some Reflections Upon Marriage* (London: Printed for John Nutt, 1700), 23. Eliza Southgate's complaint is strikingly similar: "I declare that the inequality of privilege between the sexes is very sensibly felt by us females, and in no instance is it greater than in the liberty of choosing a partner in marriage; true, we have the liberty of refusing those we don't like, but not of selecting those we do." Eliza Southgate Bowne, *A Girl's Life Eighty Years Ago: Selections from the Letters of Eliza Southgate Bowne*, ed. Clarence Cook (New York: Charles Scribner's Sons, 1887), 38. Similarly, in *The Operative's Friend, and Defence: or, Hints to Young Ladies, Who Are Dependent on Their Own Exertions* (Boston: Charles H. Peirce, 1850), the Rev. James Porter wrote that the male sex has, by common consent, been given the exclusive right of making proposals, but he encourages women to be cautious and not allow financial gain or the fear of becoming a spinster to result in a poor spousal choice, pp. 150–65. In *Birth, Marriage, and Death: Ritual, Religion, and the Life-Cycle in Tudor and Stuart England* (Oxford: Oxford University Press, 1997), David Cressy describes intimacy in courtship between Leonard Wheatcroft and Elizabeth Hawley ca. 1655–67, p. 234. Yalom, *History of the Wife*, 112. Hufton, in *The Prospect Before Her*, pp. 126–27, refers to women who are away from families and therefore more independent.

44. Ralph Thoresby, *The Diary of Ralph Thoresby*, ed. Joseph Hunter (London: Henry Coburn and Richard Bentley, 1830), vol. 1, 176–79.

45. Alice Wandesford Thornton, *The Autobiography of Mrs. Alice Thornton of East Newton, Co. York* (Durham, Eng.: Andrews and Co., 1875), viii; Lori Anne Ferrell, "An Imperfect Diary of a Life: The 1662 Diary of Samuel Woodforde," *Yale University Library Gazette* 63 (1989): 137–44. For additional firsthand accounts of courtships and the resulting marriages see Cressy, *Birth, Marriage, and Death*, 237–54 and Stone, *Family, Sex and Marriage*, 180–92; O'Day, *Family and Family Relationships*, also describes a number of individual circumstances of matches made by parental coercion and individual choice.

46. Hufton, *The Prospect Before Her*, 65–66. Mary P. Ryan discusses the same concerns in the nineteenth century in *Cradle of the Middle Class: The Family in Oneida County, New York, 1790–1865* (Cambridge: Cambridge University Press, 1981), 180.

47. Phillis Emily Cunnington and Catherine Lucas, *Costume for Birth, Marriages & Deaths* (London: Adam & Charles Black, 1972), 92.

48. Thomas Deloney, *The Pleasant History of John Winchcomb* (London: E. Crowch for Thomas Passenger, 1672), n.p. A kirtle is a tunic-like garment worn in the Middle Ages over a chemise or a smock and under the formal outer garment.

49. Cunnington and Lucas, *Costume*, 92–93. A caul was a fashionable headdress of net lined in silk and attached to a band, which covered the pinned-up hair. The custom of brides wearing their hair down seems to have lasted until the mid-seventeenth century.

50. Ibid., 75–76.

51. The philosophers of the Age of Enlightenment did not represent a single school of thought and their philosophy was less a set of ideas than a set of values. At its core was a critical questioning of traditional institutions, customs, and morals. Stone, *Family, Sex and Marriage*, 232–34, 258–67;

Stephanie Coontz, *Marriage, A History: From Obedience to Intimacy, or How Love Conquered Marriage* (New York: Viking Penguin, 2005), 145–46; Gillis, *For Better, For Worse*, 110–12.

52. James F. Traer, *Marriage and the Family in Eighteenth-Century France* (Ithaca, NY: Cornell University Press, 1980), 49, 74–75; Stone, *Family, Sex and Marriage*, 240–41; Coontz, *Marriage, A History*, 146–49.

53. Michèle Crampe-Casnabet, "A Sampling of Eighteenth-Century Philosophy," in *Renaissance and Enlightenment Paradoxes*, ed. Natalie Zemon Davis and Arlette Farge, vol. 3, *A History of Women in the West*, ed. Georges Duby and Michelle Perrot, trans. Arthur Goldhammer (Cambridge, MA: Belknap Press of Harvard University Press, 1993), 315–347, 360–61.

54. The Manufacture Royale de Beauvais was the weaving workshop that served the French monarchy and accepted commissions from the aristocracy. This tapestry is one of a set of four in the collection of the Cincinnati Art Museum that depict the de Sauvigny family.

55. Spitalfields was a rural district on the eastern outskirts of London that became a silk manufacturing center at the end of the seventeenth century. It flourished through the eighteenth century, producing the most luxurious silk fabrics of the period. Its decline began in the early nineteenth century due to laissez-faire economic policies, the failure of the weavers to adopt new industrial methods, changes in fashion, and cheaper production in nearby areas.

56. Mary Beth Norton, *Liberty's Daughters: The Revolutionary Experience of American Women, 1750–1800* (Ithaca, NY: Cornell University Press, 1996), 155–60, 171–77; Yalom, *History of the Wife*, 158–61; Coontz, *Marriage, A History*, 151.

57. Arlette Farge's essay "Protesters Plain to See," in *Renaissance and Enlightenment Paradoxes* (see note 53), 489–505, discusses the role of women in popular uprisings in France, Germany, Holland, and England. Dominique Godineau, "Daughters of Liberty and Revolutionary Citizens," in *Emerging Feminism from Revolution to World War*, ed. Geneviève Fraisse and Michelle Perrot, vol. 4, *A History of Women in the West*, ed. Georges Duby and Michelle Perrot, trans. Arthur Goldhammer (Cambridge, MA: Belknap Press of

Harvard University Press, 1993), 16–17, 24.

58. Elisabeth G. Sledziewski, "The French Revolution as the Turning Point," in Fraisse and Perrot, *Emerging Feminism from Revolution to World War* (see note 57), 36–37.

59. Godineau, "Daughters of Liberty," 28–34; Yalom, *History of the Wife*, 147; Nancy F. Cott, *The Bonds of Womanhood: "Woman's Sphere" in New England, 1780–1835* (London: Yale University Press, 1977), 82.

60. Sledziewski, "French Revolution," 34–40. Chaumette quoted on p. 39.

61. Cott, *Bonds of Womanhood*, 3.

62. American founding father Thomas Paine (1737–1809) was among many in the era of the American Revolution who wrote about marriage choices and roles. Many of these essays centered on how to achieve balance between husband and wife and defined marital companionship.

63. Quoted in Nancy F. Cott, *Public Vows: A History of Marriage and the Nation* (Cambridge, MA: Harvard University Press, 2000), 17.

64. Ibid., 17–21.

65. Nancy F. Cott, *No Small Courage: A History of Women in the United States* (Oxford: Oxford University Press, 2000), 151–54, 195–96; Cott, *Public Vows*, 21; Cott, *Bonds of Womanhood*, 101–23. See also Jan Lewis, "Motherhood and the Construction of the Male Citizen in the United States, 1750–1850," in *Constructions of the Self*, ed. George Lewis Levine (New Brunswick, NJ: Rutgers University Press, 1992), 143–63. See Norton, *Liberty's Daughters*, 256–94, for an extensive discussion of the raising of educational standards for women.

66. Greek statuary was originally painted in vibrant colors, the remnants of which had virtually disappeared. Fashions of this period falsely mimicked the unearthed colorless sculptures.

67. Barbara Welter, "The Cult of True Womanhood: 1820–1860," *American Quarterly* 18 (1966): 151–74; Linda K. Kerber, "Separate Spheres, Female Worlds, Woman's Place: The Rhetoric of Women's History," *Journal of American*

History 75 (1988): 9–39; Leonore Davidoff and Catherine Hall, *Family Fortunes: Men and Women of the English Middle Class, 1780–1850* (Chicago: University of Chicago Press, 1987), 114–15; Cott, *No Small Courage*, 180; Cott, *Bonds of Womanhood*, 64; Walter E. Houghton, *The Victorian Frame of Mind, 1830–1870* (New Haven, CT: Yale University Press, 1957), 347. Coventry Patmore's *The Angel in the House* (London: John W. Parker and Son, 1868) is a lengthy series of poems that glorifies woman, placing her on the pedestal that negated educational, political, or professional opportunities in the nineteenth century.

68. In France, divorce was not legal from 1816 to 1884. Erna Olafson Hellerstein, Leslie Parker Hume, and Karen M. Offen, eds., *Victorian Women: A Documentary Account of Women's Lives in Nineteenth-Century England, France, and the United States* (Stanford, CA: Stanford University Press, 1981), 120, 161–62; Cott, *No Small Courage*, 180, 261; Nancy F. Cott, *A Heritage of Her Own: Toward a New Social History of American Women* (New York: Simon and Schuster, 1979), 243, 251. Hellerstein, Hume, and Offen, *Victorian Women*, 161–62, reproduces the French civil codes that outline the respective rights and duties of a wife and husband. W. Peter Ward, *Courtship, Love, and Marriage in Nineteenth-Century English Canada* (Montreal: McGill-Queen's University Press, 1990), 38–39; Sir William Blackstone, *Commentaries on the Laws of England*, vol. 1, *Of the Rights of Persons* (1765; facs. ed., Chicago: University of Chicago Press, 1979), 430.

69. Cott, *Bonds of Womanhood*, 76–77; Ellen K. Rothman, *Hands and Hearts: A History of Courtship in America* (New York: Basic Books, 1984), 102–08.

70. Cott, *Bonds of Womanhood*, 76; Cott, *No Small Courage*, 180; Hellerstein, Hume, and Offen, *Victorian Women*, 93.

71. Published in Philadelphia, *Godey's Lady's Book* was an American periodical founded by Louis Godey in 1830. In print until 1887, it gained popularity in the 1840s after Sarah Josepha Hale became the editor in 1841. The *Ladies' Monthly Magazine* was published in England first under the title the *World of Fashion and Continental Feuilletons* (1824–51). It continued from 1852 to 1879 as the *Ladies' Monthly Magazine and World of Fashion* and from 1880 to 1891 as *Monde Élegant or the World of Fashion Monthly*. Jenni Calder, *Women and Marriage in Victorian Fiction* (New York: Oxford University Press, 1976), 125; see also Michael Denning, *Mechanic Accents: Dime Novels and Working-Class Culture in America* (London: Verso, 1987) for a complete discussion of romance stories in dime novels and as serials in periodicals. In the November 10, 1877 issue of *Harper's Weekly*, a serial story titled "The Open Verdict" by Miss M. E. Braddon relates the wedding of an older wealthy manufacturer to a young woman below his station. In this case, it was not only the bride, Bella, but her entire family that would rise in social class by this marriage that her parents "had striven so hard to bring to pass." The story serves the moral purpose of exposing the evils of marrying for money.

72. Cott, *No Small Courage*, 181; Ward, *Courtship, Love, and Marriage*, 107; Rothman, *Hands and Hearts*, 70–73, 156; Blanche Butler Ames, *Chronicles from the Nineteenth Century: Family Letters of Blanche Butler and Adelbert Ames* (Clinton, MA: Colonial Press, 1957), xiii.

73. Rothman, *Hands and Hearts*, 197; Hellerstein, Hume, and Offen, *Victorian Women*, 144–47.

74. Joan Perkin, *Women and Marriage in Nineteenth-Century England* (Chicago: Lyceum Books, 1989), 127; Rothman, *Hands and Hearts*, 155–56, 146–47; Ward, *Courtship, Love, and Marriage*, 158; Cott, *Bonds of Womanhood*, 80.

75. Davidoff and Hall, *Family Fortunes*, 325; Charlotte Perkins Stetson [Charlotte Perkins Gilman], *Women and Economics: A Study of the Economic Relation Between Men and Women as a Factor in Social Evolution* (Boston: Small, Maynard & Company, 1898), 71; Alexis de Tocqueville, *Democracy in America* (New York: Alfred A. Knopf, 1945), 201–02. In *Love and Power in the Nineteenth Century: The Marriage of Violet Blair*, author Virginia Jeans Laas relates the marriage of Violet Blair and Albert Janin. Married in 1874, Blair remained unusually independent (Fayetteville: University of Arkansas Press, 1998).

76. For a full discussion of this topic see Shirley Foster, *Victorian Women's Fiction: Marriage, Freedom, and the Individual* (Towata, NJ: Barnes & Noble Books, 1986); William Makepeace Thackeray, *Vanity Fair: A Novel without a Hero* (New York: Random House, 1999), 90; Calder, *Women and Marriage*, 17, 49.

77. Foster, *Victorian Women's Fiction*, 5; Hellerstein, Hume, and Offen, *Victorian Women*, 122–23, 163; Cott, *Bonds of Womanhood*, 64–74; Rothman, *Hands and Hearts*, 199; Yvonne Knibiehler, "Bodies and Hearts," in Fraisse and Perrot, *Emerging Feminism from Revolution to World War* (see note 57), 364; Davidoff and Hall, *Family Fortunes*, 327–28.

78. The silk for Queen Victoria's dress was woven at Spitalfields and was creamy, not optical, white, which would have been typical for the period. Kay Staniland and Santina M. Levy, "Queen Victoria's Wedding Dress and Lace," *Costume: The Journal of the Costume Society* 17 (1983): 1–7.

79. Elizabeth Langland, *Nobody's Angels: Middle-Class Women and Domestic Ideology in Victorian Culture* (Ithaca, NY: Cornell University Press, 1995), 63. In Chapter 3, Langland discusses at length the paradox of Victoria—a female monarch in a culture strongly demarcated along gender lines.

80. According to several sources, including her own diaries, it is clear that Victoria and Prince Albert were in love. For instance, see Cecil Woodham-Smith, *Queen Victoria: From Her Birth to the Death of the Prince Consort* (New York: Alfred A. Knopf, 1972) and Gill Gillian, *We Two: Victoria and Albert: Rulers, Partners, Rivals* (New York: Ballantine Books, 2009). Walter Bagehot is quoted in Dorothy Thompson, *Queen Victoria: The Woman, the Monarchy, and the People* (New York: Pantheon Books, 1990), 62–65, 139. Bagehot (1826–77) was a British businessman, essayist, and journalist who wrote extensively about literature, government, and economic affairs.

81. *Godey's Lady's Book*, August 1849, 156. Italics are the author's.

82. Wanamaker's was the first department store in Philadelphia. John Wanamaker (1838–1922) established his first venture, a menswear store, in 1861. In 1876, he opened Wanamaker's Grand Depot in time for the American Centennial Exposition of 1876. Alexander Turney (A. T.) Stewart (1803–76) opened the Marble Palace in New York City in the mid-nineteenth century. In 1862, he built an even larger establishment in New York, a six-story building called the Iron Palace, which employed up to two thousand people. Le Bon Marché, translated as "the good deal," was a Paris department store sometimes considered the first in the world. It was originally founded as a small shop in 1838 but had become a fixed-price department store as of 1850. London-based Harrods was founded by Charles Henry Harrod (1799–1855), a wholesale grocer whose business expanded to include dry goods and had become a large concern by 1880. In 1898, Harrods debuted the first escalator. See William Leach, *Land of Desire: Merchants, Power, and the Rise of a New American Culture* (New York: Pantheon Books, 1993) for a complete discussion of the rise of consumer culture and the department store in the United States. Tim Dale, *Harrods: A Palace in Knightsbridge* (London: Harrods Publishing, 1995) relates the history of Harrods department store.

83. Émile Zola, *The Ladies' Paradise* (Los Angeles: University of California Press, 1992), 69.

84. Stone, *Family, Sex and Marriage*, 408–09; Anne Bissonnette, "The 1870s Transformation of the *Robe de Chambre*," in Cynthia Amnéus, *A Separate Sphere: Dressmakers in Cincinnati's Golden Age, 1877–1922* (Lubbock: Texas Tech University Press, 2003), 170; John F. Kasson, *Rudeness and Civility: Manners in Nineteenth-Century Urban America* (New York: Hill and Wang, 1990), 43–45. This subject is also discussed in Langland, *Nobody's Angels*, Chapter 2.

85. Langland, *Nobody's Angels*, 47–46; Karen Halttunen, *Confidence Men and Painted Women: A Study of Middle-Class Culture in America, 1830–1870* (London: Yale University Press, 1982), 64. See S. A. Frost, *The Art of Dressing Well: A Complete Guide to Economy, Style, and Propriety of Costume* (New York: Dick & Fitzgerald, Publishers, 1870) as an example of exact descriptions of correct dress for every possible occasion.

86. For comments on simplicity or conservatism in bridal dress, particularly in France, see, for instance, *The Habits of Good Society: A Handbook for Ladies and Gentlemen* (New York: Carleton, Publisher, 1864), 424; Frost, *The Art of Dressing Well*, 65; Cecil B. Hartley, *The Gentlemen's Book of Etiquette and Manual of Politeness: Being a Complete Guide for a Gentleman's Conduct in All His Relations Towards Society* (Boston: J. S. Locke & Company, 1874), 289, and *Decorum: A Practical Treatise on Etiquette and Dress of the Best American Society* (New York: Union Publishing House, 1880), 193. Moiré, often called watered silk, is a heavier fabric with a watery appearance usually created by a finishing technique called calendaring. *Godey's Lady's Book*, August 1849, 156; *Peterson's Magazine*, July 1875, 76; *Harper's Bazar*, December 3, 1887, 831.

87. Poplin was a blend of cotton or wool with silk and therefore less expensive. *Harper's Bazar*, December 12, 1868, 93.

88. *Godey's Lady's Book*, February 1870, 476, 205; *National Era* 5, November 27, 1851, 192.

89. Mollie Dorsey Sanford, *Mollie: The Journal of Mollie Dorsey Sanford in Nebraska and Colorado Territories 1857–1866* (Lincoln: University of Nebraska Press, 1959), 109–13; Dorsey mentions her "wedding garments," but provides no description of the dress, its construction, or acquisition. She married in her

family's kitchen: "Start not! ye fairy brides. Beneath your veils and orange blossoms, in some home where wealth and fashion congregate, your vows are no truer, your heart no happier, than was this maiden's, in the kitchen of a log cabin," 112. Barbara Penner describes a typical nineteenth-century wedding in "'A Vision of Love and Luxury': The Commercialization of Nineteenth-Century American Weddings," *Winterthur Portfolio* 39 (2004): 1.

90. Sanford, *The Journal*, 113.

91. Penner, "A Vision of Love and Luxury," 5–6. See also the serial fiction story "An Open Verdict" in the November 10, 1877 issue of *Harper's Weekly*, which describes the purchasing of services from the local confectioner "to supply everything, from the tables and decorations down to the salt-spoons." Marrying below his station, the groom wished to impress his acquaintances and had no interest in the small, homemade wedding that the bride preferred. The orange blossom so prodigiously employed in bridal attire is a symbol of fertility, because only the orange tree blooms and bears fruit simultaneously. L. H. Sigourney, *Whisper to a Bride* (Hartford, CT: H. S. Parsons & Co., 1850), 10.

92. Penner, "A Vision of Love and Luxury," 6, 15. Ada M. Davis's journal is in the collection of the Cincinnati Art Museum.

93. The value of Bartlett's trousseau in 2010 currency would equal approximately $717,000. Penner, "A Vision of Love and Luxury," 12, 14. Tiffany & Co.'s jewelry was illustrated in "The Diamond Wedding," *Frank Leslie's Illustrated Newspaper*, October 22, 1859, 331; also in *Harper's Bazar*, April 18, 1863, 241–42; and June 5, 1880, 335.

94. Marian Fowler, *In a Gilded Cage: From Heiress to Duchess* (New York: St. Martin's Press, 1993), xiii. The *Chicago Daily Tribune* issue on November 25, 1900, lists American heiresses married to date. For additional information on American heiresses' marriages into the British aristocracy see also Maureen E. Montgomery, *Gilded Prostitution: Status, Money, and Transatlantic Marriages, 1870–1914* (London: Routledge, 1989); and "*She Is Now a Duchess*," *New York Times*, November 7, 1895.

95. "Trousseau for a Bride," *New York Times*, October 27, 1895. *The Pictorial Review*, April 1900, 1: 8, 14 states that brides of social prominence were concerned about being besieged by reporters regarding wedding preparations. *Harper's Bazar*, November 11, 1895, 908. Consuelo Vanderbilt's gown was designed by Parisian couturier Jacques Doucet but made by American dressmaker Mrs. Donovan.

96. "*She Is Now a Duchess*," *New York Times*, November 7, 1895; "A Duke's Bride," *Toronto Daily Mail and Empire*, November 7, 1895. The front-page coverage continues well onto the second page, and includes tongue-in-cheek first-person reportage signed "Kit," followed by the Associated Press account.

97. "Cupid: Richardson-Loveland," *Cincinnati Enquirer*, June 7, 1894; *Illustrated Business Directory and Picturesque Cincinnati* (Cincinnati: Spencer and Craig Printing Works, 1894), 394.

98. "Random Notes," *Cincinnati Enquirer*, May 27, 1906; "Random Notes," *Cincinnati Enquirer*, January 9, 1910; "Social Affairs," *Cincinnati Enquirer*, January 13, 1910.

99. *Harper's Bazar*, May 1914, 79; *Vogue*, April 15, 1914, 90. See Katherine Jellison's essay in this publication regarding the bridal industry in the post-World War II era.

100. Cott, *No Small Courage*, 369; U.S. Bureau of the Census, Dr. Leon E. Truesdell, *Sixteenth Census of the United States: 1940, Characteristics of Persons Not in the Labor Force 14 Years Old and Over* (Washington, DC: U.S. Government Printing Office, 1943), 4.

101. Cott, *No Small Courage*, 379, 425–30.

102. Cott, *A Heritage of Her Own*, 528–30. The British marriage bar applied chiefly to professional women and was based on the assumption that marriage and motherhood were incompatible with a career. Marriage bars were not formally eliminated until the end of World War II. See Jane E. Lewis, *Women in England 1870–1960: Sexual Divisions and Social Change* (Brighton, England: Wheatsheaf Books, 1984), 77, 102–03; Cott, *Public Vows*, 167.

103. Lewis, *Women in England*, 78–79.

104. *Vogue*, April 1, 1922, 53, 59–61, 120.

105. Vicki Jo Howard, "American Weddings: Gender, Consumption, and the Business of Brides" (PhD diss., University of Texas at Austin, 2000), 86–87. *So You're Going to be Married* became the *Bride's Magazine* in 1936 and *Bride's* in the early 1970s. *So You're Going to Be Married*, Autumn 1935, 70 and Autumn 1940, 111; *Ladies' Home Journal*, June 1929, 124.

106. *So You're Going to be Married*, Autumn 1935, 25. Duplon's Satin Ultra was rayon—first introduced in 1890 as "artificial silk"—and was adopted during the Depression era for bridal wear because it was less expensive than silk. Rayon was made from cellulosic fibers chemically treated to produce the hand and sheen of silk. Nylon is a manmade fiber that is exceptionally strong, abrasion-resistant, lustrous and easy-care. *Bride's Magazine*, Winter 1936/37, 3. It was not unusual during this era for working-class brides, who could not afford even synthetic white gowns, to wear a best day dress or suit.

107. *Bride's Magazine* covers of Autumn 1936, Winter 1936/37, Spring 1937, Summer 1937, Autumn 1937, and Summer 1938 featured Brissaud illustrations. *Bride's Magazine*, Spring 1940, 3.

108. Yalom, *History of the Wife*, 336–38; Cott, *No Small Courage*, 487–88; Katherine Jellison, *It's Our Day: America's Love Affair with the White Wedding, 1945–2005* (Lawrence: University Press of Kansas, 2008), 67. Betty Grable, one of the most popular pin-up girls, became even more popular after she married and had a child, reinforcing her image as everyone's sweetheart, future wife, and mother.

109. *Bride's Magazine*, Autumn 1943, 98; Spring 1942, 42; Autumn 1943, 2; Summer 1942, 51.

110. *Bride's Magazine*, Summer 1942, 33; Autumn 1943, 2.

111. *Bride's Magazine*, Autumn 1943, 59. The Historic Costume and Textiles Collection at the Ohio State University has in its collection a 1947 wedding gown made from a parachute brought home by the groom.

112. *Bride's Magazine*, Autumn 1935, 35 (tiara/diadem); Autumn 1936, 47 (coronet); Summer 1937, 52 (tiara). "Diadem" was also used to describe bridal headdresses in *Vogue*, April 1922, 52–53.

113. *Bride's Magazine*, Autumn 1936, 3.

114. Ibid., Spring 1937, 54.

115. Ibid., Summer 1937, 58.

116. Ibid., Early Fall 1950, 26; Spring 1951, 81; Spring 1957, 103.

117. Ibid., Spring 1955, 116.

118. Cott, *No Small Courage*, 497; Lois White Eck, "I Thought My Life Was Over," *Ladies' Home Journal*, April 1945, 137. TV shows like *The Adventures of Ozzie and Harriet* (1952), *Father Knows Best* (1954), and *Leave it to Beaver* (1957) exemplified the "perfect" post-World War II family. Cott, *Public Vows*, 187–88.

119. Betty Friedan, *The Feminine Mystique* (New York: W. W. Norton, 1997), 21.

120. It may have been understood by readers that the offerings of pale blue, yellow, and pink gowns for brides were targeted at older brides, divorcées, or widows, but there is no suggestion of this in the descriptions.

121. Through the mid-nineteenth century, a sheer cotton or linen chemisette would have given the appearance of a blouse worn under a gown with a low neckline, thereby making it more modest.

122. Frick, *Dressing Renaissance Florence*, 1–2, 115–16; Ronald Rothstein and Mara Urshel, *How to Buy Your Perfect Wedding Dress* (New York: Fireside, 2001), 119.

123. Kitturah B. Westenhouser, *The Story of Barbie* (Paducah, KY: Collector Books, 1999), 39. Kim Osborne posted an article on March 3, 2009, titled "Barbie doll generates discussion on body image" in the online newsletter, *The Brown and White*, of Lehigh University, stating that the clothing for *My Size Barbie* was unreasonably small for girls aged four to ten.

124. Lexi Walters, "The Buff Bride's Handbook: Get in Shape for your Wedding Day," *FitnessMagazine.com*, April 2009, http://www.fitnessmagazine.com/weight-loss/plans/get-in-shape-for-your-wedding-day/; and "Legs, Thighs, and Butt: Workouts for Buff Brides," *FitnessMagazine.com*, April

2009, http://www.fitnessmagazine.com/weight-loss/plans/legs-thighs-butt-workouts-for-buff-brides/.

125. *Bride's Magazine*, Autumn 1941, 61; Jen Schefft, "My Pre-Wedding Workout Secrets," *WeddingChannel.com*, http://weddings.weddingchannel.com/wedding-planning-ideas/jen-schefft-bridal-blog/articles/jen-schefft-wedding-workout-secrets.aspx?MsdVisit=1.

126. Quoted in Norton, *Liberty's Daughters*, 42.

127. *Pictorial Review*, April 1900, 14; *Ladies' Home Journal*, June 1891, 25.

128. *Home Journal 1846*, June 10, 1854, 2.

129. *Bride's Magazine*, Summer 1960, 111; Summer 1953, 63; Rothstein and Urshel, *Perfect Wedding Dress*, 7, 36.

130. Kamy Wicoff, *I Do But I Don't: Walking Down the Aisle without Losing Your Mind*, (Cambridge, MA: Da Capo Press, 2006), 141–44; Ali Guy, Eileen Green, and Maura Banim, eds., *Through the Wardrobe: Women's Relationships with Their Clothes* (Oxford: Berg, 2001), 10.

131. Diane Meier Delaney, *The New American Wedding: Ritual and Style in a Changing Culture* (New York: Viking Studio, 2005), 8, 78–80.

132. Marilyn J. Matelski, *Soap Operas Worldwide: Cultural and Serial Realities* (Jefferson, NC: McFarland & Company, 1999), 1.

BRIDES ON A BUDGET: 1880–1910

SARA LONG BUTLER

In 1906, *Town and Country* magazine chronicled the White House wedding of Alice Roosevelt, daughter of President Theodore Roosevelt, to Cincinnatian Nicholas Longworth.[1] The list of notable guests, the bride's gown, and the wedding itself were described in detail for eager readers.

Just a year later, Abigail Harris married John Shaw at her mother's home in the countryside near Hamilton, Ohio, twenty-five miles north of Cincinnati (fig. 20).[2] Abbie might well have read with interest accounts of the lavish society wedding while she was planning her own. Abbie, however, was a schoolteacher, and John a farmer.[3] A wedding on the scale of the Roosevelt wedding was out of the question, but perhaps it would be possible to adapt certain elements. As the *Ohio Farmer* magazine observed, "It is not strange that the country girl who reads the description of an elaborate city wedding, feels that she cannot plan a pretty, simple one, but she is greatly mistaken."[4] By the time Abigail Harris married John Shaw, rural Ohio brides could indeed emulate the weddings —and white wedding dresses—of their upper-class contemporaries. Advances in manufacturing, distribution, communication, and fashion had opened up new possibilities for brides of limited means.

WEDDING DRESSES ON A BUDGET IN THE LATE NINETEENTH CENTURY

Only twenty-five years before Abbie's wedding, in the 1880s, a new, white wedding dress would have been a less attainable goal for a young woman with few resources. A new silk dress was expensive and white was impractical. The fashionable style of the 1880s, with its tightly fitted bodice and complicated bustle skirt, required advanced dressmaking skills. Even though marriage was a seminal point in the lives of women of all social classes and the wedding dress marked the significance of the event, often frugality had to take precedence over the desire for the perfect dress. Fanny Field, writing in the *Ohio Farmer* in 1885, provided words of understanding for women of limited

Figure 21
Anna Mason and Charles Sohngen wedding, June 9, 1880.
Cincinnati Museum Center.

means: "I do want to speak a few words for the benefit of the women who cannot afford to spend much time or money on a dress—the ones who think themselves lucky if they get a new 'best dress' once in two or three years. . . . According to my way of thinking, a good cashmere [wool] of becoming color, prettily made, would be in better taste for a wedding dress than the cheap, over-trimmed silks that some folks indulge in."[5]

What were the wedding dress options for brides on a budget in the 1880s? Some women simply wore the best dress they already owned. A wedding, however, offered an opportunity to indulge in a new dress—one that would likely become a bride's best dress for the next several years. Women with the necessary skills made their own wedding dresses, often of colored fabric.[6] Paper patterns and fashion magazines provided some guidance, but constructing a wedding dress was a significant undertaking. Thurine Oleson, a Wisconsin farm bride, had apprenticed to the owner of a dress shop and learned sufficient dressmaking skills to sew her own wedding dress of brown wool sateen in 1886.[7] Maud Dinsmore in 1883 proudly described to *Washington Post* readers how she saved money by making her gray silk dress and bonnet. Along with her matching gloves, Maud spent only $12.73 on her wedding attire and $50 for the full trousseau.[8] Other women enlisted the help of family members. Mrs. H. C. Gates, the daughter of a farmer, drafted her aunt to make her 1883 wedding dress when her father refused to pay for a dressmaker. "It was up-to-date, blue, not much trimming and went to my ankles . . . it lasted a long time."[9]

Hamilton, Ohio resident Anna Mason chose the common combination of a colored wedding dress and a white veil when she married Charles Sohngen in 1880 (fig. 21).[10] Charles was just twenty-two years old at the time of their marriage and was yet to see the success he would achieve as an executive in the brewing industry.[11] Anna's father owned a boarding house and saloon and, since the bride's family was expected to pay for most of the wedding expenses, the cost of her dress was likely an important consideration. Although etiquette dictated that the veil not be worn again, Anna probably wore her wedding dress often after the wedding.

Mary Bieker was another Hamilton bride on a budget in the late nineteenth century. Mary, a domestic servant, married blacksmith William Kilfoyle in 1896 (fig. 22).[12] Mary's fashionable wedding dress seems incongruous with her working-class status, but even a working woman living in rural Hamilton had alternatives. If she were a skilled seamstress, Mary might have made her own dress. Or she could have saved her earnings to purchase fabric and employ the services of a dressmaker. Dressmakers were readily available in nineteenth-century Hamilton—ninety-three were listed in the Hamilton City Directory in 1892.[13] Hamilton dry goods stores carried a range of dress fabrics, with some offering made-to-order clothing as well. As early as the 1880s, Winter's Cheap Cash Store advertised made-to-order clothing in the "latest style and lowest prices" (fig. 23).[14]

In some cases, wealthy employers provided wedding dresses to their domestic servants. Writing to the *Ladies' Home Journal*, a woman described her servant's wedding preparations: "When she was ready to be married she told me that her money saved from the housekeeping allowance has purchased her wedding trousseau, also some bedding and table linen. I gladly supplemented this with a pretty wedding gown."[15]

As the nineteenth century drew to a close, fashion magazines directed toward women of moderate means increasingly suggested white wedding dresses of a less expensive fabric for the economical trousseau.[16] Ignoring the common practice of wearing a practical colored dress, in 1890 the *Ladies' Home Journal* declared, "From time immemorial, the bride's gown has been white; and if one could only have a simple muslin frock it seems it ought to be of that pure tone, because her own heart is thought to be as clean and white as is her gown."[17]

Working-class women desired to follow this advice as carefully as their more affluent sisters. Gertie, Elizabeth Pringle's servant, insisted her dress be of white lawn, prompting Elizabeth to write in her diary, "Fashion is as exacting with them as with the highest social layer, and not to comply with what is just the last touch of elegance for a bride would be terrible to Gertie."[18] The *Ladies'*

Figure 22
Mary Bieker and William Kilfoyle wedding, November 5, 1896.
Family photograph, by permission of Dick Scheid.

Home Journal frequently provided suggestions for low-cost white fabrics and trimmings, outlining in detail the costs associated with making a moderately priced wedding dress.[19] In 1900, *Ohio Farmer* suggested that "no prettier or more appropriate wedding dress can be selected for a youthful bride than a white one, and for people in moderate circumstances the less expensive goods, like mull, swiss, organdy, are pretty materials as can be desired."[20]

ECONOMICAL WEDDING DRESSES IN THE EARLY TWENTIETH CENTURY

By the beginning of the twentieth century, changes in the production and distribution of women's clothing presented new possibilities for cost-conscious brides. The ready-to-wear industry was growing at a rapid pace, fueled by the flood of immigrants who provided a willing workforce. As ready-to-wear grew, distribution channels in the form of department stores and catalogs expanded to enhance the flow of goods from manufacturer to consumer. When budget-minded brides around the country (like Hamiltonian Abigail Harris) read about the wedding gowns of wealthy debutantes, they could realistically imagine similar styles for themselves. As Abbie prepared for her wedding to John Shaw in 1907, a white dress of reasonable cost was feasible. Abbie selected a dress of "white polka net over white silk" in the high-necked, mono-bosom silhouette of the period.[21] The January 1906 issue of *Ladies' Home Journal* defined the "dotted and figured Swisses" as the fashion fabrics of the spring season, adding, "They will be first favorite for the graduating-gown as well as for the simple, dainty wedding-dress."[22]

Much like today's brides, Abbie may have begun her wedding preparations by consulting an etiquette book. Aimed at the middle and working classes, etiquette books provided detailed instructions on how to negotiate social life.[23] Weddings were especially public and meaningful rituals, and even women of modest means thought it important to observe the accepted post-Victorian rules of decorum. Most etiquette books included a chapter on weddings and wedding attire. Annie Randall White's book was typical of etiquette publications of the time: "The dress of the bride should be devised according to her means—but it is imperative that it is white, and may be muslin, silk or satin, according to her means or taste" (fig. 24).[24]

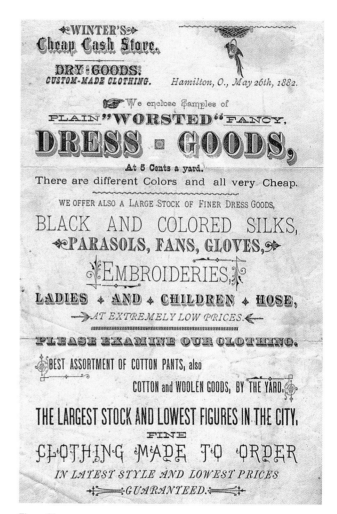

Figure 23
Advertisement for Winter's Cheap Cash Store, Hamilton, Ohio.
Butler County Historical Society.

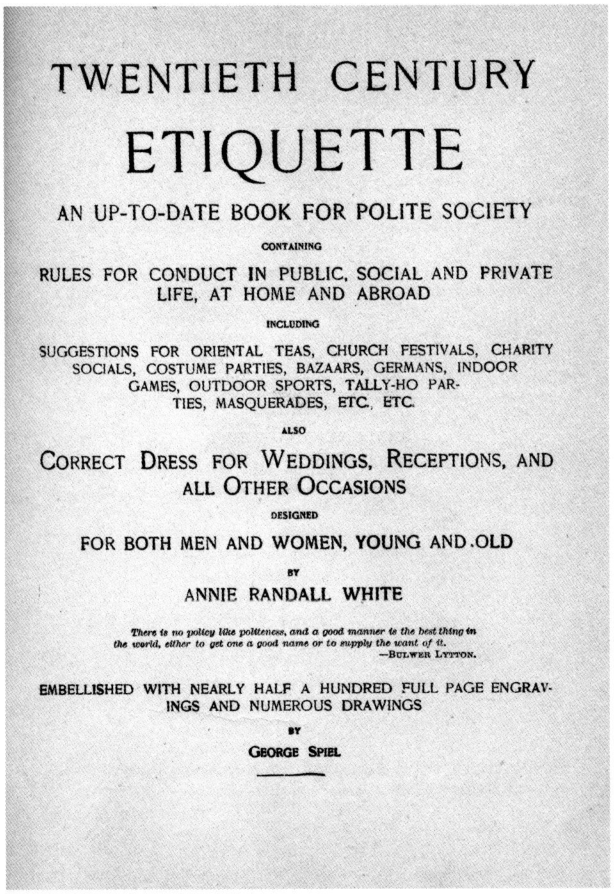

TWENTIETH CENTURY

ETIQUETTE

AN UP-TO-DATE BOOK FOR POLITE SOCIETY

CONTAINING

RULES FOR CONDUCT IN PUBLIC, SOCIAL AND PRIVATE LIFE, AT HOME AND ABROAD

INCLUDING

SUGGESTIONS FOR ORIENTAL TEAS, CHURCH FESTIVALS, CHARITY SOCIALS, COSTUME PARTIES, BAZAARS, GERMANS, INDOOR GAMES, OUTDOOR SPORTS, TALLY-HO PARTIES, MASQUERADES, ETC., ETC.

ALSO

CORRECT DRESS FOR WEDDINGS, RECEPTIONS, AND ALL OTHER OCCASIONS

DESIGNED

FOR BOTH MEN AND WOMEN, YOUNG AND OLD

BY

ANNIE RANDALL WHITE

There is no policy like politeness, and a good manner is the best thing in the world, either to get one a good name or to supply the want of it.
—BULWER LYTTON.

EMBELLISHED WITH NEARLY HALF A HUNDRED FULL PAGE ENGRAVINGS AND NUMEROUS DRAWINGS

BY

GEORGE SPIEL

Figure 24
Cover page of a typical etiquette book of the early twentieth century.
From the Walter Havighurst Special Collections, Miami University Libraries.

Like etiquette books, early-twentieth-century magazines provided advice about weddings. *Ohio Farmer* ran columns directed to the farm-wife-to-be, suggesting white wedding gowns and including recommendations for inexpensive fabrics.[25] One of the most useful national fashion magazines for women of moderate circumstances was the *Ladies' Home Journal*. Founded in the mid-1880s, the *Journal* expanded rapidly, boasting a circulation of over a million and half by 1912.[26] Subscription costs were reasonable, and single-issue copies were widely available for 15 cents at office buildings and stores. The *Journal* provided an abundance of advice on cost-effective ways of managing the home, including information on wedding planning. Brides-to-be wrote to the *Journal* for wedding suggestions, sometimes asking about economical wedding dresses: "Please suggest a suitable and inexpensive material for a gown for a June bride—something in white that she can use afterward."[27] The *Journal's* staff responded in the magazine with advice on acceptable fabrics and styles.

In 1905, *Journal* editors announced that they had received enough questions from brides-to-be to publish a special issue. "We Shall Make a Bridal Number, and the next Journal will be an out-and-out bridal issue. . . . The number will have a bridal cover, and by Howard Chandler Christy, too, showing the famous 'Christy Girl' as a bride. In fact, the whole number will have a bridal air" (fig. 25).[28]

The March bridal issue of the *Journal* included nineteen articles devoted to various aspects of a wedding, including advice for the woman on a budget.[29] Abbie Harris might well have read "The Details of a Home Wedding" and "Mrs. Ralston's Chat About an Economical Trousseau" as she prepared for her own wedding. Mrs. Ralston provided multiple suggestions for inexpensive white wedding fabrics, as well as colored fabrics appropriate for the traveling suits that also served as wedding attire. Running alongside Mrs. Ralston's column, an ad from

Figure 25
The first bridal issue of the *Ladies' Home Journal,* March 1905.
Miami University Libraries.

the National Cloak & Suit Company announced made-to-order shirtwaist suits. Although these were advertised as Easter costumes, a creative bride may have envisioned the white blouse with detailed trimmings and matching white skirt (the shirtwaist suit) as a wedding dress. The issue also included drawings of "Four Pretty Wedding Gowns" that were pictured with pattern numbers and ads for fabrics in an adjacent column. This first *Journal* bridal issue provided a wealth of information for etiquette-attentive, cost-conscious brides.

Armed with advice from etiquette books and the *Journal,* Abbie may have done what her nineteenth-century budget-conscious predecessor did—either make the dress herself or hire a dressmaker. In contrast to the complicated fashions of the 1880s, however, early-twentieth-century styles were simpler and less precisely fit. A woman with moderate sewing skills could make a presentable dress using the dependably sized paper patterns now widely available. The *Delineator,* originally a catalog for Butterick patterns, had evolved into a more general ladies' magazine, though it continued its focus on home sewing.[30] Articles included illustrations of dresses, some much like Abbie's, accompanied by pattern numbers and step-by-step instructions on how to use the pattern and construct the dress (fig. 26).[31] Wedding dresses were a regular *Delineator* feature. Holbrock Brothers in Hamilton carried Butterick patterns and a variety of dress fabrics, and Abbie would have been able to purchase both the fabric and the pattern close to home.[32]

Despite the relative simplicity of turn-of-the-century gowns, however, sewing the wedding dress and trousseau oneself was still an onerous task. The multitude of tucks, pleats, lace and decorative insertions fashionable at the time meant many a long hour over the sewing machine. In a *Youth's Companion* story of wedding preparations, an overwrought bride exclaims to her husband-to-be: "O Dick, it's no use! I can't marry you! It's—it's—oh, it's too much work!"[33] Shifting the burden to

A pretty afternoon frock of batiste

a dressmaker would probably have been tempting to Abbie. Although declining in number, more than seventy dressmakers were still listed in the 1906 Hamilton city directory, and Abbie could have purchased one of the many low-cost fabrics available at Holbrock's or Winter's and paid a dressmaker to do the work.[34]

The most noteworthy new option for the cost-conscious bride of the young century was a ready-made dress. Just a few months before the Harris-Shaw wedding, *Ladies' Home Journal* fashion and wedding columnist Mrs. Ralston touted the advantages of ready-to-wear: "Hoping that they may be of help to prospective brides I am going to give a few items and price-lists for very modest and practical trousseaux; all of the prices given for these garments apply to the 'ready-to-wear' clothes that are found in any of the large department stores." Mrs. Ralston's list included a wedding dress priced at $6.[35]

One of the most popular ready-to-wear dress styles of the early twentieth century was the so-called "lingerie" dress. The high-necked, long-sleeved lingerie dress was constructed of lightweight fabrics with dainty trimmings of lace, embroidery, and tucks, and was often white. Abbie may have seen a dress of this style as an appropriate, low-cost option. Unfortunately, underwear, outerwear, and suits appear to have been the only ready-made garments available to Hamilton women in the first decade of the twentieth century.[36] Cincinnati, however, was less than two hours away by train. Big-city department stores offered ready-to-wear merchandise in a range of prices. The bride on a budget could take advantage of wide selections, sales or seasonal clearances, and free alterations. Abbie might have taken a day for a shopping excursion, searching among the

Figure 26
Illustration of a dress accompanying an article titled "Dressmaking Made Easy," *Delineator*, July 1908. From the Collection of the Public Library of Cincinnati and Hamilton County.

ready-made lingerie dresses available at Rollman's, McAlpin's, or Kline's.[37] In May 1907, just a month before Abbie's wedding, Rollman's offered "dainty lingerie dresses" constructed of the same fabrics recommended by fashion magazines as inexpensive wedding dress material (fig. 27).[38]

If a day trip to Cincinnati were too much for Abbie, she could have found a ready-made lingerie dress in the Sears catalog. Sears began offering women's clothing at the end of the nineteenth century, and by 1907 the catalog presented a wide range of women's apparel. Abbie may have found the page of white lingerie dresses in her Sears catalog an appealing, low-cost solution for a wedding dress that could be worn later. A shirtwaist suit in the Spring/Fall catalog of 1907 was described as "appropriate for weddings and parties." Shirtwaist suits offered more wearing options as separates, a plus for the cost-conscious bride wanting to wear her wedding garments again. Two years after Abbie's wedding, a 1909 Sears catalog advertised a lingerie dress as a "beautiful one-piece party or wedding dress." Sears continued to promote lingerie dresses as wedding gowns throughout the teens, eventually including veils on models to make the lingerie dress option crystal-clear to brides searching for inexpensive solutions (fig. 28).[39]

MARY BATT'S ECONOMICAL TRAVELING SUIT WEDDING

Only four months after Abbie's wedding, Mary Batt married Henry Bergedick in Hamilton (fig. 29). Children of German immigrants, Mary and Henry were also among the working class of Hamilton after the turn of the century. In contrast to Abbie, Mary opted to wear the more practical tailored suit for her wedding. Etiquette books and magazines had recommended marrying in a traveling dress or suit even during the final decades of the nineteenth century if cost was a factor.[40] In 1902, Mrs. Ralston of the *Ladies' Home Journal* made clear that "there is no

Figure 27
Advertisement for Rollman & Sons department store, *Cincinnati Enquirer*, May 5, 1907. From the Collection of the Public Library of Cincinnati and Hamilton County.

question but that it is far wiser and more economical for the girl who has only $75 to spend on her trousseau to be married in a street or traveling gown—preferably a tailor suit in some dark

Figure 28
Advertisement for lingerie dresses, Sears catalog, 1913. As reprinted in JoAnne Olian, ed., *Everyday Fashions 1909–1920 as Pictured in Sears Catalogs*. New York: Dover Publications, Inc. 1995.

color—than in the conventional wedding gown of white. . . . All of the articles mentioned in the list which is given for this trousseau are presumably 'ready-made' clothes, which have reached a truly wonderful point of prettiness and cheapness combined."[41] Mrs. Ralston lists the wedding suit at $15. Suits or "tailor-mades" were among the early items of ready-to-wear available to women, and by 1907 they were widely available at department stores or through catalogs. Holbrock Brothers in Hamilton advertised tailored suits in a variety of prices (fig. 30).[42] Mary could have purchased her flowered hat, shirtwaist, and gloves at Holbrock's at the same time. Although the fit was not as precise as a dressmaker suit, a ready-made tailored suit—a garment that could see a great deal of wear following the wedding—offered a practical alternative.

ABIGAIL HARRIS'S 1907 WHITE WEDDING

By the early twentieth century the newest styles were no longer the privilege of the wealthy; the democratization of fashion had taken place for women across the country, including those in Hamilton, Ohio. Although

Figure 29
Mary Batt and Henry Bergedick wedding, October 22, 1907.
Frank R. Snyder Photography Collection.
Smith Library of Regional History, Lane Public Libraries.

the single-use, white wedding dress common today was yet to come, the new century offered new possibilities. Hamilton bride Abbie Harris had options for economical wedding attire that had not been available to Anna Mason and Mary Biecker a few short decades earlier. The most significant transformation was the increased availability of low-cost, ready-to-wear clothing. A notable shift had taken place in the way clothing was produced and distributed in the U.S. The mass production of women's apparel prompted the expansion of department stores and catalogs. By 1907, brides anywhere could easily purchase the popular white lingerie dress at big-city department stores and from catalogs at lower prices and with trims and details appropriate for a wedding dress. At the same time, ladies' magazines such as the *Delineator* and the *Ladies' Home Journal* provided more information targeted to the cost-conscious home sewer. Seamstresses continued to be readily available in big cities and small towns alike to provide sewing assistance to the bride choosing to make her own dress or alter a ready-made dress. Dressmakers, too, continued to create fashionable dresses at a considerable savings over custom-made gowns. The options available to Abigail Harris in 1907 serve as examples of the choices open to women of modest means in small towns across America.

It is difficult to determine which of these alternatives Abbie used, but it is clear that she wore a fashionable white wedding gown when she married John Shaw at her mother's farm home. Like the Roosevelt wedding, the Harris-Shaw nuptials were described in the press—in this case the *Hamilton Telegraph*. "The bride, who is a decided brunette, wore a wedding gown of white polka net over white silk, and carried a shower boquet [sic] of bride's roses." The maid of honor wore a "stunning gown of white organdie with real lace trimmings" while the groom and his attendant wore "conventional black." A "sumptuous two course supper" followed the ceremony. After a wedding trip to Cincinnati and Lexington, the newlyweds settled down at Pleasant View Farm outside Hamilton.[43] Although schoolteacher Abigail Harris could never have fully duplicated the elaborate affairs of the upper class, the social and technological advances of the time allowed Abbie and women of similar circumstances to plan weddings that, in a modest way, reflected the lavish society weddings they read about in *Town and Country*.

Figure 30
Advertisement for Holbrock Bros. store, *Hamilton Telegraph*, April 11, 1907. Smith Library of Regional History, Lane Public Libraries.

1. "A Wedding of World-Wide Interest: The Marriage of Miss Alice Roosevelt and Mr. Nicholas Longworth," *Town and Country*, February 24, 1906, 23.

2. *Hamilton Telegraph*, June 13, 1907. Hamilton was the county seat and a center for manufacturing in 1909, yet was still predominantly rural. Hamilton was located twenty-five miles north of Cincinnati on the Cincinnati, Hamilton, and Dayton railroad line. *Greater Hamilton: A Review of Its Manufacturing, Merchantile [sic] Commercial Industries and Enterprises*, 1909.

3. U.S. Census Bureau, Twelfth Census of the United States, 1900, Milford Township, Butler County, Ohio.

4. May Ellis Nichols, "A Pretty Home Wedding," *Ohio Farmer*, September 20, 1900, 208.

5. Fanny Field, "Hints About Dress," *Ohio Farmer*, November 14, 1885, 318. During the nineteenth and early twentieth century, cashmere was defined as "a closely woven, soft, fine and light dress fabric made with single cotton or wool warp and fine botany wool weft in a 2-1 filling-faced twill." Phyllis G. Totora and Robert C. Merkel, *Fairchild's Dictionary of Textiles* (New York: Fairchild Publications, 2000), 97–98.

6. Barbara Penner, "A Vision of Love and Luxury": The Commercialization of Nineteenth-Century American Weddings," *Winterthur Portfolio* 39 (Spring 2004): 1–20. Penner writes that brides of various religions, the less affluent, and those from rural areas married in colored gowns in the nineteenth century.

7. Erna Oleson Xan, ed., *Wisconsin, My Home* (Madison: University of Wisconsin Press, 1950), 155.

8. "Dress and Dollars: Extravagance and Economy in Female Attire," *Washington Post*, April 22, 1883. Dinsmore explains that the standard expectation for trousseau cost was $200. As the third daughter of a large family of girls, $50 was all that could be budgeted for her. Her trousseau included not only wedding attire, but the underclothing, bonnets, dresses, wrappers, and incidentals needed for the first two years of marriage.

9. Mrs. H. C. Gates, of Hastings, NE, interview by Frederick W. Kaul and Louis Rollins, October 1938, in *American Life Histories: Manuscripts from the Federal Writers' Project, 1936–1940*, http://memory.loc.gov.

10. Marriage record, Charles E. Sohngen and Anna G. Mason, Lane Public Library; Smith Library of Regional History, Lane Public Libraries.

11. *Memorial Record of Butler County, Ohio* (Chicago: Record Publishing Company, 1894).

12. Dick Schied, personal communication to the author, August 8, 2007.

13. *Hamilton City Directory* (Cincinnati: Williams & Co., 1892–93).

14. "Winter's Cheap Cash Store advertisement," Business File Drawer, Retail and Dry Goods File, Butler County Historical Society.

15. Frances A. Kellor, "The Housewife and Her Helper," *Ladies' Home Journal*, April 1907, 42; Harriet S. Blaine Beale, ed., *Letters of Mrs. James G. Blaine* (New York: Duffield & Co., 1908), vol. 1, 309. In a letter written in 1882, Blaine suggested that she would have given her servant, Fagie, her wedding dress herself, but thought she should give her something less perishable. Blaine was the daughter and wife of prominent national politicians and was writing from her home in Washington, DC in 1882. Fagie had presented two samples of dress fabric, one red and one black, to her employer, but Blaine considered the fabrics too cheap to be worth the cost of "making up."

16. Isabel A. Mallon, "Belongings of a Bride," *Ladies' Home Journal*, June 1891, 9; "Answers to Correspondents," *Harper's Bazar,* July 8, 1893, 555; Emma M. Hooper, "The Complete Bridal Outfit," *Ladies' Home Journal*, April 1895, 18.

17. *Ladies' Home Journal*, November 1890, 24.

18. Cornelius O. Cathey, ed., *A Woman Rice Planter* (Cambridge, MA: Macmillan & Co., 1922), 253.

19. Mallon, "Belongings of a Bride," 9; "Answers to Correspondents," 555; Hooper, "The Complete Bridal Outfit," 18; "Fashionable Dress Fabrics," *Ladies' Home Journal*, November 1891, 24; Emma M. Hooper, "Making a Moderate Wedding Outfit," *Ladies' Home Journal,* March 1898, 20 and "Wedding and Traveling Outfits," *Ladies' Home Journal*, May 1893, 20.

20. "Home and Fireside: For Country Weddings," *Ohio Farmer*, April 26, 1900, 377.

21. "Shaw-Harris," *Hamilton Telegraph,* June 13, 1907.

22. Emily La Farge Claxton, "New White Materials for Spring," *Ladies' Home Journal,* January 1906, 62.

23. Kenneth Cmiel, "Refined Dining in the Nineteenth Century," in *The Ladies' Etiquette Handbook: The Importance of Being Refined in the 1880s*, ed. David E. Schoonover (Iowa City: University of Iowa Press, 2001), viii–ix; John F. Kasson, *Rudeness and Civility: Manners in Nineteenth-Century Urban America* (New York: Hill and Wang, 1990), 54, 57. Cmiel indicates that while rules of etiquette originated with the urban upper classes, etiquette books were available to rural Americans of modest circumstances. Kasson agrees that

etiquette advisors spoke to the upper levels of the working class. He suggests that many etiquette books "stressed that one could observe the forms of gentility on an extremely modest budget."

24. Annie Randall White, *Twentieth Century Etiquette: A Ready Manual for All Occasions* (1900). Nineteenth- and early-twentieth-century etiquette books often provided advice in absolute terms, leaving little decision-making to the reader. By the early twentieth century a white dress was proper etiquette, hence White's declaration that it was "imperative" that the wedding dress be white.

25. See, for example, "Home and Fireside: For Country Weddings," *Ohio Farmer,* April 26, 1900, 377.

26. Mary Ellen Zuckerman, *A History of Popular Women's Magazines in the United States, 1792–1995* (Westport, CT: Greenwood Press, 1998), 29.

27. *Ladies' Home Journal,* May 1903, 56.

28. *Ladies' Home Journal,* February 1905, 1.

29. *Ladies' Home Journal,* March 1905.

30. Zuckerman, *Popular Women's Magazines,* 29. Zuckerman indicates that Butterick tissue paper patterns were sized as early as 1867, and became available in stores by 1869. The *Delineator* continued to publish patterns and sketches of clothing at the end of the nineteenth century, but included general-interest articles as well.

31. Eleanor Chalmers, "Dressmaking Made Easy," *Delineator,* July 1908, 70–73, 148–49.

32. Holbrock Bros. advertisement, *Hamilton Telegraph,* April 11, 1907.

33. "Too Much Work!" *Youth's Companion,* July 28, 1904, 357.

34. *Hamilton Directory* (Cincinnati: Williams & Co., 1906). As ready-made dresses became available, and simpler styles meant more women could make their own dresses, the demand for dressmakers decreased. See Cynthia Amnéus, *A Separate Sphere: Dressmakers in Cincinnati's Golden Age, 1877–1922* (Lubbock: Texas Tech University Press, 2003).

35. Mrs. Ralston, "The Journal's Department of Clothes: A Talk About Spring Styles," *Ladies' Home Journal,* April 1907, 89. Public school teachers such as Abigail Harris made about $431 a year in 1907. Scott Derks, *The Value of a Dollar: Prices and Incomes in the U.S. 1860–2009,* 4th ed. (Amenia, NY: Grey House Publishing, 2009). Estimates of clothing expenditures indicate approximately thirteen percent of income (or $56 in Abigail Harris's case) was spent annually on clothing in 1907–08. Scott Nearing, *Financing the Wage-Earner's Family* (New York: B. W. Huebsch, 1913), 51. Families usually assumed the cost of the wedding dress and trousseau, however, which may have been the case with Harris's dress. To get a sense of wedding dress costs from another perspective, a $6 dress in 1907 would have cost about $142 in 2008, as calculated at http://measuringworth.com/.

36. A review of the *Hamilton Telegraph* and advertising flyers and cards in 1906 and 1907 indicated no advertising for ready-made women's dresses.

37. In the spring of 1907 the *Cincinnati Enquirer* ran advertisements for ready-to-wear lingerie dresses. Rollman's, McAlpin's, and Kline's were major department stores in downtown Cincinnati. In addition to the Rollman's ad, McAlpin's listed "New Silk Dresses" and "New White Princess Dresses" in

a March 11 advertisement. In an April 25 illustrated advertisement, Kline's promoted "Silk Jumper Suits" at a special clearance price of $9.95.

38. Advertisement for Rollman & Sons Co., *Cincinnati Enquirer,* May 5, 1907.

39. Sears offered fabrics and trimming suitable for wedding dresses as early as 1897, but it appears that the first reference to ready-made dresses described as wedding dresses appeared in the Spring/Fall catalog of 1907 (p. 1355). By Fall 1911, Sears advertised lingerie-type dresses specifically as wedding dresses (p. 167) and by 1913 included an illustration of a model in a lingerie dress with a veil (p. 25). Philadelphia: Sears, Roebuck and Company.

40. "Fashion Department: Fashion Notes," *Arthur's Home Magazine,* November 1884, 663. A tailor-made is described as a favorite for a "quiet" wedding, a tactful way of defining an economical wedding. Mallon in "Belongings of a Bride" emphasizes a perfect fit for a traveling dress and in the June 1892 issue of the *Journal* also suggests suits (which she says are now called "going-away gowns"). In response to a reader's query, the *Ladies' Home Journal* describes a "pretty walking suit" as the best choice for a quiet wedding, November 1890, 32.

41. Mrs. Ralston, "Moderate Trousseaus for Spring Brides," *Ladies' Home Journal,* March 1902, 46.

42. Advertisement for Holbrock Bros., *Hamilton Telegraph,* April 11, 1907.

43. "Shaw-Harris," *Hamilton Telegraph.*

THE COMMERCIALIZATION OF WEDDINGS IN THE TWENTIETH CENTURY

KATHERINE JELLISON

Grace Larew was the archetypal postwar bride. Walking down the aisle of an Iowa City church only a few days after the bombings of Hiroshima and Nagasaki, the nineteen-year-old University of Iowa student represented her generation's middle-class ideal: Clad in a white gown and veil purchased at a local department store, she was about to marry her childhood sweetheart and become a helpmate on his family farm. As her mother Vera watched Grace make her way down the aisle on that late summer day in 1945, she remembered her own wedding twenty years earlier, when she had worn a homemade dress to marry in the minister's parlor. Now, Vera Larew and her husband were able to provide their only daughter with stylish attire and a church setting for what they hoped would be "the outstanding wedding of the year." Only ongoing rationing restrictions dictated that some aspects of the celebration be on a small scale or of the do-it-yourself variety. A local caterer served cake and coffee at a modest reception on the church premises, the bridesmaids wore homemade dresses, and friends and relatives donated the wedding flowers from their gardens. Nevertheless, the 250-guest wedding cost the Larew family $1,000—"a lot of money then."[1]

In 1983, when Grace's daughter Joan Young married in an Iowa City church ceremony, she too represented the middle-class bridal ideal—of the next generation. The 32-year-old bank vice president married a fellow banker in a celebration featuring a designer gown, a dinner-dance for 220 people at a private club, and a honeymoon in Cancun. Nearly a decade and a half older than her mother had been when she became a bride, Joan

Figure 31
Typical of the times, the 1930 wedding of Ella Bischoff and A. W. Winkelmann featured both purchased and home-produced items. The bride's family purchased the white gown and floral arrangements, but her mother and sister prepared the wedding banquet themselves and served it in their home.
Collection of the author.

Figure 32
Shown here at their 1938 wedding, Cecile Dunckley and Harvey Sigle were typical of many Depression-era couples in their lack of bridal finery. Collection of the author.

was already established in a well-paying career. Social mores and gender-role prescriptions had changed dramatically in the four decades since her mother's nuptials, but Joan's festivities demonstrated that the American wedding basically remained the same. It was still a celebration highlighted by the best costumes and party that money could buy.[2]

Both Grace Larew and her daughter Joan Young embraced with equal enthusiasm a ritual that was unavailable to Grace's mother Vera. When Vera married in the 1920s, and certainly during the Great Depression of the 1930s, most weddings were a small-scale patchwork of home-produced goods and a few purchased items (figs. 31, 32, 33). Weddings that featured an elaborate multi-tiered cake, abundant hothouse flowers, and a white gown had been fashionable for several decades, but only the nation's wealthiest brides could afford all the accoutrements of a so-called "white wedding." When Vera's daughter Grace married in 1945, businesses that provided non-elite brides with all the goods and services of a formal wedding were just beginning to emerge, and Grace took advantage of the few products they offered. But by the time Grace's daughter Joan married in the 1980s, a nationwide network of jewelers, printers, clothiers, florists, photographers, videographers, caterers, bakers, hoteliers, restaurateurs, musicians, limousine drivers, and travel agents had appeared to serve the nation's brides. For brides of Joan Young's generation, a catered banquet, professional musicians, and travel to a distant honeymoon resort had become standard components of the American wedding. And as expectations increased, so did the price tag. In the years leading up to World War II, the

Figure 33
In contrast, by the time they posed for this 1962 snapshot, Cecile and Harvey could afford a fashionable wedding gown for their daughter Peggy, as well as stylish bridesmaid dresses for her sisters Jody and Linda.
Collection of the author.

average cost of a formal wedding, including engagement and honeymoon, represented about one-third of the annual mean American family income; by 1967, it was half the average family income; and by the 1990s, it was a little less than two-thirds.[3]

A variety of factors prompted the emergence of the elaborate, capital-intensive wedding as the new American norm, but the most significant was the democratization of the formal wedding gown. Only a few years before Grace Larew married, a handful

of enterprising individuals in the Northeast and Midwest established firms to design and manufacture wedding dresses on a large scale, using new, inexpensive synthetic fabrics. These innovators based their enterprises on smaller-scale operations already in existence in the Italian neighborhoods of several U.S. cities, where immigrant seamstresses custom-made bridal gowns piece by piece, with one woman making the sleeves, another the bodice, a third the skirt, and the trio then assembling the dress. Moving this process into a factory setting allowed several copies of a gown to be produced quickly and shipped out to retail establishments, where shoppers could try on their favorite designs. Once a customer determined which sample gown she liked the best, store personnel measured her and ordered a custom-fitted gown. This ingenious method of producing and marketing luxurious wedding dresses for the masses resulted in the establishment of a national bridal wear business that would become the centerpiece of a postwar wedding industry.[4]

To promote their interests, members of the fledgling bridal wear business created a professional organization, the Association of Bridal Manufacturers, to wage a successful campaign equating middle-class marriage and gender roles with the formal white wedding. Claiming that World War II was being fought to protect hallowed American institutions, like marriage, the Association persuaded Congress and the War Production Board—in the interest of national morale—to exempt the bridal industry from restrictions on the use of scarce silks, satins, and synthetics. After all, they argued, "American boys are going off to war and what are they fighting for except the privilege of getting married in a traditional way? They're fighting for

Figure 34
When this twenty-two-year-old World War II veteran married his twenty-year-old bride, they did so in high white wedding style—even though he had grown up on a small Kansas farm and she was the daughter of small-town school teachers. Collection of the author.

our way of life, and this is part of our way of life . . ."[5] By the specious invocation of tradition to justify their exemption from wartime restrictions, the Association in reality promoted a new cultural norm. The Association's wartime argument served two of the chief purposes of an invented tradition: It established the legitimacy of a particular institution, and it socialized the public in the values and conventions of that institution. According to the Association's argument, bridal clothing was so meaningful,

Figure 35
Posing in front of the backyard barbecue, bride, groom, and parents
demonstrate family togetherness at a 1960 wedding reception.
Collection of the author.

during the war and flourish after the war. War-era advertising promised better times to come by heavily relying on the image of the formal wedding and the idealization of marriage and family that it represented. Product tie-ins helped publicize wedding industry goods at a time when rationing restrictions, rushed wartime ceremonies, and the belief that lavish celebrations in wartime were unpatriotic still prevented most Americans from having white weddings. For example, the extensive Woodbury soap campaign featured well-to-do real-life brides ("Woodbury Debs") wearing full white wedding regalia, cutting into huge wedding cakes, carrying ornate bouquets, and posing with their exquisitely dressed bridesmaids. These sumptuously attired brides clearly symbolized marriage. And happy marriages would be the foundation of a prosperous and secure postwar society free from the worries of depression and armed conflict and ready for the full realization of the American dream.[7]

so integral to cultural values that its manufacturers should be exempt from the rules that applied to other members of the garment industry. Without a factory-produced bridal gown, a "real" wedding simply could not take place, and the Association made a commitment to place the "formal wedding . . . within the reach of every Bride."[6]

Given concern that wartime conditions imperiled American domesticity, the white wedding gown seemed to preserve the traditions of marriage and family life so that they could survive

The young wedding industry's wartime advertising whetted Middle Americans' appetite for the white wedding, while the strong postwar economy and the era's emerging domestic ideal provided consumers with the financial resources and the ideological rationale to satisfy their hunger. Returning from war to establish households in a revived economy, young Americans in 1946 wed at an extraordinary pace: 16.4 marriages per every 1,000 persons, or 2.2 million couples, more than double the number of any prewar year. For the next decade and a half—as national income increased by sixty percent, and the number of Americans with discretionary income doubled—Americans continued to marry at a high rate and at a young age. Women's median age at first marriage, which was 21.5 years in 1940,

"Dream Wedding" for Miss America 1960

And a dream wedding it must be, since a Miss America may not marry before her year's reign is over. But in her dreams she wears this blush pink gown of Ban-Lon bridal lace, its scalloped and scooped neckline embroidered in seed pearls, its bell skirt caught up with taffeta roses. Edyth Vincent for Alfred Angelo. about $175. Crown, Angelo. • Dresses, both pages, at Macy's, N. Y., Roosevelt Field, White Plains; Carson Pirie Scott, Chicago; Horne's, Pittsburgh and stores on page 177.

fell to only 20.3 years by 1950. For men, median age dropped even more—from 24.3 to 22.7. In the fifteen years following Pearl Harbor, the percentage of men who married in their early twenties doubled, as did the fertility rate for women in their early twenties. The postwar baby boom was underway. And with Social Security easing fears of poverty in old age and veterans' mortgages facilitating home ownership, for the first time many Americans could afford the extras that improved a young family's social status. In the first five years following World War II, when consumer spending in general increased sixty percent, the money spent on household furnishings and appliances rose 240 percent (fig. 34).[8]

Postwar abundance and the increased emphasis on consumption gave new strength to the old myth that America was a classless society. In a society where white-collar workers were indeed beginning to outnumber blue-collar workers and a middle-class identity was becoming the national norm, seemingly everyone could now aspire to and eventually become members of the middle class. Heeding the messages of consumer culture became a full-time commitment. The middle class purchased consumer items to demonstrate their success, and those making the transition from the working class to the middle class announced their arrival through appropriate purchases. Automobiles, single-family dwellings, and formal weddings were particularly popular signifiers of middle-class status and stability. Consumers in the immediate postwar era used these purchases not only to advertise their families' class status but to enhance their families' emotional well-being. At a time when psychologists, educators, social workers, clergy members, and the press promoted the notion of family "togetherness," family members exhibited their solidarity by gathering around the

Figure 36
Miss America 1960 models a bridal gown of synthetic Ban-Lon lace.
Hagley Museum and Library, Wilmington, Delaware.

television set or backyard barbecue pit, piling into the station wagon for a family vacation, or standing next to one another smiling in the receiving line at an elegant wedding reception (fig. 35). New housing developments, shopping centers, car dealerships, and vacation resorts sold themselves by reflecting the ideals of the financially and emotionally stable middle class.[9]

The wedding industry made its products particularly alluring by emphasizing these ideals. Recognizing the child-centered nature of the middle-class family, the industry sold its wares by stressing that good parents owed their daughters the splendor of a formal wedding. It also emphasized middle-class notions of romantic marriage by promoting the exchange of objects, such as rings, that symbolized fidelity and affection. Most significantly, the industry played on middle-class concerns about proper appearances. By hosting just one event—a white wedding—a family could project an image of respectability, material success, and domestic happiness that would live eternally in photographs. While certain regional, ethnic, religious, and individual family variations in wedding celebrations existed, most professionally orchestrated weddings now hewed closer to a generic script that reflected the traditional values of the white, native-born, urban/suburban middle class.[10]

Among the middle-class standards that the postwar wedding both reflected and promoted were Middle America's gender-role prescriptions: the adult male as household provider and the adult female as household consumer. The formal wedding provided a training ground for young women in their upcoming consumer role. Capitalizing on the dramatic increase in the nation's marriage rate and family-oriented spending, department stores around the country began establishing bridal service sections. In March 1949, Philadelphia's Strawbridge and Clothier opened its bridal shop, staffed by consultants whose main task was to provide the bride with her wedding gown and clothe the other female wedding players. But the store's management also encouraged the bridal shop staff to engage in "interselling." Bridal consultants accompanied prospective brides to the store's other departments, encouraging each young woman to buy items not only for the wedding day, but also for the honeymoon trousseau and her new home. In the home furnishings department, the interior decorator advised the bride on color schemes, and an expert in the engraved stationery department counseled her on the appropriate wording of her invitations and announcements. By the mid-1950s, the store's management estimated that if sales personnel did their jobs correctly, a single bride and her entourage would spend $3,300—$25,915 in current dollars—at Strawbridge and Clothier.[11]

As the example of Strawbridge and Clothier indicates, postwar retailers enthusiastically joined bridal wear manufacturers to idealize the white wedding. And distinctly middle-class notions of gender and family shaped this strategy. Marketers deemed women the primary consumers of the goods and services that enhanced marriage and family life, so they rarely addressed men in their campaigns. Stores even promoted products that the groom purchased, such as a diamond engagement ring, as items to be selected by the bride. And because retailers, like the rest of American society, assumed that a "woman walked up the aisle a bride and back down it a housewife, whether or not she continued to work or study," they sought to capture her permanent business. On the mandatory trek through the entire store to purchase goods for the wedding, the department store acquainted brides with the elements of both the perfect wedding and the idealized middle-class household.[12]

By the mid-1960s, the American wedding industry was so successful in its campaign to take the lavish wedding to the masses that eighty-five percent of brides purchased formal wedding gowns. The fact that the first baby boomers had now reached marriageable age contributed to the popularity of the

expensive formal wedding. Members of this large cohort, whose entire life experience occurred amidst postwar prosperity, were accustomed to disposable family income. Teenage girls spent approximately one-tenth of the average family income on themselves. While comprising only twelve percent of the country's female population, they purchased twenty-seven percent of all cosmetics and fifty percent of all phonograph records. And, together with their male peers, they purchased a full twenty percent of the nation's new and used cars. For these young women, buying expensive items for a one-day wedding celebration was merely an extension of their lifelong behavior.[13]

In one of the most successful wedding industry ad campaigns of the early and mid-1960s, the makers of Ban-Lon employed Miss Americas to model wedding dresses made of their artificial fabric, thus transforming the fantasy figure of single womanhood—the virginal American beauty queen—into the accessible fantasy of every American bride (fig. 36). But with the rise of second-wave feminism, the feminine ideal that Miss America represented soon came under attack. In 1968, radical feminists descended on the Atlantic City pageant and denounced Miss America as a "Degrading Mindless-Boob-Girlie Symbol" whose idealized virginity contributed to a Madonna–whore complex that demeaned all women. Protestors deposited false eyelashes, curlers, wigs, girdles, bras, and other symbols of "female oppression" into a Freedom Trash Can. And a year later, one product endorsed by Miss America—the white wedding dress—received similar treatment when radical feminists raided a Madison Square Garden bridal fair wearing black veils and carrying placards that read "Always a Bride, Never a Person." Singing "Here Comes the Slave, Off to Her Grave," they proclaimed that marriage "oppress[ed] everyone, and particularly women."[14]

In addition to feminist protesters condemning Miss America, the American bride, and the American family, social surveys indicated that few young women conformed to their mothers' sexual mores and gender prescriptions. In the 1950s, polls indicated that only a quarter of Americans found no fault with premarital sex. By the 1970s, however, three-quarters of the population tolerated the practice. Historical circumstance contributed to this change in attitudes. The introduction of an oral contraceptive in 1960 and subsequent U.S. Supreme Court decisions overturning state bans on birth control allowed young women opportunities for sexual expression without the fear of unwanted pregnancy. The counterculture's "If it feels good, do it" mantra, along with feminist criticism of patriarchy and the sexual double standard, made it acceptable for fewer brides to reach the altar as sexual innocents. And whether or not they themselves were enthusiastic adherents of 1960s and 1970s feminism, young women were able to take advantage of new job and educational opportunities that feminist reformers procured through Title VII of the Civil Rights Act of 1964 and Title IX of the Higher Education Act of 1972. Women's increased participation in higher education—from thirty-eight percent of college-aged women enrolled as full-time students in 1960 to forty-nine percent in 1970—often resulted in delayed marriage, contributing to the greater likelihood of sexual activity before marriage. And, once married, women were more likely to continue paid employment than pursue full-time domesticity.[15]

During roughly the same time that the premarital sex and female employment rates were increasing, the nation also witnessed a steep rise in divorce: between 1960 and 1980, the divorce rate increased ninety percent. A major reason for rising divorce numbers was the heightened expectations that Americans now held for marriage. If a marriage did not match the romantic, sexual, and emotional needs that Americans now believed it should provide, they more readily ended it.

In conformity with changing social standards, several states began to reform their divorce laws. Most significantly, on New Year's Day 1970, California became the first state to allow divorce on non-adversarial grounds, ending the practice of one spouse assuming guilt or fault for the end of a marriage. Other states quickly followed suit. By August 1977, only three states continued to practice an adversarial system of divorce in which one party always assumed guilt for the end of the union. This no-fault revolution helped dismantle the idea that marriage was a contract in which the husband automatically assumed economic support of the wife. When a marriage ended with neither partner at fault, the law could no longer require a cruel, adulterous, or otherwise guilty spouse to pay his ex-wife alimony, and the U.S. Supreme Court rendered the concept of alimony gender-neutral when it ruled in the late 1970s that women as well as men could be potentially liable for the financial support of an ex-spouse.[16]

In the new cultural landscape, a white gown did not necessarily symbolize a woman's virginity or her lifelong commitment to the man she married. Nevertheless, the white wedding had become so central to the act of getting married that brides in the 1970s were more likely than ever to buy a formal white gown. In the early 1970s, eighty-seven percent of American brides wore floor-length gowns; ninety-four percent of those garments were white or ivory. At an average cost of $164 ($865 in current dollars), a gown and accompanying headpiece upheld "traditional fashion" in the early 1970s at a significant but not excessive price. Most American brides wanted a glamorous white gown and had little trouble accessing it.[17]

In the 1970s and 1980s, young women were adopting a new version of the marriage fairy tale. As one sociologist noted at the time: "Earlier generations of young girls grew up on Cinderella and Snow White, dreaming of princes to carry them off so they too could live happily ever after. Young girls today dream a different plot. There is still the prince, but happily-ever-after now includes a career."[18] Young men of the period

Figure 37
The father of the bride dances with his daughter at an African American
wedding celebration of the early 2000s.
Courtesy of Michael DiBari, Jr.

Figure 38
A lesbian couple visit a Massachusetts bridal salon to choose the white
gowns for their 2004 wedding.
Courtesy of Robert Spencer.

also expressed a greater desire to marry partners who were
significant wage earners. In order to afford the upper-middle-
class lifestyle that most young people aspired to, a two-wage
family was virtually mandatory in the era's economy.[19]

Economic realities and black popular culture taught African
American baby boomers, in particular, that men and women
shared wage-earning responsibility within marriage. Like other
well-to-do Americans, elite and upper-middle-class urban
blacks had hosted white weddings since the late nineteenth
century. But the significant growth of the black middle class
that resulted from desegregation laws and affirmative action
policies, and the decoupling of the white wedding ceremony
from the notion of a breadwinner–housewife marriage, meant
that more and more African Americans could now afford and

were opting to hold such celebrations. At a time when most
members of American society still automatically associated
African Americans with the poor or working classes, members
of the black middle class often worked diligently to display the
indicators of middle-class status, and the white wedding was
one such hallmark. The author of a 1978 article in *Essence*, the
leading black women's magazine, urged the African American
bride to think of herself as a Cinderella: "It's your show and
you're the potential superstar. . . . You ask yourself: What is my
lifelong wedding fantasy?" Like other segments of American
society, members of the black middle class remained firm adherents
of the white wedding into the twenty-first century (fig. 37).[20]

In contrast to its developing efforts to woo black customers,
the wedding industry made no attempt in the 1970s and 1980s

to acquire the patronage of gays and lesbians. As a business that exploited the heterosexual Cinderella fantasy as its chief marketing strategy, the wedding industry could not afford to acknowledge gay and lesbian couples as potential customers. Nevertheless, after gay patrons of New York's Stonewall Inn bar rebelled against police harassment in 1969 and launched a high-profile gay and lesbian liberation movement, more same-sex couples chose to announce their partnerships in public commitment ceremonies. Lacking any other paradigm for the occasion, gay and lesbian couples frequently modeled their celebrations on the middle-class, heterosexual weddings they had known since childhood, acquiring floral bouquets, wedding gowns, and tuxedos from the usual sources.[21] So when Massachusetts became the first U.S. state to legalize same-sex marriage in 2003, the wedding industry built on couples' existing familiarity with white wedding products to begin actively marketing them to lesbian and gay customers (fig. 38).

Regardless of race, class, or personal politics, the typical late-twentieth-century bride continued to envision herself as a white-swathed princess. But she was a different Cinderella from the one who had fantasized about fairy princess dresses a generation earlier. In many ways, she was actually a throwback to the more assertive Cinderella who existed before her domestication in late-nineteenth-century picture books and twentieth-century film treatments. As folklorists have noted, in the versions of the Cinderella story prior to the late Victorian era, the protagonist was a young woman actively involved in her own transformation from house servant to princess. She went looking for her own magical tokens, invoked her own spells, or, at the very least, advised the fairy godmother on how to go about converting a ragged girl into a beautiful lady. Brides of the late twentieth century reclaimed that agency, but they used their own purchasing power—rather than magical amulets or incantations—to effect the transformation from ordinary woman to princess bride. By the early 1990s, the median first-time

Figure 39
The bare-shouldered sheath was the preferred wedding-gown style for brides of the early twenty-first century.
Courtesy of Michael DiBari, Jr.

marriage age for American women was 23.9 years. As a bride with more maturity, the prototypical bride of the 1990s did not want—in the words of an industry old-timer—a wedding dress covered in "froufrou" and instead preferred the sleek styles popularized by Vera Wang and other well-known late-century designers. And the trend toward bare-shouldered sheath dresses continued into the twenty-first century (fig. 39). Even brides who chose to wear heirloom gowns often modified them to fit the new fashion standard. One way in which a bride could achieve "a greater sense of family connection" at the turn of the twenty-first century was to refashion and re-wear her grandmother's postwar gown, a process that could cost as much as $4,000 (fig. 40).[22]

In the late 1990s, a Roper Organization survey found that seventy-two percent of women planning formal weddings worked full time. Forty-one percent of them earned as much as or more than their grooms. Eighty-four percent said that they never wanted to be financially dependent, and almost a third reported that they would maintain their own separate bank accounts after marriage. The average age of survey respondents was twenty-six. Sixty-five percent were college graduates; in fact, respondents were twenty percent more likely than their fiancés to have attended college or graduate school. Studying the poll's results, Nina Lawrence, the publisher of *Modern Bride* and commissioner of the survey, observed that women marrying in the late 1990s were more affluent than previous brides because they had had time to develop independent careers and earning power. Thus, when it came time for their weddings, these women felt that they deserved "the best of everything."[23]

For this generation of "have-it-all" women, "the best of everything" still meant the Cinderella fantasy. After trying on and rejecting fifty-nine different dresses at the annual bridal gown sale at Filene's Basement in Boston, one hard-to-please bride told a reporter exactly what she was looking for in a bridal dress: "I want the fairy tale."[24] As the 1990s ended, most American brides still wanted the fairy tale. They wanted to travel by limousine (a modern-day version of Cinderella's ornate coach), to surround themselves with fragrant flowers, and to be feted by hundreds of guests at an elaborate party.

Among those attracted to this extravaganza were women who explicitly proclaimed a feminist identity—a development that surprised many second-wave feminists. In the late 1960s and 1970s, radical feminists had criticized the obsession with beauty and narcissism, attempted to minimize the differences between men and women, and questioned the idea of an all-consuming romantic love. To them, the white wedding flew in the face of these feminist crusades. It was, after all, a ceremony that promoted traditional standards of female beauty and stereotypical gender roles. But attempts to undermine the

wedding industry through acts of civil disobedience, such as the Madison Square Garden protest in 1969, had little long-term impact. The equity branch of second-wave feminism had secured greater workplace equality for women, transforming Cinderella into a woman who combined employment and marriage. Radical feminism, however, had not succeeded in dismantling the Cinderella myth altogether. By the turn of the twenty-first century, the white wedding was more popular than ever. As feminist journalist Susan Weidman Schneider observed, "Even staunch advocates of women's equality seem comfortable, at least for a few hours, enacting what appears to be a classic sexist drama—bride in virginal white, 'given away' or handed off from her family of origin to her husband."[25]

When Grace Larew married in 1945, middle-class consumer values were ascending to new prominence. A consumer culture in which participants defined themselves by the products they purchased had existed in the United States for several decades, but only in the post-World War II period did "consumer culture . . . crowd out all other cultural possibilities."[26]

In contrast, by the time Grace's daughter Joan Young wed in 1983, the values of the white middle class had been under siege for a decade and a half. By the late 1960s, the counterculture, the civil rights movement, and organized feminism had all challenged the standards on which the postwar wedding and wedding industry were based. The nation's "wedding industrial complex," however, adapted to changing times. During the last three decades of the twentieth century, businesses marketed the props of the formal wedding to a wider variety of consumers, including more non-whites, divorced women, and even people in same-sex relationships. Yet, the real reason the wedding remained so popular in the midst of sweeping social change was that the central purpose of the white wedding remained the same. Regardless of the participants' race, previous marital history, or sexual orientation, it remained a ritual that allowed

Figure 40
As satirized in this 2008 "For Better or For Worse" comic strip, the skin-baring wedding gown styles of the early twenty-first century made the fashions of an earlier generation look hopelessly out of date.
Courtesy of Universal Press Syndicate.

those involved to experience and project a sense of stability, emotional security, and success.[27]

Although the chief customers for formal weddings in the late twentieth century remained young heterosexual women, their experiences and expectations differed in part from their mothers'. Most brides of the post-Vietnam War era earned an income both before and after their marriages and thus shared the role of household provider with their spouses. Nevertheless, like their mothers, these women would become their families' chief household purchasers, and their experiences as wedding consumers reinforced that identity as women embraced the ritual's promise of picture-perfect domesticity while choosing china, crystal, and silver patterns. At the same time, the wedding industry now told women that their bridal purchases would enable them to express and enhance their individual personalities and achievements—

coveted goals in this new age. By buying the right accoutrements, a bride could show the world that she was a modern, successful woman. Her selection of wedding gown style and reception and honeymoon sites communicated her personal tastes, lifestyle choices, and—at a time when more brides paid for at least a portion of their own weddings—the health of her bank account. The fantasy the wedding industry had long promoted—that purchasing the right goods and services transformed an ordinary woman into the star of the perfect wedding—continued to appeal to even well-educated, politically astute late-twentieth-century brides. Wedding and celebrity magazines, movies and television shows, bridal fairs and advice books all reinforced the idea that the American bride would—in the words of a popular song—both "bring home the bacon and fry it up in a pan." And she would do it all in grand style as she accessorized her happy home.[28]

Examining changes and consistencies in wedding celebrations between 1945 and 2000 reveals how successfully values forged in the postwar era of expanding suburbs, youthful marriage, high birth rates, and family togetherness survived to the end of the century. Although she lived in a period of high divorce rates, extensive female employment, rising marriage ages, and numerous alternatives to the heterosexual two-parent family, the late-century bride ultimately possessed attitudes toward marriage, family life, and social class that differed little from those of her mid-century counterpart. Whether she married at mid-century or at the century's end, the American bride assimilated consistent messages as she shopped for her wedding. The essence of those messages was this: An elaborate wedding publicly demonstrated the stability and happiness of a woman's relationships with her family and mate, commemorated a committed partnership that would succeed (even against increasing odds), and allowed her to hold center stage on what was supposedly the most important day of her life. Despite the many dramatic changes that occurred in American society in the decades following World War II, the history of the formal wedding indicates that the most basic values and expectations underlying the institutions of marriage and the family remained largely intact—even as the outward characteristics of those fundamental institutions continued to evolve. Regardless of the political Right's oft-expressed concern about the demise of family values in the aftermath of the sexual revolution, the white wedding's continuing popularity as the twentieth century ended indicated that the nation's mid-century faith in the importance of marriage and the American family—however those entities were now defined—remained in place as the country prepared for a new millennium. Americans continued to invest in the elaborate white wedding as a means to ensure acceptance in a culture that placed a heavy premium on consumption, class status, and the image of a happy family.

1. Grace Larew Young, interview with the author, North Liberty, IA, June 15, 1996; Grace Larew Young, e-mail communication with the author, July 12, 2001; Katherine Jellison, "From the Farmhouse Parlor to the Pink Barn: The Commercialization of Weddings in the Rural Midwest," *Iowa Heritage Illustrated 77* (Summer 1996): 59. In current dollars, the Larew-Young wedding cost $11,867. All dollar-value conversions in this essay were determined via the American Institute for Economic Research Cost-of-Living Calculator (www. aier.org/research/cost-of-living-calculator).

2. Grace Larew Young interview and e-mail communication.

3. Elizabeth H. Pleck, *Celebrating the Family: Ethnicity, Consumer Culture, and Family Rituals* (Cambridge, MA: Harvard University Press, 2000), 218. An exact accounting of the particular goods and services that Americans purchased with their increasing investment in weddings is difficult to reconstruct. National statistics about the types of weddings that Americans participated in are not available for the pre-1960 period, and, even for the post-1960 period, those numbers only reflect which ceremonies were religious (and therefore more likely to be "formal") and which ones were civil (and therefore more likely to be "informal"). Information regarding the specific kinds of wedding apparel and other goods that Americans purchased for their nuptial celebrations is fragmentary at best for the period prior to the 1950s, and, even when such data is available for later decades, it largely reflects statistics gathered by wedding industry boosters eager to demonstrate the popularity of their wares and services.

4. Maria McBride-Mellinger, *The Wedding Dress* (New York: Random House, 1993), 99; Marcia Seligson, *The Eternal Bliss Machine: America's Way of Wedding* (New York: William Morrow & Company, 1973), 132; Willie Dolnick, Bridal Originals sales representative since 1947, interview with the author, Chicago, IL, October 14, 1995. For further discussion of the development of the wedding gown business and the larger wedding industry, see material throughout Cele C. Otnes and Elizabeth H. Pleck, *Cinderella Dreams: The Allure of the Lavish Wedding* (Berkeley: University of California Press, 2003) and Vicki Howard, *Brides, Inc.: American Weddings and the Business of Tradition* (Philadelphia: University of Pennsylvania Press, 2006).

5. Kitty Hanson, For Richer, For Poorer (New York: Abelard-Schuman, 1967), 114. Although the Association of Bridal Manufacturers was ultimately successful in persuading the government to ease some fabric restrictions, silk in particular remained in short supply for civilian use, limiting the number of formal wedding gowns manufactured during the war. See McBride-Mellinger, *The Wedding Dress*, 34, 37.

6. Eric Hobsbawm, "Introduction: Inventing Traditions," in Eric Hobsbawm and Terence Ranger, eds., *The Invention of Tradition* (New York: Cambridge University Press, 1995), 1–14. Quotation taken from Bridal and Bridesmaid's Apparel Association advertisement, *Bride's Magazine*, Spring 1959, 146.

7. Nancy Cott, *Public Vows: A History of Marriage and the Natio*n (Cambridge, MA: Harvard University Press, 2000), 187–88; McBride-Mellinger, *The Wedding Dress*, 34, 37; Woodbury advertisement, *Life*, July 5, 1943, 55; Woodbury advertisement, *Life*, September 4, 1944, 43; Woodbury advertisement, *Life*, February 11, 1946, 5; Woodbury advertisement, *Life*, March 4, 1946, 23. For discussion of wartime advertising strategies in general, see Juliann Sivulka, *Soap, Sex, and Cigarettes: A Cultural History of American Advertising* (Belmont, CA: Wadsworth Publishing Company, 1998), 230–36.

8. Elaine Tyler May, *Homeward Bound: American Families in the Cold War Era* (New York: Basic Books, 1988), 165–66; Susan M. Hartmann, *The Home Front and Beyond: American Women in the 1940s* (Boston: Twayne Publishers, 1982), 165; Beth L. Bailey, *From Front Porch to Back Seat: Courtship in Twentieth-Century America* (Baltimore: Johns Hopkins University Press, 1988), 41–42; Loren Baritz, *The Good Life: The Meaning of Success for the American Middle Class* (New York: Harper & Row Publishers, 1990), 193–94.

9. Wini Breines, *Young, White, and Miserable: Growing Up Female in the Fifties* (Boston: Beacon, 1992), 4; Nancy A. Walker, *Shaping Our Mothers' World: American Women's Magazines* (Jackson: University Press of Mississippi, 2000), 114. For discussion of postwar domestic consumerism and its relationship to the concepts of family security and togetherness, see May, *Homeward Bound*, 165–66, 181; Karal Ann Marling, *As Seen on TV: The Visual Culture of Everyday Life in the 1950s* (Cambridge, MA: Harvard University Press, 1994), 96, 132, 134–35; Walker, *Shaping Our Mothers' World*, 151. See

also material throughout Lizabeth Cohen, *A Consumers' Republic: The Politics of Mass Consumption in Postwar America* (New York: Vintage, 2004) and Susan Sessions Rugh, *Are We There Yet?: The Golden Age of American Family Vacations* (Lawrence: University Press of Kansas, 2008).

10. For thoughtful analysis of the creation of a distinctive middle-class culture in nineteenth-century America and discussion of its unique values and characteristics, see Chapters 2–4 of Clifford Edward Clark, Jr., *The American Family Home, 1800–1960* (Chapel Hill: University of North Carolina Press, 1986); Chapters 1–2 of Margaret Marsh, *Suburban Lives* (New Brunswick, NJ: Rutgers University Press, 1990); Chapters 1–5 of Carl N. Degler, *At Odds: Women and the Family in America from the Revolution to the Present* (New York: Oxford University Press, 1980); and material throughout Stephen M. Frank, *Life with Father: Parenthood and Masculinity in the Nineteenth-Century American North* (Baltimore: Johns Hopkins University Press, 1998).

11. "Spring Weddings and Our Bridal Service," *Strawbridge and Clothier Store Chat*, March 1949, 2; "The Curtain Lifts on Our New Bride's Shop: Glimpses of the Shop and Its Personalities," *Strawbridge and Clothier Store Chat*, April–May 1949, 10–12; "Wedding Gift Service," *Strawbridge and Clothier Store Chat*, February 1954, 8; "A Bride Is Worth $3300 to a Department Store," *Strawbridge and Clothier Store Chat*, February 1956, 6. *Store Chat* was Strawbridge and Clothier's in-house publication for its employees. The magazine is available to researchers at the Imprints Department, Hagley Museum and Library, Wilmington, DE.

12. Quotation from Jessica Weiss, To Have and *To Hold: Marriage, the Baby Boom, and Social Change* (Chicago: University of Chicago Press, 2000), 31.

13. Hanson, *For Richer, For Poorer*, 15, 28. For further discussion of teenage consumerism and marketing campaigns that focused on female baby boomers, see Joan Jacobs Brumberg, *The Body Project: An Intimate History of American Girls* (New York: Vintage Books, 1998), 85–90, 113–16.

14. "'Dream Wedding' of Miss America 1960" brochure and page from "'Dream Wedding' for Miss America 1960" layout, *Modern Bride*, Holiday 1959, in Miss America 1960 Dream Wedding promotional campaign scrapbook; press release from Everglaze marketing division, November 18, 1960, in Miss America 1961 Dream Wedding promotional campaign scrapbook; advertisements and promotional card included in folder labeled "1964–Pictures and Pamphlets–Miss America and 'Ban-Lon,'" Box 6. All included in the Joseph Bancroft and Sons Company Collection, Accession 72.430, Pictorial Collections, Hagley Museum and Library, Wilmington, DE; "No More Miss America," in Alexander Bloom and Wini Breines, eds., *"Takin' It to the Streets": A Sixties Reader*, 2nd ed. (New York: Oxford University Press, 2003), 404–06.

15. John D'Emilio and Estelle B. Freedman, *Intimate Matters: A History of Sexuality in America*, 2nd ed. (Chicago: University of Chicago Press, 1997), 307–18, 333–34; Blanche Linden-Ward and Carol Hurd Green, *Changing the Future: American Women in the 1960s* (New York: Twayne Publishers, 1993), 68.

16. D'Emilio and Freedman, *Intimate Matters*, 331; Glenda Riley, *Divorce: An American Tradition* (New York: Oxford University Press, 1991), 156–57, 159, 163; Cott, *Public Vows*, 206–07; Karla B. Hackstaff, *Marriage in a Culture of Divorce* (Philadelphia: Temple University Press, 1999), 28–31.

17. Seligson, *The Eternal Bliss Machine*, 1, 126.

18. Rosanna Hertz, *More Equal Than Others: Women and Men in Dual-Career Marriages* (Berkeley: University of California Press, 1986), 2.

19. Barbara Ehrenreich, *Fear of Falling: The Inner Life of the Middle Class* (New York: Pantheon Books, 1989), 212–19.

20. Seligson, *The Eternal Bliss Machine*, 65–66, 269–74; Jacqueline Jones, *Labor of Love, Labor of Sorrow: Black Women, Work, and the Family from Slavery to the Present* (New York: Basic Books, 1985), 269–74; Liz Gant, "The Lowdown on Costs," *Essence*, June 1978, 98.

21. Seligson, *The Eternal Bliss Machine*, 282–87.

22. Jane Yolen, "America's Cinderella," in Alan Dundes, ed., *Cinderella: A Casebook* (Madison: University of Wisconsin Press, 1988), 294–306; Robert Kerr, "Older Brides, Bridegrooms See the New Trends Trailing Along," *Memphis Commercial Appeal*, February 9, 1992; Dolnick interview; Jay Molishever, "Bridal Gowns That Draw Oohs a Second (or Fifth) Time Around," New York Times, July 28, 2002.

23. Marshall Hood, "Say 'I Do' to Simplicity," *Columbus [OH] Dispatch*, January 13, 1998.

24. Sara Rimer, "Searching for a Fairy Tale Wedding Gown, at a Bargain Price," *New York Times*, May 20, 1997.

25. Susan Weidman Schneider, "Isn't It Ironic . . . Retro Weddings in a Feminist Age," *Lilith*, Spring 2000, 16. For a first-person account by a feminist bride who held an elaborate white wedding in 2000, see Kamy Wicoff, *I Do But I Don't: Walking Down the Aisle Without Losing Your Mind* (Cambridge, MA: Da Capo, 2006).

26. Ehrenreich, *Fear of Falling*, 35.

27. Sociologist Chrys Ingraham has coined the term "wedding-industrial complex," which refers to "the close association among weddings, the . . . wedding industry, marriage, the state, religion, media, and popular culture." See Ingraham, *White Weddings: Romancing Heterosexuality in Popular Culture* (New York: Routledge, 1999), 26.

28. For further discussion of the influence of motion pictures, television programs, and other forms of popular culture in perpetuating the white wedding idea, see material throughout Katherine Jellison, *It's Our Day: America's Love Affair with the White Wedding, 1945–2005* (Lawrence: University Press of Kansas, 2008). For discussion of the marketing of the "perfect wedding," see Otnes and Pleck, *Cinderella Dreams*, 18–19, 42–43 and material throughout Rebecca Mead, *One Perfect Day: The Selling of the American Wedding* (New York: Penguin, 2007).

CATALOG

1 / DRESS IN TWO PARTS (DRESS AND PETTICOAT)

ABOUT 1735, RESTYLED 1763
UNITED STATES (BOSTON, MASSACHUSETTS)

STOMACHER

MID 18TH C.
ENGLAND OR EUROPE

In 1740, when Mary Waters married Anthony Sigourney in Boston, she chose a fashionable gown of the finest silk. Unlike those of most brides today, however, her dress was constructed of rich green silk woven with a polychrome design of flowers, leaves, and fruit. The large-scale pattern in salmon, pink, gold, olive green, and blue is distinctive against the dark background. Waters chose not only a beautiful textile but a costly one. Imported from England, the fabric was woven at Spitalfields, where the finest silks of the period were produced. In 1763, Mary Waters's daughter married James Butler in the same dress.[1] Although the choice may have been sentimental in nature, the gown's second use prolonged the life of this exorbitant expenditure.

Dress styles of the mid-eighteenth century emphasized a cone-shaped torso, a small waist, and full skirts that exaggerated the width of the hips, sometimes outrageously. Mary Waters's gown does not depart from these fashionable parameters. The low square neckline is edged with linen bobbin lace. The three-quarter-length sleeves end in a wide flounce of the same trim. Beneath the gown, a pair of boned stays creates the rigid shape of the upper body. Constructed in the English style—*à l'anglaise*—deep box pleats fall from the center back neckline and are stitched close at the waist. The lacing at the center front of the bodice is hidden by the stomacher—a triangular inset embellished with metallic thread embroidery. Pleated to the bodice, the voluminous skirt is open at the center front, revealing a separate petticoat of the same fabric. The skirt extends modestly over the hips, resting on *paniers*—structured hoops that support the shape.

Colorful wedding gowns were not unusual in the eighteenth century. Although some women undoubtedly chose white (see fig. 7), there was no prevailing preference. Mary Waters's polychromatic gown, however, was far more serviceable than a white dress. Soil or a stain could easily disappear amid the bold floral pattern or against the darker background, whereas a single mishap could abruptly ruin a white garment in a period when modern cleaning processes were not available. Waters's lavish choice proved to be a profitable investment some twenty years later, when the textile was still fresh enough for the dress to be modified and worn again.

1. Biographical information is from the curatorial files of the Museum of Fine Arts, Boston. Spitalfields was a rural district on the eastern outskirts of London that became a silk manufacturing center at the end of the seventeenth century. It flourished through the eighteenth century, producing the most luxurious silk fabrics of the period.

American (Boston, MA),
fabric English
*Dress in two parts
(dress and petticoat)*,
about 1735, restyled 1763
Silk; brocaded plain
weave
Museum of Fine Arts,
Boston
Gift of
Mrs. (or Miss) H. L.
Campbell
1990.513a-b

with

English or European,
Stomacher, mid 18th c.
Silk embroidered with
metallic yarns
Museum of Fine Arts,
Boston
The Elizabeth Day
McCormick Collection
43.1914

Photograph © 2010
Museum of Fine Arts,
Boston

2 / WEDDING DRESS

1801
UNITED STATES

During the French Revolution, fashion was employed to make political statements, and the heavy silks and structured gowns of the aristocracy (see cat. 1) were banished with those who had worn them. By the final years of the eighteenth century, fashionable styles were based on classical dress that revealed the body.

There were philosophical, artistic, and political reasons for this abrupt change to such a severe style. The philosophers of the Enlightenment, particularly Jean-Jacques Rousseau (1712–78), advocated a return to the purity of nature. The excavation of the Roman ruins at Herculaneum in 1738 initiated an interest in classicism. A preoccupation with perfect beauty as espoused by the ancient Greeks and Romans inspired a rejection of ornate embellishment in favor of austere geometric forms. Gowns of the period resembled attenuated Greek columns; the high waistline pushed the bust upward, echoing the form of the capital. Plain white cotton or linen fabrics were chosen for their simplicity and resemblance to the marble sculptures found in ancient ruins.[1]

The slim silhouette of this stark gown is characteristic of its period. The skirt is gathered in the back, where the fullness is accentuated by a small bustle pad. Slightly trained, the skirt falls from a high or Empire waistline that defines the bust. The cut of the bodice tended to draw the shoulders backward, pushing the chest forward and compelling the elbows to bend. Although the dress gives the impression of lightness and comfort, in actuality it enforced a constricting posture.[2]

The dress is embellished at the hemline with French knot and satin stitch embroidery of feathers, grape bunches intersected with ribbonlike swags, and curved leafy branches circling large dots. The embroidery motifs on the bodice and sleeves, although worked in the same stitches, are somewhat different in design. This reinterpretation of the motifs, along with the set of the sleeves and the cut of the back, indicate that the bodice may have been replaced—an easy alteration, as it was sewn to the skirt by hand.[3] The fabric, however, looks identical in weave structure, texture, and density, as does the weight and type of thread used for the embroidery. If the bodice were in fact replaced, it would have been within no more than ten years of its original making, as styles would have changed enough to make the dress quite unfashionable.

Ruhamah Smith of Worcester married James Davis, Jr. (b. 1772) on September 12, 1801, in Holden, Massachusetts. The Davis family had settled in and around Holden in 1722. They were a prominent family, some of considerable wealth; many of the Davis men held office in the town. Little else is known about Ruhamah and James except that by 1815 they had two children, James Sullivan Madison (b. 1810) and Ruhamah Lusana (b. 1815). Their descendants prospered and continued to live in the area.[4] Ruhamah and James's granddaughter, Ada M. Davis, was married in nearby Worcester, Massachusetts, in 1874 (see cat. 10).

1. Akiko Fukai, "Rococo and Neoclassical Clothing," in Jean Starobinski et al. *Revolution in Fashion: European Clothing, 1715–1815* (New York: Abbeville Press, 1990), 114–16.

2. *Yester-Morn to Yester-Eve: In and Out of Fashion in the 19th Century* (Boston: National Society of the Colonial Dames of America in the Commonwealth of Massachusetts, 1991), 4.

3. Nancy Bradfield, *Costume in Detail 1730–1930* (Boston: Plays, Inc., 1968). See p. 96 for an illustration of a similar back bodice construction, although the opening in Ruhamah Smith's dress is in the center back. The sleeves are set well into the back of the bodice and pleated only along the back neckline and armseye seam, creating a fullness not generally seen in the earliest years of the century. The back bodice seams extend in a diagonal line from the armseye to the waistline rather than in the severe curve characteristic of 1801. The dissimilarity in the embroidery patterns between bodice and skirt is obvious. The skirt patterns are unusual in that the feather and grape-bunch motifs run the circumference of the skirt. They do not intersect or even seem to relate to the leaf and dot motifs, which also encircle the skirt closer to the hem. The French knot technique is much more prominent on the skirt, although it is incorporated into the embroidery on the bodice and sleeves, perhaps a later attempt at making a visual connection with the earlier embroidery. It is possible Ruhamah or the dressmaker had extra fabric and embroidery thread with which to orchestrate alterations, and the gown was reworked either for Ruhamah herself or for a family member.

4. Family History Library, Salt Lake City, UT, Film #0721196; David Foster Estes, *The History of Holden Massachusetts, 1684–1894* (Worcester, MA: Press of C. F. Lawrence & Co., 1894), 165, 253–54; *Vital Records of Holden, Massachusetts to the end of the year 1849* (Worcester, MA: Franklin P. Rice, 1904), 31–32, 120; Nicholas Zook, *Holden: The Evolution of a Town* (Holden, MA: Holden Bicentennial Commission, 1976), 35.

United States
Wedding Dress, 1801
Linen
Gift of
Madeleine King
Short
in memory of
Ethel Heald King
1999.233

Figure 1
Detail of embroidery
on skirt.

United States
Wedding Dress: Bodice and Skirt,
1838
Silk
Gift of Mrs. Charles J. Livingood
1935.116, 117

3 / WEDDING DRESS: BODICE AND SKIRT

1838
UNITED STATES

Mary Barr Denny Muhlenberg (1807–93) wore this dress for her wedding to Richard Hubbell Hopkins (1798–1863) on December 11, 1838, in New York City.[1] Despite the fact that this was her second marriage—Muhlenberg had been a widow since 1831—she chose a fashionable white satin gown. The low décolleté, puff sleeves, and bell-shaped skirt were characteristic of gowns of the late 1830s, a transitional period in women's dress. Just a year or two earlier, a more extreme sleeve design would have widened the neckline generously and a shorter hemline would have revealed the ankles. Although the sleeves are short, they still exhibit the fullness that was beginning to be pushed down the arm in this period. The gown is accessorized with detachable sheer undersleeves or *engageantes* that cover the forearm for modesty.

By 1838, women's fashions had begun to exhibit the more reserved look that would dominate the 1840s. In particular, the fan-shaped pleating that converges at the center front of the bodice is characteristic of the slimming vertical lines of the upcoming decade. Similarly, the pleats falling from the waistband to the hem of the skirt emphasize this same linear quality.

Richard and Mary Hopkins had two children together. The first, Mary Muhlenberg Hopkins, was born December 19, 1844. Her sister Isabella Frances was born four years later. Richard Hopkins was a dry goods merchant; the family lived in New York, in a prestigious neighborhood near Washington Park. In 1862 they moved to Cincinnati, Ohio, not far from the Circleville/Chillicothe area where Mary Hopkins's father, General James Denny, had been a pioneer settler.[2]

The Hopkins's elder daughter Mary (1844–1927) married Thomas J. Emery (1830–1906) on May 24, 1866, in St. John's Church at Seventh and Plum Streets in Cincinnati.[3] She, too, wore the white satin wedding dress first worn by her mother. By the mid-1860s dress styles had changed significantly, but Hopkins, like many women, chose to wear her mother's wedding gown rather than a more fashionable dress. Hopkins and her mother must have been similar in size, as there are no

Figure 1
The wedding
dress with the net
chemisette as Mary
Hopkins would have
worn it in 1866 when
she married Thomas
J. Emery.

visible signs of alteration in the dress itself. However, when the dress was donated to the Cincinnati Art Museum's collection, a net chemisette with silk satin detailing accompanied it. Presumably, this was worn by Mary Hopkins to affect a more modest neckline.

Thomas J. Emery was a successful businessman, and when he died in 1906, his widow became one of Cincinnati's wealthiest women. A generous philanthropist, devoted patron of the arts, and supporter of diverse social causes, Mary Emery is perhaps best known as the founder of the planned community Mariemont just east of Cincinnati.[4]

1. Millard F. Rogers, Jr., *Rich in Good Works: Mary M. Emery of Cincinnati* (Akron, OH: University of Akron Press, 2001), 7; New York City Marriages, 1600–1800s and the New York Genealogical and Biographical Record, 1932, both at http://www.ancestry.com/.

2. Rogers, *Rich in Good Works*, 7–8.

3. Ibid., 14; *The National Cyclopaedia of American Biography* (New York: James T. White Company, 1935), vol. 24, 127–28.

4. *National Cyclopaedia of American Biography*, vol. 24, 127–28.

This gold-colored silk dress was worn by Abigail Holmes (1822–1901) when she married Clark S. Potter (1811–75) on October 3, 1839, in Albion, New York.[1] It is a fashionable dress for the period, with a wide neckline, bell-shaped skirt, and corseted waist. The distinctive sleeves are pleated tightly to the upper arm, balloon out just above the elbow, and are caught in a tight cuff at the wrist. This rather peculiar style represents a transitional phase. If Holmes had married a few years earlier, her sleeves would have been voluminous to the shoulder, making the breadth of the neckline seem even wider.

By 1839, however, sleeves were being "banded down" or pleated on the upper arm. They were transformed into a narrow sleeve, the length of the entire arm, in the early 1840s. Many women compressed the full sleeves of their older dresses with pleating, thereby extending the gowns' fashionable life. The sleeves of this dress, however, have not been altered, indicating that Holmes probably had this gown made specifically for the occasion.

The bride chose an unassuming, colored day dress for her wedding. The trims, constructed of the same fabric as the dress, are restrained and subtle. Narrow piping outlines the bottom edge and seams of the bodice; the sleeve bands, seams, and cuffs; and the top edge of the skirt embellishment. Self-fabric festoons are draped asymmetrically around the skirt and on the upper sleeve, with a pleated version across the bust. A pleated tab holds each point of the swags.

While colored gowns were not unusual in this period, Holmes's choice stands in contrast to that of Mary Barr Denny Muhlenberg, who had selected a white satin gown for her wedding just one year earlier (see cat. 3). Little is known about Holmes's family of origin. Perhaps she could not afford the more expensive satin, or she may simply have been a very practical bride, opting for a gown that she could wear as long as it

was fashionable after her wedding. The young bride also had a matching pelerine, or short cape, made for going away. Perhaps her fabric choice was dictated by the fact that the couple intended to embark on a trip immediately after the ceremony. A gold-colored dress would have been far more practical for traveling, given the inevitable dust and dirt the couple would encounter on the road.

If the Holmes family was not affluent, Mr. and Mrs. Clark Potter seem to have prospered. In the 1860 U.S. Federal Census, they were living in Albion with their eight children, ranging in age from nineteen to one, and employed one servant—a young Irish woman, Mary Florin. Clark Potter was employed by the Revenue Office.[2]

1. Birth and death dates, http://www.rootsweb.ancestry.com/~nyorlean/mtal6p4.htm; Cincinnati Art Museum curatorial files.

2. U.S. Federal Census, 1860.

Figure 1
Holmes's wedding gown with the matching pelerine. There is no hook and eye at the center front of the cape. Multiple pin holes indicate it was held closed by a brooch as shown here.

5 / WEDDING DRESS AND VEIL

1840
UNITED STATES

When the young Queen Victoria married in 1840, her wedding dress was the subject of much attention. Victoria chose not to follow tradition and was married in a fashionable gown rather than her coronation robes. Her dress was constructed of lightweight silk satin woven at Spitalfields, where the finest European silks were being produced at the time.[1] A creamy rather than optical white, it was simple in design. The bodice had a wide, low neckline with full, double puff sleeves similar to those on the 1838 wedding gown of Mary Muhlenberg Hopkins (see cat. 3). The waist was pointed at the center front. The separate skirt was constructed of seven widths of fabric fit to the twenty-five-inch waistband with deep forward-facing pleats. Narrow piping finished the neck, sleeve, and waist edges. The gown was trimmed with English-made lace at the neckline and sleeve ends, with a lace flounce on the lower half of the skirt (see fig. 9).

Married just six weeks after Queen Victoria in 1840, Angelina Russell's wedding dress is similar in style to the British monarch's gown. Woven with a delicate floral damask pattern, it is made of the lightweight silk popular at the time. Russell, too, trimmed the wide neckline and sleeve ends of her gown with handmade lace worked with floral patterns, in addition to narrow piping along the seams.[3] Her bodice is pointed at the waist and she chose to emphasize this with a row of five self-fabric bows down the center front. Her sleeves are pleated tight to the arm—a choice that was as fashionable in 1840 as Victoria's puff sleeves. The pleating is a design device that is carried through across the bust. Only four panels wide, Russell's skirt is gathered into a waistband that measures only twenty-two and three-quarters inches in diameter.[4]

Angelina Russell (1817–98) and her family were residents of Columbus, Ohio. She married James J. Faran (1808–92) on March 26, 1840, and moved to Cincinnati, her husband's native city. Faran became a successful lawyer, statesman, and editor. For twenty-three years, he served as editor-in-chief of a leading newspaper, the *Cincinnati Enquirer*, which he purchased in partnership with Washington McLean in 1844. The couple lived in a fashionable section of downtown Cincinnati, at 122 East Third Street, where they raised five children and enjoyed more than fifty years of married life.[5]

1. J. F. Flanagan, *Spitalfields Silks of the 18th and 19th Centuries* (Leigh-on-Sea, Eng.: F. Lewis, Publishers, 1954), 5–23.

2. Kay Staniland and Santina M. Levey, "Queen Victoria's Wedding Dress and Lace," *Costume: The Journal of the Costume Society* 12 (1983): 1–5.

3. The laces at the neckline and sleeve ends are not the same pattern. The finer lace of the two is on the sleeves. It is a French blonde or bobbin lace with both a honeycomb and Star of David ground. It is worked as a continuous lace, meaning the ground, motifs, and picot edge are made in one piece. The lace at the neckline, also a bobbin lace, has a point ground—a more common style. It too is a continuous lace. For the detailed information about the lace, I am indebted to Elizabeth Davis, whose doctoral dissertation from Cornell University is titled "All of Them Ladies of Taste and Refinement: How Lace Democratized Fashion in Late Victorian Women's Dress, 1870–1890."

4. The dress has been altered slightly. The skirt and bodice are stitched together and the waistband appears to have been replaced.

5. Charles Theodore Greve, *Centennial History of Cincinnati and Representative Citizens* (Chicago: Biographical Publishing Company, 1904), vol. 1, 291–92, 654; *History of Cincinnati and Hamilton County, Ohio: Their Past and Present* (Cincinnati: S. B. Nelson & Co., Publisher, 1894), 494–95; *The City of Cincinnati and Its Resources* (Cincinnati: Cincinnati Times Star Co., 1891), 157, 181; *Cincinnati Society Blue Book and Family Directory* (Cincinnati: Peter G. Thomson, 1879), 184–85; Last Will and Testament of Angelina R. Faran, 1898; Last Will and Testament of James J. Faran, 1892; U.S. Federal Census 1860 and 1880; *Williams' City Directory* (Cincinnati: Williams Directory Company, 1849–89).

United States
*Wedding Dress and
Veil*, 1840
Silk
Gift of Jane R. Faran
1986.1220a,b

Figure 1
Detail of damask
fabric.

United States
Wedding Dress:
Bodice and Skirt, ca.
1862
Silk
Gift of Miss Julie
Caroline O'Hara
1938.8, 9

6 / WEDDING DRESS: BODICE AND SKIRT

CA. 1862
UNITED STATES

Although there is no information about the bride who wore this wedding gown, it clearly dates to the first half of the 1860s. Prior to the invention of the hoop skirt or cage crinoline in the late 1850s, skirt size had been limited by the number of cumbersome petticoats that could be layered beneath. With the crinoline as a lightweight alternative, however, skirts began to grow larger. In the early 1860s, skirts became more elliptical in contrast to the bell shape of the preceding decade. This gown, with its flatter front and extended silhouette in back, exhibits the changing form. It also illustrates the increasing use of deep knife and box pleats to reduce the extreme circumference of the skirt panels to fit the waistband.[1] The breadth of the shoulder line extended by the puff sleeves, the expanse of the skirt hemline, the angled bust darts, the center front point of the bodice at the waist, and the diverging pleats of the skirt all conspire to make the woman's waist appear smaller.[2]

As in this design, many 1860s dresses left the skirt fabric unadorned, while the bodice was the focus of embellishment. Here, pleated silk net forms a V at both front and back. The net is trimmed with yellow-gold silk cording and tassels.

The October 1859 issue of *Godey's Lady's Book* illustrated two similarly decorated examples, accompanied by text explaining this was a new style, with many variations having been introduced in the previous year (fig. 1). The tasseled design mimicked the Hussar jacket—a military garment trimmed with similar cording. The shoulder decorations were described as epaulettes.[3]

Etiquette manuals and women's periodicals of the day (and for decades thereafter) frequently asserted that modesty in bridal attire was most appropriate. Although the high neckline of this dress is a properly reserved choice, the embellishment draws the eye directly to the bust, suggesting a lower décolletage. This placement was called *en berthé* in reference to the bertha collar, a low round style that extended from shoulder to shoulder. Similarly, the short puff sleeves leave the arms bare—an immodesty that would have been deemed inappropriate for a church wedding. The bride might have worn sheer white cotton or linen undersleeves (see cat. 3), but, as evidenced by extant garments, women did not necessarily heed the advice of etiquette manuals when it came to wedding gown design.[4]

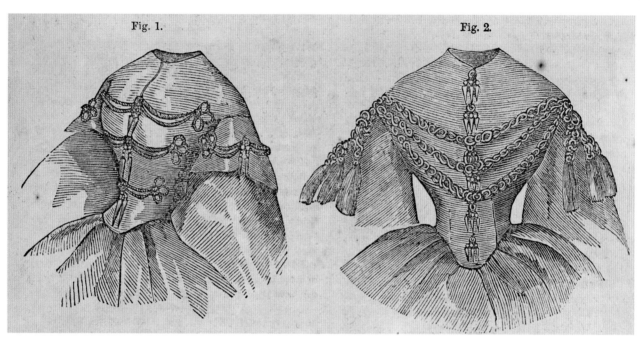

Figure 1
Two bodices with similar cord and tassel embellishment from *Godey's Lady's Book*, October 1859.

To modern eyes, this gown may seem to have been made for a single use. The fact that it was trimmed so sparingly, however, provided ample opportunity for detaching the original embellishments and replacing them. The dress could then be retrimmed and worn on other occasions. In fact, the pleated net and cording had been removed from the dress before it was donated to the Cincinnati Art Museum collection. Only careful examination revealed the stitch marks that indicated its original placement.

1. The skirt could also be gored—a new type of construction that became popular in the 1860s for this very reason. A gored skirt was constructed of shaped panels that were narrow at the top and wide at the bottom. The large circumference was maintained at the hemline, while the top of the skirt could be fitted to the waistband without any pleating or gathering.

2. The actual waist measurement is twenty-four inches. The hemline circumference is one hundred sixty-eight inches.

3. *Godey's Lady's Book*, October 1859, 383–84.

4. The *en berthé* style of bodice trimming is referred to in a *Godey's Lady's Book* (April 1861) description of the colored fashion plate, p. 383. Undersleeves or *engageantes* were separate from the dress and served to protect the more costly silk or fine cotton dress fabric from body oils and perspiration. They were basted into a garment and removed frequently for laundering. *Engageantes* were most often worn in this period with the pagoda-style sleeve. Although sheer, the undersleeves covered the forearm sufficiently for modesty and were gathered into a cuff at the wrist.

7 / WEDDING DRESS

1866
UNITED STATES

Elizabeth Kissam (1844–1902) was the daughter of James A. and Adeline Kissam of Brooklyn, New York, where her father was a merchant. We can only speculate how Elizabeth met Henry DeBus (1844–89), her future husband, who was an Ohio native. Henry's father, Louis DeBus, operated his own business manufacturing stills, tubs, and cisterns in Cincinnati as early as the late 1840s. Henry seems to have taken over the company in 1866, shortly after he returned from fighting in the Civil War—the same year he and Kissam were married. By 1868, the business took on the name DeBus Tub and Cooperage Co., with offices on Elm Street in downtown Cincinnati.[1] Coopering was a lucrative business in Cincinnati in the mid-nineteenth century; the city was growing rapidly. More than thirty-five breweries were located in Cincinnati's Over-the-Rhine district in the 1860s.

Elizabeth Kissam's choice of wedding gown immediately reveals that she was a fashion-forward young woman. Her expansive skirt, with a hem circumference of 220 inches, is most impressive. The late 1850s invention of the cage crinoline or hoop skirt had allowed designers to increase the size of skirts to enormous proportions. Crinolines, constructed of lightweight wire, maintained the fashionable shape of the skirt without the heavy petticoats that had previously been required, allowing women to move more freely. Consequently, 1860s skirts became more voluminous than ever before. The shape evolved into an ellipse, with the front rather flat and the bulk of the skirt projecting behind the wearer. By 1866, when Kissam and DeBus married, skirts were at their largest.

Kissam's substantial skirt stands in pronounced contrast to her small waist, which measures only twenty inches in diameter. She was a petite woman, standing just over five feet, to be maneuvering in such a massive gown. However, she must have possessed tremendous poise, as she chose a design with rather unusual construction. Most gowns of this period were made in two pieces—the bodice separate from the skirt. Although the gored construction that Kissam chose, in which the skirt and bodice are cut in one, was featured in fashion magazines as early as 1859, not many garments of this style have survived. This may indicate that few were actually made or worn. The fabric was cut and seamed to fit the garment closely over the torso and waist, then widened to form the skirt. It was a style that mimicked the shape of the body underneath and many women may have considered it a bit too revealing.[2]

In January 1866, *Peterson's Magazine* illustrated and described just such a gored dress, explaining, "These are made quite plain in front and on the hips, but with three box-pleats at the back." Kissam's wedding gown is constructed in exactly this manner, with a deep box pleat on the left and right sides of the back and a smaller one in the center. The fashion notes in *Peterson's* in August 1861 also noted that dresses with the bodice and skirt made in one piece were generally very long behind, as is this gown.

The color of this bridal dress is as arresting as the construction. Rather than white, Kissam chose a gold and rose changeable silk taffeta that was referred to in fashion magazines as

United States
Wedding Dress, 1866
Silk, linen
Gift of Mrs. Robert
W. Knauft
1964.54

Figure 1

This bridal gown illustrated in the January 1860 issue of *Godey's Lady's Book* depicts a gored construction. It is similar in its simplicity to Elizabeth Kissam's dress, although she chose less embellishment and a more revealing cut, with a low neckline and short sleeves.

maize or corn-colored.[3] The bride astutely heeded the advice of etiquette manuals, which insisted that simplicity was most tasteful for wedding gowns. This garment is sparsely embellished with a narrow handmade bobbin lace stitched just inside the neckline and a wider piece draped below the bust and over the shoulders. A twist of two yarns—one of gold-colored chenille and the other a white satin cording—embellish the bodice and diminutive puff sleeves. The buttons at the center front opening are domed and covered with fine crochet—a popular style in the period.

1. Edward Kissam, *The Kissam Family in America from 1644 to 1825* (New York: Dempsey and Carroll's Art Press, 1892), 79–80; National Park Service, U.S. Civil War Soldiers, 1861–1865, http://www.ancestry.com/; Obituary for Elizabeth Kissam, *New York Times,* February 28, 1902; *Williams' City Directory* (Cincinnati: Williams Directory Company, 1849–89); U.S. Federal Census, 1870 and 1880.

2. *Godey's Lady's Book* in December 1859 illustrated two gored dresses on pp. 484 and 485 that were described on p. 567: "A new style of gored dresses has been introduced . . . the skirt and waist are in one entire piece, gored at the sides."

3. *Peterson's Magazine,* January 1866, 84, and August 1861, 160. The "Fashions for January" section of *Peterson's Magazine* (January 1866) mentions corn-colored silk and *Godey's Lady's Book* (May 1863) in "ChitChat Upon New York and Philadelphia Fashions for May" describes a maize-colored silk.

Although Mary Dayton Richards (1842–1921) and Milton Brayton Graff (1841–77) were married in 1869 in Manhattan, the bride's birthplace, the couple returned to Graff's native Cincinnati, where he was a practicing physician. Initially, they resided with Milton's parents, Jacob and Mary Ann Graff, who lived at 129 Dayton Street, which was situated west of the downtown area.[1] Between 1850 and 1890, the city's wealthy beer brewers and pork packers erected impressive Italianate townhouses along Dayton Street and the adjoining avenues in a neighborhood that came to be known as Millionaire's Row. Although the Graffs were certainly not millionaires, Jacob was an auctioneer specializing in real estate and he may have had a hand in the establishment of this important, now historic, district.[2]

Unfortunately, the couple's marriage was cut short by Milton's death in 1875. By 1880, Mary had built her own house in Glendale, Ohio, a planned community fifteen miles north of Cincinnati on the commuter railway. Glendale was established in 1855, as wealthy Cincinnatians built summer residences away from the noise and pollution of the city.[3] Its sedate setting, with wooded acres and tree-lined curvilinear avenues, must have appealed to this young widow with two small children to raise. Graff built an impressive home on Congress Avenue and lived in Glendale until her death in 1921.

In 1869, when Richards and Graff married, skirt styles, although still large and elliptical, had begun to diminish in size. The petite, twenty-seven-year-old bride must have looked angelic in her snow-white tarlatan dress—a model of nineteenth-century modesty and submission.[4] Her gown consisted of multiple components. The bodice or blouse had a round neckline and buttoned up the center front. Because tarlatan is a sheer fabric, the bodice was lined with opaque cotton. The long transparent sleeves were made more modest with an elbow-length inner sleeve with dainty eyelet trim. The skirt consisted of an underskirt, skirt, and shorter overskirt—all supported by a cage crinoline

and trimmed effusively with undulating horizontal rows and diagonal lines of box-pleated self-fabric. The overskirt was fashionably asymmetrical—pulled up on the side back, perhaps with a fragrant bunch of orange blossoms. In contrast to Elizabeth Kissam's gown (see cat. 7), this dress indicates a movement toward increased embellishment.

1. Graff biographical information, http://www.springgrove.org/sg/genealogy/stats/99316.tif.pdf and http://www.springgrove.org/sg/genealogy/stats/29488.tif.pdf; *The Cincinnati Directory, for the Year 1834* (Cincinnati: E. Deming, 1834); Charles Cist, ed., *The Cincinnati Directory for the Year 1842* (Cincinnati: E. Morgan and Company, 1842); *Williams' City Directory* (Cincinnati: Williams Directory Company, 1875–83).

2. A brief description and history of Dayton Street can be found at http://www.cincinnati-oh.gov/cdap/pages/-6743-/. Dayton Street is listed on the National Register of Historic Districts. Also see Zane L. Miller and Bruce Tucker, *Changing Plans for America's Inner Cities: Cincinnati's Over-the-Rhine and Twentieth-Century Urbanism* (Columbus: Ohio State University Press, 1998).

3. Glendale's Historic District is listed on the National Register of Historic Places. More comprehensive histories can be found in *Glendale's Heritage: Glendale, Ohio* (Cincinnati: Young & Klein, 1976) and *The Village of Glendale, 1855–2005* (Cincinnati: Glendale Heritage Preservation, 2004).

4. Tarlatan or tarlatane was a somewhat coarse, open-weave cotton fabric with a plain weave structure, heavily sized, and often used for ball gowns. It is frequently referenced in fashion descriptions of the 1860s, although it appears earlier and is described or mentioned in nineteenth- and early-twentieth-century textile dictionaries. For instance, see *Godey's Lady's Book*, June 1859, 573; June 1860, 544; May 1861, 68; and *Harper's Bazar*, October 1871, 635. Also C. M. Brown and C. L. Gates, *Scissors and Yardstick; or, All about Dry Goods* (Hartford, CT: C. M. Brown and R. W. Jacqua, 1872), 56 and George S. Cole, *A Complete Dictionary of Dry Goods and History of Silk, Cotton, Linen, Wool and other Fibrous Substances* (Chicago: W. B. Conkey Company, 1892), 348.

United States
*Wedding Dress:
Bodice, Overskirt,
Skirt, and
Underskirt,* 1869
Cotton
Gift of Milton and
Kathryn Graff
2001.105a–d

Figure 1
Detail of bodice
front.

Figure 2
Mary Dayton Richards Graff.

Figure 3
Milton Brayton Graff.

9 / COURT PRESENTATION DRESS: BODICE, SKIRT, AND TRAIN

1871
MRS. JAMES (ACTIVE 19TH C.)
ENGLAND

The 1871 census for London lists Florence Carlisle residing at the St. James Hotel on Jermyn Street. She is one of a group of more than forty Americans, including her mother and two older sisters, who seem to have been traveling together. Perhaps the group of mostly young adults, along with some parental chaperones, was on a Grand Tour. In the nineteenth century, the final stage of an upper-class education included traveling in Europe to learn the intricacies of French high society, study ancient ruins in Rome, and view first-hand Renaissance painting and sculpture in Florence. In London, it seems, the group was being presented at the court of Queen Victoria. The St. James Hotel was just a few blocks from St. James's Palace, where afternoon presentations took place in the Drawing Room.

Court presentation was originally reserved for those of high rank. By the late nineteenth century, however, Lady Violet Greville, author of *The Gentlewoman in Society*, bemoaned the fact that many of those presented at Court were "people of no estimation except . . . their own." Being presented at Court had become a passport to "Good Society," and many Americans traveling abroad participated in the ritual to ensure social approbation.[1]

Court presentation was fraught with strict regulations regarding dress. In 1871, when Florence Carlisle went to London, ladies were required to wear fashionable evening dress with a low décolleté and short sleeves. The skirt was constructed of ruched netting and the obligatory train was to be attached at the waist and extend a specific length from the hem of the dress. A headdress of three curled ostrich plumes and a veil were required. Carlisle's gown bears the label of the London dressmaker Mrs. James, one of many in the West End who specialized in court dress. It is clear from the original photographs taken in London that Mrs. James provided Carlisle with a regulation dress.[2]

Like bridal attire, court dress was a specialized costume made for a specific occasion in which to be seen and presented. It was not uncommon for new brides to wear their wedding gowns to be presented at Court—or vice versa, if the two events fell within close proximity. When Florence Carlisle's daughter donated the gown to the Cincinnati Art Museum's collection, she identified it as her mother's court dress and wedding gown. However, Carlisle did not marry until June 1884, and by this time the dress would have been woefully out of style. Carlisle may have worn it just as Mary Emery wore her mother's 1838 wedding dress twenty-eight years later (see cat. 3), but it is less likely that a court presentation gown would have held the same sentimental attachment.

1. Nigel Arch and Joanna Marschner, *Splendor at Court: Dressing for Royal Occasions since 1700* (London: Unwin Hyman, 1987), 10.

2. Ibid., 56–57, 68–69.

Figure 1
Detail of
bodice front.

Figure 2

These photographs, inscribed on the back, are of Florence Carlisle in her court dress in 1871. They were taken by the London Stereoscopic &
Photographic Company. Founded in 1856 by George Swan Nottage, the firm operated two London studios and was well known for its stereo
photographs and *cartes de visite*.

10 / WEDDING DRESS: BODICE AND SKIRT

1874
UNITED STATES

In 1870, schoolteacher Ada Maria Davis (1845–99) was living as a boarder in the home of George and Mary Hudson in Rutland, Massachusetts. At the time, she was twenty-five years old. Her mother had died when she was three, and her father when she was twenty. Teaching was a common occupation for many single nineteenth-century women who chose to be employed until they married. With both her parents deceased, however, teaching was Davis's livelihood, and residing with the Hudsons was far more respectable than living alone—a thought she simply would not have entertained. The man Davis was to marry, Timothy Sibley Heald (1832–1920), was born and lived in Hubbardston, Massachusetts, just north of Rutland. His father owned a sawmill.[1]

By 1874, Davis had moved to Worcester, Massachusetts, where she was teaching at the Adams Square School. On September 4 of that year, she began keeping a journal of her purchases for her wedding, which was to take place just six weeks later, on October 21. In all, Davis spent $667.16 for articles specifically related to the wedding. She recorded that a large portion of the money was "from proceeds of wood sold in Holden." One might speculate that Davis had inherited wooded property upon the death of her father or that he had worked in the lumber business. This might have been the connection between the Heald and Davis families that resulted in Timothy and Ada becoming acquainted.

Davis was meticulous in recording her wedding- and trousseau-related purchases; in her journal she documented everything from an embroidered nightdress to the invitation postage. She patronized numerous shops along Main Street in Worcester, acquiring fabric, lace and other sewing supplies, kid gloves, stockings, orange blossoms, a hoop skirt, and a bustle, among other necessities. She was conscious of every penny she spent.

The wedding gown must have been constructed of the eighteen yards of white satin Davis bought from dressmaker Mrs. G. W. Aldrich for $45. She purchased this fabric on October 13, just eight days before she was to be married. It is unclear who actually made the gown, however, as Davis recorded dealings with Mmes. Knowles, Bachelder, Garfield, and Dunlap—all dressmakers in Worcester.[2]

The *cuirass* bodice, which was cut to fit down over the hips, had just been introduced in 1874, and some fashion editors were still debating its longevity. Ada Davis chose a compromising style that was neither the short-waisted version of 1873 nor a full *cuirass*. This transitional period also saw the beginnings of a slimmer skirt and abandonment of excessive bustling of fabric at the back waist. Even so, Davis's skirt is surprisingly narrow for 1874. The deep box pleats at the back flow smoothly over the half hoop skirt she wore underneath, providing ample fabric for the train.[3] These new skirt and bodice designs inspired a desire for asymmetry, which Davis's dressmaker successfully incorporated into the gown. A diagonal line of gathered self-fabric and rows of pleated silk netting travel across the front of the skirt, ending in a bow on the left side.[4]

Ada Davis and T. Sibley Heald were married between eight and nine o'clock in the evening at the fashionable Bay State House. The hotel, built in 1856, stood in the heart of Worcester's business district. According to Davis's journal, the couple invited 239 guests, mostly friends and relatives from Worcester and the surrounding area, although some came from as far away as Chicago and Cincinnati. It was quite a fashionable event and one hundred guests enjoyed the handiwork of local confectioner Hannah Hemenway, who specialized in wedding cakes.[5]

United States
*Wedding Dress:
Bodice and Skirt*
1874
Silk
Gift of Madeleine King
Short in memory of
Ethel Heald King
1999.234a,b

On September 4th 1874 I Ada M. Davis of Worcester, commenced purchasing articles preparatory to my wedding, which was to occur in the month of October. The following is a list as nearly as I can recollect of articles purchased and their prices.

1	Set of Cambric Under-clothes	$ 2.00
1	" " Chemise and Drawers	5.25
1	Skirt with two ruffles	3.00
1	" " one flounce	2.75
1	Chemise	2.50
6 Yd	Cotton Flannel	2.10
2 "	Hamburg Edge	.55
2 "	" Insertion	.65
12 "	" Edge	3.00
2 "	" Insertion	.50
2 "	Embroidered Flannel	6.00
30 "	Cotton Flannel	60.05

Figure 1
The first page of Ada Davis's wedding journal.

Figure 2
This illustration from *Godey's Lady's Book* in November 1874 depicts the fuller skirt style that was more common the year Ada Davis married. Davis's skirt is surprisingly narrow and lacks the bustled fabric at the back. The gown on the right features a typical *cuirass* bodice that was cut to fit well over the hips. The length of the *cuirass* varied from quite short, as in Davis's gown, to as long as the top of the thigh in the late 1870s and early 1880s.

In 1876 T. Sibley Heald was listed in the Worcester city directory as a conductor on the Boston, Barre & Gardner Railroad traveling out of the Union Depot on Madison Street. This new line opened in 1871 but was shut down just seven years later, an event that may have been the impetus for the couple and their growing family to move to Rutland in 1880.[6]

1. The relationship between Ada M. Davis and the Hudsons is not clear. George Hudson is listed as a bootmaker in the 1870 census. In 1900 Hudson was employed as a day laborer and Arthur Ashton Heald (b. 1876), the son of Ada Davis and T. Sibley Heald, a schoolteacher like his mother, was boarding with the Hudsons. This implies that there may have been a personal connection of some kind between the families. On the other hand, Lillian C. Brooks, schoolteacher, boarded with the Hudsons at the same time as Arthur A. Heald, indicating that the couple may have taken in boarders regularly to supplement their income.

2. Charles Nutt, *History of Worcester and its People* (New York: Lewis Historical Publishing Company, 1919), 705. Ada M. Davis's journal is in the collection of the Cincinnati Art Museum.

3. The February 1875 issue of *Milwaukee Monthly Magazine* dismissed the *cuirass* "as a novelty, not to recommend to our readers." A similar transitional style is seen in an evening gown illustrated in *Harper's Bazar*, January 1873, 60. Davis's half hoop skirt was donated with the dress. It is constructed of cotton with boning running horizontally from top to bottom. Secured around the waist, it laces down the inside center back behind the legs. The hoop skirt takes on a rounded or half circle form as the lacing is pulled tighter.

4. Stella Blum, ed., *Victorian Fashions and Costumes from Harper's Bazar, 1867–1898* (New York: Dover Publications, 1974).

5. Ada Davis journal, 1874, n.p.; Nutt, *History of Worcester*, 1039; *The Worcester Directory* (Worcester, MA: Drew, Allis & Co., 1876), 4.

6. *The Worcester Directory*, 1876, 122; Nutt, *History of Worcester*, 988–89.

11 / WEDDING DRESS: BODICE AND SKIRT

1874
UNITED STATES

Like Ada M. Davis, Virginia Palmer Reynolds (1855–1922) had an important decision to make in April 1874, when she was preparing to wed William Griffith (1846–1920). Fashionable styles were in a transitional phase, moving from the higher-waisted, fussier designs of the early 1870s to the slimmer silhouette of the latter years of the decade. Reynolds's choices resulted in a gown quite different from that worn by Ada Davis (see cat. 10).[1]

Both brides chose a V neckline, which was considered immodest for a church ceremony but appropriate for a home wedding. Unlike Davis's bodice, which was quite short on the sides, Reynolds's choice was a moderate version of the *cuirass*, cut to cover the top of her hips, with extended V shapes at the center front and back. The dress, with its effusive trimmings, was quite fashionable for 1874, but in contrast to the forward-looking spareness of Davis's dress. The box-pleated silk net trim at the neckline, sleeve ends, and across the front of the skirt unifies the design, as does the use of gathered self-fabric. The vertical ruching of the three-quarter-length sleeves echoes the inflated nature of the bustle. Like most wedding gowns of the period, Reynolds's dress is trimmed with wax orange blossoms—a symbol of fertility since ancient times—both on the bodice and extensively on the skirt.

The rosy beige color of Reynolds's gown is most interesting. Although colorful wedding dresses were not unusual in the nineteenth century, these were often modest dresses meant for traveling soon after the ceremony, or worn by brides with limited means. This was not the case for Reynolds. Her father, Edmund Reynolds, was a physician who had relocated to Cincinnati from New York.[2] The dress cannot be mistaken for anything other than a formal bridal gown, and the fact that the original orange blossoms remain intact indicates it was probably never worn again. This rosy shade, however, was not an uncommon color for dresses of the period, including wedding attire (see cat. 9).[3]

Virginia and William Griffith purchased a home on Ashland Avenue in East Walnut Hills, a fashionable neighborhood just north of downtown Cincinnati, where they lived throughout their married life. William Griffith worked with his father and two brothers in the family business, James T. Griffith & Sons, one of the oldest and largest building contractors in the city. Employing hundreds of workmen, the company built some of the city's most important edifices, including Music Hall, the John Shillito block, the Alms & Doepke buildings, the Ohio National Guard Armory, and many prominent suburban residences. William Griffith became president of the company in 1911. The couple had two children.[4]

1. Obituary of William Griffith, *Cincinnati Commercial Tribune*, November 18, 1920.

2. U.S. Federal Census, 1870.

3. In addition to Florence Carlisle's 1871 court presentation dress (see cat. 9), there are two other wedding gowns of the same color in the Cincinnati Art Museum collection, dated 1871 and 1879.

4. U.S. Federal Census, 1880, 1900, and 1910; *Williams' City Directory* (Cincinnati: Williams Directory Company, 1849–89); *Cincinnati Commercial Tribune*, Griffith obituary; John William Leonard, *The Centennial Review of Cincinnati: One Hundred Years of Progress in Commerce, Manufactures, the Professions, and in Social and Municipal Life* (Cincinnati: J. M. Elstner, 1888), 72.

Figure 1
Virginia Reynolds in
her wedding gown,
1874.

Figure 2
Virginia Reynolds's wedding gown followed fashionable trends, as evidenced by this color plate from *Godey's Lady's Book*, April 1874. Note the effusive use of orange blossoms on the bodice, sleeves, and skirt, similar to that on Reynolds's gown.

12 / WEDDING DRESS: BODICE AND SKIRT

1874
CHARLES FREDERICK WORTH (1825–95)
ENGLAND, WORKED IN FRANCE

The wedding gown worn by Katherine Phillips (1848–1911) when she married Robert Fulton Leaman (1841–87) on April 22, 1875, was created by Charles Frederick Worth (1826–95).[1] English by birth, Worth became the most sought-after Paris couturier of the nineteenth century; his reputation was established through the patronage of the Empress Eugénie. Like many wealthy American women, Phillips traveled to Paris to shop for her wedding gown and trousseau. She probably patronized a number of high-quality dressmakers for specific articles of clothing, but no other couturier would suffice for this most important gown. Surely, she was not disappointed by this very fashion-forward example of Worth's design skills.

In January 1874, a fashion plate in *Harper's Bazar* illustrated a low-cut evening gown with puff sleeves and a similarly draped flounce near the hemline of the skirt. In fact, Worth's thoughts about wedding dresses were recorded in detail. "Worth forbids all lace on bridal robes, and trims the richest faille and satin with tulle. . . . Soft dull faille dresses are preferred to those of glossy satin . . . the front and sides [of the skirt] cling to the figure, [and] are fastened to the [waist] band without pleats or gathers, and all the fullness is in box-pleats behind, affording a graceful sweep for the fan-shaped train."[2]

As dictated by Worth, Katherine Phillips's dress is constructed of silk faille—a finely ribbed fabric that lacks the sheen of satin. In keeping with his reported disdain for lace, Worth embellished the skirt with an overlay of sheer silk formed into swags and caught up with rosettes of the same transparent fabric. The gored skirt fits smoothly over the hips, with the pleated fullness at the back falling into the rounded or fan-shaped train. Worth's treatment of the bottom edge of the bodice is most distinctive. Deep scallops ornament this new style, called the *cuirass*—a term derived from a piece of medieval armor that appeared to be molded to the body.

Fitting over the hips, this shape pushed the fullness downward, creating a narrower skirt silhouette that, according to *Harper's Bazar*, would "cling to the figure."

Katherine Phillips, a Cincinnati native, was the daughter of Sarah (neé Samson) and Thomas Phillips, a prominent iron merchant. Katherine's husband, Robert Fulton Leaman, was born in Bucks County, Pennsylvania, but he moved to Ohio, just north of Cincinnati, as a child. Leaman interrupted his study of law to serve in the Civil War with the 131st Regiment, Ohio Volunteer Infantry Division. After the war, he made his fortune in book publishing but died at the early age of forty-six, leaving his wife to care for their four children.[3]

1. Charles Theodore Greve, *Centennial History of Cincinnati and Representative Citizens* (Chicago: Biographical Pub. Co., 1904), vol. 2, 499–500; Last will and testament of Robert Fulton Leaman, 1887; Ohio Deaths, 1908–1932, http://www.ancestry.com/; Jeffrey G. Herbert, ed., *Restored Hamilton County Marriages 1870–1884* (Cincinnati: Hamilton County Chapter of the Ohio Genealogical Society, 1994). For more information on Charles Frederick Worth see Diana De Marly, *Worth, Father of Haute Couture* (New York: Holmes & Meier, 1990) and Elizabeth A. Coleman, *The Opulent Era: Worth, Doucet, and Pingat* (New York: Thames and Hudson, 1989).

2. *Harper's Bazar*, January 24, 1874, 58.

3. Greve, *Centennial History of Cincinnati*, 499–500.

Charles Frederick
Worth (1825–95)
England, worked in
France
*Wedding Dress:
Bodice and Skirt,*
1874
Silk
Gift of Mrs. John
Tytus
1988.144a,b

13 / WEDDING DRESS: BODICE AND SKIRT

1875
UNITED STATES

While Louisa Uphoff's 1875 bridal gown does not have the avant-garde flair of Katherine Phillips's Worth creation of the previous year (see cat. 12), her dressmaker provided her with a very fashionable dress. Uphoff's gown is perhaps the more correct of the two, according to etiquette manuals of the day. The neckline is high and the sleeves are long; the gown is the picture of modesty—perhaps because Uphoff was married in St. Francis de Sales Roman Catholic Church.[1]

Uphoff also chose to wear white satin, therefore following the firm advice of S. A. Frost in *The Art of Dressing Well*. "From the millionaire's daughter to the mechanic's child, there is always one rule, that the bride must be white throughout. Dress, veil, gloves, slippers, wreath, or bonnet, all must be of pure white for a full dress bridal."[2] Both Frost and her fellow etiquette writer, Cecil B. Hartley, lamented the extravagant trims lavished on American wedding dresses. Hartley advised that simplicity is the wiser choice. "In France it is always remembered, with better taste, that when a young lady goes up to the altar, she is '*encore jeune fille*;' her dress, therefore, is exquisitely simple."[3]

One might say Uphoff did excessively embellish her gown, with rows of self-fabric ruffles, lace at the neckline, and multiple strands of orange blossoms around the skirt and festooned from her elaborate headpiece. While she probably could not have afforded Phillips's elegant Parisian gown, it is safe to assume that Uphoff aspired to Katherine Phillips's station. Louisa's father, George H. Uphoff, owned a livery stable; the family resided in the East Walnut Hills neighborhood of Cincinnati and was probably middle class. Desiring a dress as fashionable as Phillips's, however, Uphoff would have studied popular ladies' magazines to decide upon a stylish design. Although her dress bears no label, she probably employed a local dressmaker as Ada Davis did in 1874 (see cat. 10).[4]

Louisa Uphoff (1853–1933) married Francis (Frank) Xavier Bernard Homan (1851–79) in May 1875. Frank managed the family business after the death of his father in 1865. Homan & Co., established in 1847, was a manufacturer of silver-plated and Britannia ware. Frank's early death from typhoid fever in 1879 occurred while Louisa was pregnant with their third child. Louisa and her brother-in-law, Henry Korf, owned and operated Homan & Co. until Margaret Homan, Frank's mother, purchased the firm from her.[5]

1. Regarding the fashionableness of Uphoff's gown see, for instance, *Frank Leslie's Lady's Magazine*, May and November 1875. Both of these color fashion plates illustrate brides. Genealogical research was provided by the Homan family.

2. S. A. Frost, *The Art of Dressing Well: A Complete Guide to Economy, Style and Propriety of Costume* (New York: Dick & Fitzgerald, Publishers, 1870), 64–65.

3. Cecil B. Hartley, *The Gentlemen's Book of Etiquette, and Manual of Politeness; Being a Complete Guide for a Gentleman's Conduct in All His Relations Towards Society* (Boston: J. S. Locke & Company, 1874), 289. The author makes the distinction between "full dress" or a formal bridal gown and a going-away dress, which would most often be made of colored fabric.

4. U.S. Federal Census, 1860, 1870; New York Passenger Lists, 1820–1957, http://www.ancestry.com/.

5. Homan family genealogical information.

Figure 1
Louisa Uphoff Homan in her wedding gown, 1875.

United States
*Wedding Dress:
Bodice and Skirt,*
1875
Silk
Gift of Elizabeth
Busse Schulenberg
2004.126a,b

United States
Wedding Dress, 1879
Silk
Gift of Elizabeth
Busse Schulenberg
2004.127

14 / WEDDING DRESS

1879
UNITED STATES

Comparing the bridal photos of Rose Uphoff (b. abt. 1858) and her older sister Louisa (see cat. 13), Rose appears to be the coquette of the two. She looks coyly at the camera with a rather teasing smile. For her June 11, 1879 wedding to Frank Hackmann (b. abt. 1852), Rose chose the "decidedly fashionable" princess cut for her gown. According to *Godey's Lady's Book*, this cut only suited the well-proportioned figure, which Rose Uphoff shows to good effect in her profile photograph. The white satin from which the gown is constructed has a faint pink tinge, which is also mentioned in the lady's magazine as the latest trend.[1]

Rose Uphoff's wedding dress perhaps epitomizes the overstated trimmings of which American etiquette writers complained: "The French bridal costume is simple; in England it is more elaborate, while in this country it is very apt to be an occasion of ostentatious extravagance painfully absurd."[2] Although calling Uphoff's gown absurd may be going too far, it is rather extreme in the amount of box-pleated self-fabric, lace, and especially orange blossoms that embellish it. Careful examination of Rose Uphoff's wedding photo (see fig. 1) reveals copious amounts of gathered lace around the neckline and down the center front of the dress, almost to the knees. Between these central rows of lace is what appears to be a continuous strand of orange blossoms. Bunches of flower buds encircle Uphoff's wrists. These wax facsimiles also decorate the skirt at intervals and form the prodigious headpiece. Long vines of blossoms appear and disappear within the netting of the veil. Perhaps Uphoff had seen an illustration of this type of ornamentation: The January 1872 issue of *Godey's Lady's Book* describes a bridal hair wreath of orange blossoms "with long pendants and tendrils floating gracefully over the shoulders and brow of the destined bride, helping to hide the glad face, as 'love transfigures life.'"[3]

Although Rose Uphoff's husband, Frank Hackmann, seems to have earned his living as a wholesale grocer, his father Henry was a partner in Hackmann & Duesterberg, Undertakers and Livery Stable. Rose's father also owned a livery stable, which explains how the couple probably met. Little else is known about them.[4]

1. U.S. Federal Census, 1870; Jeffrey G. Herbert, ed., *Restored Hamilton County Marriages 1870–1884* (Cincinnati: Hamilton County Chapter of the Ohio Genealogical Society, 1994), 991; *Godey's Lady's Book*, December, 1875, 577. There are several alternate spellings of Frank Hackmann's name in the city directories and census, including Hakman, Hackman, and Hackmann, as used here.

2. S. A. Frost, *The Art of Dressing Well: A Complete Guide to Economy, Style and Propriety of Costume* (New York: Dick & Fitzgerald, Publishers, 1870), 65.

3. *Godey's Lady's Book*, January 1872, 299–300.

4. U.S. Federal Census, 1880; *Williams' City Directory* (Cincinnati: Williams Directory Company, 1849–89).

Figure 1
Rose Uphoff Hackmann in her wedding gown, 1879.

Ellen Curtis (1850–
1923)
United States
(Lexington,
Kentucky)
*Wedding Dress:
Bodice and Skirt*,
1879
Silk
Gift of Anita Keller
Dodd in memory of
her grandmother,
Ellen Curtis Scott
1986.943a,b

15 / WEDDING DRESS: BODICE AND SKIRT

1879
ELLEN CURTIS (1850–1923)
UNITED STATES (LEXINGTON, KENTUCKY)

It can be taken for granted that Ellen Curtis (1850–1923) would have worn the most fashionable of wedding gowns when she married Louis A. Scott in April 1879. Ellen, however, was not a socialite from a prominent family. She was a dressmaker in Lexington, Kentucky. Dressmakers were in an exceptional position when it came to their own wardrobes. Most were working-class women who struggled against overwhelming odds to acquire and retain a reliable client base. At the same time, they had the finest fabrics at their disposal and a finger on the pulse of fashion. Some were successful enough to hire a team of seamstresses to work for them. Others were able to travel periodically to New York City and Europe to purchase fabric and trims.[1]

It is clear by the stylish mode of her gown that Ellen Curtis was a dedicated student of fashion trends. By the time she made her wedding dress, the *cuirass* bodice was ubiquitous and skirts had continued to narrow. In June 1877 *Harper's Bazar* discussed Paris trends, noting that fashion demanded that "women . . . be sheathed from neck to feet in a garment stretched on the figure, giving them the appearance of a pencil with a train attached." Although Curtis did not make her gown as pencil thin as the exaggerated fashion plates she undoubtedly scrutinized (see fig. 2), the silhouette is decidedly slimmer than that of Virginia Palmer Reynolds, for instance, five years prior (see cat. 11).[2]

The late 1870s *collant* or close-fitting skirts were made so by pairs of linen tapes sewn inside the back side seams. These were tied behind the legs, pulling the skirt close in front and isolating fullness at the back. The result was such a narrow silhouette that women were forced to walk with short mincing steps. These sheathlike skirts were widely criticized. As early as 1875, *Godey's Lady's Book* disparaged the style: "There has been much good-natured satire about fashionably-dressed women not being able to sit on their chairs except sideways and with extreme caution, otherwise the elastic, strings, and other cunning devices for tying back [skirts] would suddenly break away. But with the new skirts the difficulty does not rest with the sitting down; the problem is how to walk at all."[3]

Curtis incorporated a number of fashionable ideas into her wedding dress design. One, credited to Paris couturier Charles Frederick Worth, was the draped fabric around her hips, called *paniers*, a revival of an eighteenth-century style.[4] She constructed her dress from two silk fabrics in a monochromatic color scheme: fine ribbed faille and satin woven with a subtle scrollwork pattern. The varying textures of the materials each accentuate a different section of the garment. The high neckline was not only stylish, but appropriately modest for her wedding at St. Paul's Roman Catholic Church. The gown would have served Curtis well after her wedding as a dress in which to consult with her wealthiest customers. She would have impressed them with her stylishness, as the tailored bodice with faux lapels and military-style cuffs were design elements frequently seen in contemporary fashion illustrations.

1. See Wendy Gamber, *The Female Economy: The Millinery and Dressmaking Trades 1860–1930* (Urbana: University of Illinois Press, 1997) and Cynthia Amnéus, *A Separate Sphere: Dressmakers in Cincinnati's Golden Age 1877–1922* (Lubbock: Texas Tech University Press, 2003) for a full discussion of the dressmaking trade.

2. *Harper's Bazar*, June 2, 1877, 343.

3. Ibid.; *Godey's Lady's Book*, May 1877, 469 and December 1875, 577.

4. *Harper's Bazar*, November 10, 1877, 715 and October 1879, 328.

Figure 2
The gowns in this fashion plate exemplify the exaggerated slimness of fashionable 1879 styles. *Peterson's Magazine*, October 1879.

16 / WEDDING DRESS

882–83
GEORGE HENRY LEE AND CO. (ACTIVE LATE 19TH C.)
ENGLAND (LIVERPOOL)

The princess style, in which the bodice and skirt of a gown were cut in one, returned to favor in the early 1870s. This construction enjoyed continued popularity throughout the decade, and in November 1877 *Harper's Bazar* declared it was quite fashionable for wedding gowns.[1] When well-fitted, the style outlined the body perfectly, displaying the desired hourglass figure that could only be achieved with corsetry.

Despite the widely accepted notion of tight-laced Victorian morality, many design elements in this dress seem to be deliberately alluring. For the princess style to be successful, the gown had to be cut to fit the torso like a glove—a feat that could only be achieved by a talented and technically skilled dressmaker. Equally close-fitting in this period, the sleeves encased the upper arms and might, as in this dress, flare at the elbow and reveal the forearm. The low round neckline was designed to display the bosom. For a wedding, however, it was filled in with sheer fabric or lace ruffles, as seen here. These trims were intended to be removed and replaced with a narrow lace edging. A revealing décolleté was *de rigueur* for evening or dinner gowns, and many brides planned to wear their wedding attire again.

Fashions of the 1880s favored a rounded belly rather like those in the Rubenesque images of the baroque. Cinching the waist tightly pushed flesh both upward and downward, and corsets of the period were constructed to cup the abdomen. In this gown, the dressmaker draws the eye to the belly and hips with the use of horizontally pleated fabric that converges in ruching at the center front. The billowing fabric on the back of the dress focuses the viewer's eye on the derrière and forecasts the expansive bustle that appeared around 1883. In this dress, the asymmetrical puffs of fabric are playfully appealing, and there is no doubting the sensual nature of the design. Below, the train spreads out in a perfectly pleated fan shape.

According to the donor, Ida Peltz Rost wore this gown for her marriage in Gettysburg, Pennsylvania. The dress bears the George Henry Lee & Co. label. By the 1880s, this shop had developed into a department store that, like many large retail establishments, operated a custom dressmaking salon.[2] Rost must have traveled to England to be fitted for this superbly crafted gown. Perhaps, like Florence Carlisle (see cat. 9), it was the bride's court presentation gown that also served as her wedding dress.

1. *Harper's Bazar*, November 1877, 707; see also *Godey's Lady's Book*, May 1877, 469.

2. George Henry Lee & Co., founded in 1853 by Henry Boswell Lee, began as a bonnet warehouse at 12 Basnett Street in Liverpool. See http://www.johnlewis.com/Shops/DSTemplate.aspx?Id=19.

George Henry Lee
and Co. (active late
19th c.)
England, (Liverpool)
Wedding Dress,
1882–83
Silk, linen
Anonymous Gift
1965.589

Figure 1
Back view.

17 / WEDDING DRESS: BODICE AND SKIRT

1883
UNITED STATES

Katherine Burton Pease (1859–1928) could not have been more elegantly attired for her October 1883 wedding. Unlike the bride in cat. 16, Pease chose a more traditional yet very fashionable style of dress with a separate bodice and skirt. Still, the gown fits her perfectly.

The design of Pease's gown is thoughtfully unified. With the damask fabric as inspiration, the dressmaker made use of the pointed perimeter of the woven pattern, as well as the contrast between the sheen of the rose-and-leaf motif and the matte ground. Pointed triangles formed of reflective satin frame the neckline. The skirt front, also satin, has a crenellated edge echoing the leaf design. This motif is carried through most effectively in the train, which divides into three pointed sections — a design device that Paris couturier Charles Frederick Worth introduced in the late 1870s.[1]

Like many wedding gowns, both contemporary and historical, this design references past styles. Here, the skirt splits at the center front and is swept to the sides to reveal what in the eighteenth century would have been called the petticoat. Like Ellen Curtis's gown (see cat. 15), the damask is tucked to form *paniers* over the hips.[2] Spanish lace and fashionable faux pearls decorate the gown at the neckline, bust, and sleeves. The lace is cleverly used to conceal the upper arm, where the sleeve design is rather revealing.[3]

Although Pease may have been wealthy enough to wear this gown only once, it seems she expected to make further use of it after her wedding. The square neckline has been filled in with a lace modesty panel, probably for a church wedding. This would have been removed later and the gown worn as an elegant evening or dinner dress for which a low neckline was preferred.

Katherine Burton Pease was the eldest child of David Harlow Pease (1826–72) and Sarah Anne Burton (d. 1907), residents of Norwalk, Ohio. David Pease was a merchant. Katherine graduated from music school in Boston and served for several years as the organist at the Hyde Park Presbyterian Church in Chicago. On October 24, 1883, Pease married Charles B. Tourtelotte, who was the cousin of her Boston roommate.

Tourtelotte died suddenly in 1885 and their son, Charles Burton Tourtelotte, was born two months later. Katherine remarried in 1893. She lived in Chicago until about 1924, when she moved to Cincinnati to live with relatives.[4]

1. *Harper's Bazar,* November 1877, 707.

2. *Godey's Lady's Book*, September 1884, p. 304 references this style of skirt. A similar effect is described with a *basque* in the "Fashion Chat" in the *Saturday Evening Post*, July 23, 1881, 16.

3. Spanish lace was popular, especially in the last quarter of the nineteenth century. It was a dense machine-made lace, usually in repetitive floral designs. The faux pearls on this gown and that worn by Frances Amelia White (see cat. 19) are hollow glass globes coated on the interior, probably with a pearlescent pigment in a binder. A description of a wedding gown trimmed with Spanish lace over white gros grain fabric is referred to in *Harper's Bazar*, October 8, 1881, 642. The use of pearl embellishments is mentioned in *Peterson's Magazine*, March 1881, 249, and *Harper's Bazar*, September 27, 1884, 611.

4. Pease family genealogical information, Cincinnati Art Museum curatorial files.

Figure 1
Detail of damask fabric.

United States
*Wedding Dress: Bodice
and Skirt,* 1883
Silk, linen, faux pearls
Gift of family of Charles
Harlow and Fanny Peters
Pease
1964.647a,b

United States
Wedding Dress:
Bodice and Skirt,
1883
Silk
Gift of Janet S.
Humphrey
1988.222a,b

18 / WEDDING DRESS: BODICE AND SKIRT

1883
UNITED STATES

Margaret A. Means (b. 1853) was an extraordinary nineteenth-century woman. In 1910, at the age of fifty-five, she was a single woman living in a Manhattan hotel. She seems to have spent the 1880s and 1890s traveling and living in Europe, probably returning to the United States to see family from time to time.[1] If the one piece of her wardrobe that survives in the Cincinnati Art Museum's collection is any indication, she certainly had the means to do so. The French couture house Moret & Moncuit created a fashionable gold and pink silk gown for her.[2]

The relationship between Margaret Means and Eliza Isabelle Means (1858–1942) is unclear. Margaret may have been Eliza's aunt. Nevertheless, their relationship was close enough for Eliza to have seen the Moret & Moncuit gown, because she had it copied for her wedding on September 17, 1885, to William Biggs Seaton (1855–1927).[3]

Margaret's dress is quite exceptional. The French fabric is deep gold with a woven pattern of delicate pink flowers with green leaves. It laces up the bodice front and is trimmed with a high-quality machine-made lace. The same pink silk satin that forms the stylish *paniers* falls in flat panels down the front of the skirt. The bodice is trimmed asymmetrically with a large ribbon corsage on one side and flowers on the other (fig. 1 and 2).

Eliza's dressmaker must have been delighted to have the opportunity to examine a French couture gown so closely. She carefully reproduced the style with minor adjustments that were probably requested by the bride. The asymmetry of the bodice embellishments is less exaggerated, and it fastens up the front with a style of crocheted button that was popular during the period. Most noticeably, the cut and drape of the *paniers* is more conservative.

Eliza Means chose to have her gown made in shades of white, although this would not have precluded wearing it again: The September 25, 1880 issue of *Harper's Bazar* illustrates and describes a creamy white satin bridal toilette that was equally suitable for dinner or evening wear.[4]

It is somewhat surprising that Eliza did not go to Europe herself and have her gown made by a Parisian couturier. Eliza's father was a highly successfully businessman in Ashland, Kentucky—certainly wealthy enough to send his daughter along on such an excursion with Margaret. Nevertheless, Eliza's gown stands as an interesting example of a practice that was not uncommon in the nineteenth century, particularly for women of lesser means.

1. U.S. Federal Census, 1910; U.S. Passport Applications, 1795–1925, http://www.ancestry.com/.

2. See Otto Charles Thieme, *With Grace and Favour: Victorian and Edwardian Fashion in America* (Cincinnati Art Museum, 1993), 65 for additional description of Margaret A. Means's gown.

3. Oren Andrew Seaton, ed., *The Seaton Family, with Genealogy and Biographies* (Topeka, KS: Crane & Company, 1906), 308.

4. *Harper's Bazar*, September 25, 1880, 1.

Figure 1
Margaret A. Means's
reception dress (left)
and Eliza Isabelle
Means's wedding
gown (right)

Figure 2
Margaret A. Means in her Mmes. Moret & Moncuit gown.

19 / WEDDING DRESS

1887
UNITED STATES

On the evening of June 22, 1887, friends and family joined Mordecai Morris White (1830–1913) and Hannah Amelia Coffin White (1838–1934) to witness the marriage of their eldest daughter, Frances Amelia (1859–1926), to John Gates (1853–1927) at the White home on Auburn Avenue in Cincinnati. Without doubt it was both a decorous and posh event, as befitted a family of wealth and station in the city.[1]

When Mordecai White died in 1913, his estate was estimated at between fifteen and twenty million dollars. White had earned his fortune primarily as a leading financier in the Midwest, serving as president and chairman of the board of the Fourth National Bank from 1875 until 1908. Other business ventures included a partnership in A. H. Wells & Co., a wholesale grocer, and interests in railways and insurance companies in and around Cincinnati. White was known as a man with the highest principles, a broad vision, and a kind and gracious manner—traits no doubt nurtured by his Quaker beliefs.[2]

His daughter's wedding gown is both fashionable and opulent, as one would expect given Mordecai White's financial status. The dress is cut in the popular princess style in the back. Instead of lace, the bride chose to trim her dress with silk tulle ornamented profusely with dangles of seed beads and faux pearls. The fashion periodicals between 1885 and 1887 frequently mention this type of beaded trim. *Harper's Bazar* in October 1887 reported that "beads are threaded and attached to the net in loops," describing exactly the embellishments that ornament the net overlay at the neckline and on the skirt of Frances White's gown.[3] Here, the loops are enhanced with faux pearls in an overall pattern. The net overlay divides at the center, where the skirt is heavily laden with wax orange blossoms. The train is long and bound with a substantial piping that maintained the fabric's square shape. Although a full bustle was still in fashion in 1887, Frances either chose a more conservative style or was fashion-forward enough to realize that its demise was just around the corner.

Frances and her husband raised three children in their home on Oak Street in the fashionable neighborhood of Clifton. John Gates and his brother James assumed control of their family business—John Gates & Co., a manufacturer of boots and shoes—upon their father's death.[4]

1. The original wedding invitation has been preserved by the donor.

2. Obituary of Mordecai Morris White, *Cincinnati Enquirer*, October 1, 1913; *The National Cyclopaedia of American Biography* (New York: James T. White & Company, 1932), 238–39.

3. *Harper's Bazar*, October 31, 1887, 699. Additional references to beaded trims on net can be found in *Arthur's Home Magazine*, November 1886, 870; *Harper's Bazar*, January 17, 1885, 43; October 6, 1886, 655; June 25, 1887, 447; April 23, 1887, 291; and January 8, 1887, 23.

4. *Williams' City Directory* (Cincinnati: Williams Directory Company, 1856–89); Charles Frederic Goss, *Cincinnati, The Queen City, 1788–1912* (Cincinnati: S. J. Clarke Publishing Company, 1912), 537–38.

United States
Wedding Dress, 1887
Silk, beads, faux
pearls
Gift of Mrs. Frances
Lamson Eaton, Mr.
and Mrs. Alfred
W. Lamson, Mr.
and Mrs. Benjamin
Whitney Lamson, Jr.
1971.320

Figure 1
Detail of dress
embellishment.

PRINCESS BEATRICE IN HER WEDDING GOWN.—From a Photograph.—[See Page 506.]

Figure 2
This frontispiece of *Harper's Bazar*, August 1885, depicts a gown that is surprisingly similar to that
worn by Frances Amelia White in 1887.

20 / WEDDING DRESS: BODICE AND SKIRT

1891
LANOUETTE (ACTIVE LATE 19TH C.)
UNITED STATES

By the early 1890s, fashions had changed dramatically. The oversized bustles and tight sleeves of the previous decade were gone. Corsetry still cinched the waist, but skirts were slimmer and less cumbersome. In 1891, when Olive Douglas Perkins (1858–1930) married, the Directoire and Empire styles, which featured a higher waistline, were popular.[1] Although Perkins's gown does not actually have an Empire waist, the wide band of trim set around the midsection gives that appearance. In fact, Perkins's dress is rather unusual in design. It conforms to fashion trends with its leg-of-mutton sleeves—large at the shoulder and narrow on the forearm. It is stylish in the straighter skirt design, but the bodice construction was not commonly seen in fashion illustrations.[2]

The body of this dress is constructed of a creamy colored faille—a finely ribbed fabric that, in this case, is surprisingly soft to the touch. The upper bodice is overlaid with gathered and pleated sheer silk. The peplum that falls over the hips is sheer in front and opaque silk faille in back. It lengthens the line of the bodice, creating the look of a long jacket.[3] Most distinctive is the wide band of metallic braid, studded with faux pearls and seed beads, around the waist. The braid narrows as it moves under the arms, creating an inverted V shape at the back neckline, again reinforcing the illusion of a higher waistline by focusing the eye upward (fig. 1 and 2).

Olive Perkins may have been influenced in her choice by the growing criticism of women's constrictive fashionable dress. Although advocates of dress reform were active beginning in the 1850s, the movement gained strength in the latter decades of the nineteenth century. Early proponents of aesthetic dress included members of the Pre-Raphaelite Brotherhood—a group of painters who admired the work of medieval artists. Not only did the Pre-Raphaelites depict period clothing in their paintings, they encouraged their wives, models, and friends to wear medieval- or Renaissance-style fashions. This trend toward less constraining designs was advanced by the development in the 1870s of the tea gown, a specialized dress worn for late afternoon entertaining. Tea gowns were often constructed to appear loose-fitting, though few women would have abandoned their corsets underneath.[4] Perkins's wedding gown does not specifically fall into the category of reform dress. It is not constructed to be loose on the body, but only to suggest a period look. Nevertheless, choosing such a design for her wedding gown was a bold move at the time.

Olive Perkins, of Warren, Ohio, married Cincinnati native Samuel Watson Smith, Jr. (1859–1930) on October 20, 1891. Smith was a lawyer and later a judge of the Common Pleas Court of Hamilton County, Ohio. The couple had one child.[5]

1. The Directoire and Empire styles are discussed in *Godey's Lady's Book* in the January 1889 issue, 72. Directoire references the high-waisted dresses worn during the post-Revolution French Directory governance (1795–99). Similar styles continued into the Empire period during the rule of Napoleon I, the First French Empire. The designs reference classical modes of dress (see cat. 2).

2. Two similar examples are seen in *Ladies' Home Journal*, June 1891, 25 and *Harper's Bazar*, August 19, 1893, 672.

3. For examples of extended bodices in this same style see *Harper's Bazar*, April 20, 1889, 288–89 and October 18, 1890, 812–13.

4. Patricia Cunningham, "Healthful, Artistic, and Correct Dress," in Otto Charles Thieme, *With Grace and Favour: Victorian and Edwardian Dress in America*, (Cincinnati Art Museum, 1993), 14–25.

5. *History of Cincinnati and Hamilton County, Ohio; Their Past and Present* (Cincinnati: S. B. Nelson & Co., Publisher, 1894), 626; Charles Theodore Greve, *Centennial History of Cincinnati and Representative Citizens* (Chicago: Biographical Pub. Co., 1904), vol. 2, 579–80.

Lanouette (active
late 19th c.)
United States
*Wedding Dress:
Bodice and Skirt,*
1891
Silk, beads, metallic
thread
Gift of Mrs. Russell
Wilson
1940.1092a,b

Figure 1
Back view of Perkins's
gown alongside the
1892 wedding dress of
Minnie Crosby Emery.
See cat. 21.

A BRIDAL GOWN (Illus. No. 3)

Figure 2
A similar peplum-style gown in *Ladies' Home Journal*, June 1891.

21 / WEDDING DRESS

1892
UNITED STATES

Like Olive Perkins (see cat. 20), Minnie Crosby Emery (b. 1865) chose an alternative style for her wedding gown. Emery, too, was influenced by the ideas of dress reform that were flooding the pages of women's magazines in the late nineteenth century. The criticism of corseting, in particular, reached a peak in the 1880s. Numerous articles, sermons, and lectures condemned tight lacing—the practice of cinching the waist so tightly that it constricted breathing and potentially deformed the ribs and internal organs. Though advocates of dress reform shared a common goal—to modify women's fashionable dress—there were two philosophical camps. The aesthetes promoted artistic dress; the athletics endorsed bifurcated garments. Both, however, turned to classical Greek garments as the ideal. The Venus de Milo was often referenced as a perfect example of the natural female form—a far cry from the wasp-waisted shape of the fashionable nineteenth-century woman.

Corsetry aside, dress reformers were concerned with other aspects of women's clothing that they considered unhealthful. Long trains collected filth from the street, the narrow cut of skirts impeded movement, and the weight of the skirts and petticoats suspended from the waist put undue stress on the body. Overall, it was believed that women's clothing deprived them of their health. Dress reformers reasoned that styles based on classical Greek dress eliminated these issues. Classical fashions were light, shorter in length, untrained, and what weight there was fell from the shoulders. Reformists looked to styles of the Directoire and Empire periods as examples of stylish dress that promoted health. In particular, the high waist—just under the bust—precluded the evils of tight lacing.[1]

Minnie Emery, together with her dressmaker, created a gown that would have been recognized as artistic dress or called a tea gown in the period. Tea gowns were a more relaxed style of dress originally designed for informal entertaining. The "Watteau pleats" that fall from the back neckline were a particularly common design device that suggested looseness. Bordering on the negligee, both artistic dress and tea gowns were originally intended to be worn only in the privacy of one's home. Bolder aesthetes, however, began to wear these dresses in public.[2]

Despite its attributes of reform style, Emery's wedding gown does incorporate boning in the waist and is a particularly heavy garment due, in great part, to the beaded trim. Although little is known about the bride, the fact that she wore such an avant-garde gown for her wedding suggests she was quite self-assured and perhaps artistic.

Minnie Emery married Charles Churchill Pickett (b. 1862) in Chicago on June 1, 1892. Pickett was a lawyer and law professor. The couple had one daughter.[3]

1. For a complete discussion of dress reform in Europe and the United States see Patricia A. Cunningham, *Reforming Women's Fashion, 1850–1920: Politics, Health, and Art* (Kent, OH: Kent State University Press, 2003).

2. For a complete discussion of the origin and design of tea gowns see Anne Bissonnette, "The 1870s Transformation of the *Robe de Chambre*," in Cynthia Amnéus, *A Separate Sphere: Dressmakers in Cincinnati's Golden Age, 1877–1922,* (Lubbock: Texas Tech University Press, 2003), 169–73.

3. U.S. Federal Census, 1870–1930. The original wedding invitation has been preserved by the donor.

United States
Wedding Dress, 1892
Silk, faux pearls,
beads
Gift of James and
Betty Sutherland
2003.127

A VERY BECOMING HOUSE GOWN (Illus. No. 1)

Figure 1
The Watteau pleats and the embellishment on the back of this house gown are quite similar to those of Minnie Crosby's wedding gown. *Ladies' Home Journal*, November 1892.

Figure 2
Minnie Crosby Emery.

Figure 3
Charles Churchill Pickett.

22 / WEDDING DRESS: BODICE AND SKIRT

1894
MISS CARRIE (ACTIVE LATE 19TH C.)
UNITED STATES (LOUISVILLE, KENTUCKY)

Writing in *Ladies' Home Journal*, Isabel A. Mallon describes the art of dressing the bride as follows: "There are some things that a bride must remember: her bodice must be high in the neck; her sleeves reach quite to her wrist, and her gown must fall in full, unbroken folds that show the richness of the material, and there must not be even a suggestion of such frivolities as frills or ribbons of any kind."[1] Blanche Richardson's wedding gown fits Mallon's description of appropriate bridal attire perfectly except for the sleeves. Instead, Richardson chose a shorter style of sleeve and for modesty wore long gloves that she might remove after the ceremony, perhaps because she expected warm June weather.

Far more traditional in her choice of wedding attire than Olive Perkins and Minnie Emery (see cats. 20 and 21), Blanche Richardson (1866–1952) married Franklin Olds Loveland (1861–1915) on June 6, 1894, at the bride's Glendale, Ohio, family home. The event was described in the *Cincinnati Enquirer*: "The large and spacious mansion was brilliantly illuminated and profusely decorated with rare flowers. The bride is one of Glendale's most charming and accomplished young ladies. . . . The groom is one of the bright legal lights of the Cincinnati bar."[2]

Richardson's gown follows Mallon's suggestions for appropriate dress, but did not neglect fashionable trends of the mid-1890s. The "huge sleeves," as described in *Harper's Bazar*, are "the familiar balloon puff to the elbow." The neckline is high, with a stand-up collar that covers the neck itself. The bodice is the stylish "full round waist . . . now even used for wedding-gowns," indicating that there is no point at the center front that drops below the waistline. The plain skirt is gored, making it smooth at the waist with pleated fullness that falls in rich folds at the back. Fashion commentary in ladies' magazines of the time repeatedly extolled the use of rich white satin and extreme simplicity for wedding gowns, as exemplified here.[3]

Blanche Richardson was on the mark. Her dress is embellished only with a modest overlay of pleated netting on the shoulders, a gathered lace flounce on the sleeves, and the pleats that form a large faux bow on the bodice front. This shape settles the eye

Figure 1
Blanche Richardson
in her wedding
gown, 1894.

directly on the bust—an interesting design device for such a modest gown.[4]

Blanche and Franklin Loveland enjoyed an extended trip after their wedding. Unfortunately, Franklin's death in 1916 cut their married life short. Blanche returned to Glendale in 1927 to live with her daughter Angeline, who was married to James J. Faran III (1892–1956).[5] The 1840 wedding gown of Mrs. James J. Faran—née Angelina Russell, grandmother of Angeline's husband—is shown in cat. 5.

1. Isabel A. Mallon, "The Art of Dressing the Bride," *Ladies Home Journal*, March 1894, 17.

2. "Cupid: Richardson-Loveland," *Cincinnati Enquirer*, June 7, 1894.

3. *Harper's Bazar*, September 22, 1894, 755; March 24, 1894; September 15, 1894, 735; April 1, 1893, 251; August 26, 1893, 691.

4. A similar bodice treatment can be seen in the *New York Fashion Bazar*, April 1896, 25.

5. "Cupid: Richardson-Loveland," *Cincinnati Enquirer*; U.S. Federal Census, 1900; *High on a Hill: The Story of Christ Church, Glendale, 1865–1964* (Cincinnati: T. H. Carruthers, 1965), 126.

23 / WEDDING DRESS: BODICE AND SKIRT

1903
UNITED STATES

The "Fashions for Brides" article in *Harper's Bazar* of June 1901 advises brides on a point that had been made for decades: "Fads are not much followed in the matter of bridal gowns. They need not be conventional, but each bride-to-be tries naturally to have her gown original and yet not bizarre and odd."[1] Throughout the nineteenth century, most etiquette manuals recommended not only simplicity but conservatism when selecting a wedding gown. Similarly, the *Harper's Bazar* April 1903 issue counsels brides that fashion illustrations are attractive but gowns should be "toned down by good common sense. There are few women to whom these picturesque styles are becoming. . . . It is not possible merely to say that this or that gown will be the thing to wear because it is fashionable; it must be becoming."[2]

Like other adventurous brides before her, however, Mattie Riddell (1884–1978) chose an extreme version of fashionable trends. While her gown incorporates stylish elements, some are quite exaggerated. By the time Riddell married Charles Richard Brown (d. 1955) in November 1903, lighter fabrics such as lace and chiffon were being recommended to brides even for winter weddings, and high necklines were considered most appropriate. However, if the bride wanted her gown to be a bit more revealing but still modest, she could choose a transparent yoke made of net or lace.[3] Riddell's version is made of vertically set bands of netting connected with silk embroidery thread in a feather-stitch pattern. This design element is carried through on the skirt and sleeves. The eye is drawn to the bodice yoke, however, which is delicately embellished with faux pearls. Riddell's bodice is cut in the fashionable mono-bosom style that began to appear in the late 1890s. By 1903, this fuller bodice style allowed the fabric to blouse downward over the waist. Riddell's bodice, however, is extreme and is made more so because her gown is constructed of a stiff voile.

Similarly, her sleeves follow fashion trends. Long sleeves were preferred, but, like sheer yokes, they might be transparent. "Nothing could be more becoming to the arm than this soft flowing sleeve which half conceals and half reveals." Styles demanded fullness below the elbow that was then gathered tightly at the wrist.[4] Here again, Riddell chose an extreme design with a tight cuff that extends almost to the elbow. The elongated cuff and stiff fabric make the fullness seem even more excessive and there is nothing "soft" or "flowing" about it. Although the skirt may seem immoderately tight, it too actually follows fashionable trends. Set on a yoke, it conforms to the body, then flares like a fluted blossom. The front of the skirt curves inward toward the knees, as illustrated in many women's magazines.

It is hard to say what would have caused Riddell to choose such an extreme design for her wedding gown. She was quite tall—about five feet, nine inches—and slim. Despite its eccentricities, the gown must have been striking on her elongated, slender frame.

1. Kentucky Marriage Records, 1852–1914, http://www.ancestry.com/; *Harper's Bazar,* June 1901, 123, 128 and May 1902, 431.

2. *Harper's Bazar,* April 1903, 291.

3. *Harper's Bazar,* April 6, 1901, 880 and May 1902, 433.

4. *Harper's Bazar,* April 1903, 296, 327.

24 / WEDDING DRESS

1906
UNITED STATES

"One of the most beautiful of May Day weddings, uniting in marriage Miss Bessie Ryan, daughter of Mr. and Mrs. Matthew Ryan, of Avondale, and Mr. Charles F. Williams, was celebrated at old St. Xavier's with all the grandeur of the Roman Catholic Church." So stated the *Cincinnati Enquirer* social pages regarding the May 26, 1906 event. Charles Finn Williams (1873–1952) was a prominent young lawyer—the assistant attorney general of Ohio. The bride, Elizabeth Gertrude Ryan (1879–1972), was "a petite brunette, noted for her beauty and accomplishments."[1] She wore a princess-style gown of handmade Duchesse lace over pale yellow pleated silk—far more characteristic of the period than the gown worn by Mattie Riddell (see cat. 23).

Matthew Ryan (1830–1909), Bessie's father, was an immigrant success story. Born in County Kilkenny, Ireland, he immigrated to the United States in 1850. Having learned butchering as a youth, he established his own business in Cincinnati—Matthew Ryan & Brothers. Cincinnati was a center for hog farming, slaughtering, and packing, and many businessmen like Ryan made their fortunes at it.[2] Matthew Ryan's success enabled him to provide his daughter with a beautiful wedding. After the service, guests were invited to the Ryan home for breakfast, where an orchestra played amid elaborate, but tasteful, decorations. The newly married couple left immediately for an extended trip abroad.[3]

Charles F. Williams became a successful businessman who was highly respected in the community for his philanthropic work. He was president and later chairman of the board of Western and Southern Life Insurance Co. Williams supported the Cincinnati Zoo and Botanical Gardens; led the founding of the Institutum Divi Thomae, which in the 1930s undertook cancer research; and was dedicated to church activities. Bessie and Charles had five children.[4] The 1935 wedding gown of their daughter, Mary Elizabeth Williams, is also illustrated in this publication (see cat. 32).

1. "Random Notes," *Cincinnati Enquirer*, May 27, 1906.

2. Mary Russell, "Matthew Ryan 1830–1909," *Ryan Family Newsletter: Newsletter for the descendants of Matthew Ryan and Mary Sullivan, County Kilkenny, Ireland,* June 1998, 1–13.

3. "Random Notes," *Cincinnati Enquirer*.

4. Gerald E. Moore, *Make An Idea Succeed: The Western-Southern Story* (Cincinnati: Western and Southern Life Insurance Co., 1988); "Cincinnati Scientists United in Fight to Conquer Human Ills," *Cincinnati Times-Star*, April 25, 1940; "Who's Who of Catholics Lists 87 From City," *Cincinnati Post*, March 4, 1938.

Figure 1
Bridal photo of Elizabeth Gertrude Ryan, 1906.

United States
Wedding Dress, 1906
Silk, linen
Gift of the children
of Mrs. Charles F.
Williams
1972.335

25 / WEDDING DRESS

1910
UNITED STATES

ENGAGEMENT DRESS

1910
UNITED STATES

Ethel J. Page (1882–1976) was a modern bride. Three days before her 1910 wedding to William Leo Doepke (1883–1934), her photo was published in the newspaper.[1] This type of public display would have been considered unthinkable in the nineteenth century. Businessmen, politicians, monarchs, and actors had their photos published, but the newspaper, where anyone and everyone could see her image, was not the place for a proper lady.

Times, however, were changing. Women had been struggling for decades for equal political, legal, and educational rights, but in the early twentieth century they were, literally, marching in the streets picketing for suffrage. Women were far more visible and bolder in public than the previous generation had ever been.

Women of 1910 were also more audacious in their dress styles. Page's mother, who had married around 1880, would have worn a dress similar to Ellen Curtis's (see cat. 15), with multiple layers of heavy fabric, a petticoat, and a bustle. Her daughter's gown of soft fabric that skimmed over the body was far more revealing. In fact, women's magazines reported that the 1910 bride was especially fortunate. "Fashion puts practically no restriction upon her, so long as hard shiny satin surfaces are avoided. . . . Long slender lines, which are at their best when worn by young lithe figures, are preserved in the present season's wedding dress."[2] Fashion forecasters rejected the stiff satins that had dominated wedding gowns of the 1890s (see cat. 22).

Page's fashionable one-piece dress is constructed of soft ribbed silk. Handmade Brussels lace—perhaps a family heirloom—forms the V neckline, which is modestly filled in with pleated silk net. The slim skirt is layered with a shaped overskirt that is gathered into weighted self-fabric flowers at the hemline on each side. A square train falls from the waistline—a style that was considered "to be in general favor."[3]

While Page's gown is stylish, it is rather conservative in comparison with her engagement gown. Also a one-piece dress, it is constructed of unbleached linen voile. The novelty of this gown is in the surface embellishment. Leaf and flower patterns are printed and appliquéd asymmetrically on the bodice and skirt. Each motif is edged with a raised chain stitch and the flowers are made subtly three-dimensional with the addition of crushed fabric (fig. 3). The right side of the gown is ornamented with a soft pale green tasseled sash that falls from the underarm to the floor.[4]

Although the bride presented herself to the public in the newspaper to announce her marriage, the wedding took place in the privacy of her parents' home on Cameron Avenue in Norwood, Ohio. The society page gave a full review, describing the bride as "a young woman of culture and rare beauty, a Gibson type." According to the newspaper, the Page home "had been transformed into a veritable garden. All of the ceilings had canopies of garlands of Southern smilax, with hundreds of electric lights glistening among the foliage. . . . The bridal couple took their places in a central drawing room, a great bank of palms and white roses forming the background."

One wonders if Mr. Page, a manager at the telegraph company, spent beyond his means for this grand event. Following the wedding there was a reception for two hundred guests and a bridal supper of twelve courses, which was undoubtedly catered. Ethel Page was, indeed, a modern bride. Rather than rely on family and friends, she utilized the services of professional caterers, florists, and musicians to provide the necessities for her wedding.[5]

Page and her husband took an extensive honeymoon to China and Japan by way of San Francisco and Honolulu. They continued on to Europe for a period of four months. The groom's profession is notable; William Doepke's father co-founded the Alms & Doepke Company, one of the most successful department stores in Cincinnati during the first half of the twentieth century.[6] The Doepkes were quite wealthy; upon her husband's death in 1934, Ethel was to be paid an annual allowance of $12,000 a year.[7]

1. "Random Notes," *Cincinnati Enquirer*, January 9, 1910. Page's photograph is captioned, "Miss Ethel J. Page, Who on Wednesday next will become the bride of Mr. William L. Doepke."

2. *Harper's Bazar*, January 1910, 282.

3. A round weight is enclosed in the fabric to maintain the line of the overlay. These weights were increasingly common as lighter fabrics came into favor. *Harper's Bazar*, January 1910, 282.

Left:
United States
Wedding Dress, 1910
Silk, linen
Gift in memory
of Mrs. William
Leo Doepke (Ethel
Page) by her
granddaughter, Sara
Doepke
2003.25

Right:
United States
Engagement Dress,
1910
Linen, silk
Gift in memory
of Mrs. William
Leo Doepke (Ethel
Page) by her
granddaughter, Sara
Doepke
2003.26

Figure 1
Bridal photo of Ethel
J. Page, 1910.

Figure 3
Detail of engagement dress fabric.

Figure 4
This photograph of Ethel J. Page accompanied the announcement of her upcoming marriage to William Leo Doepke. *Cincinnati Enquirer,* January 9, 1910.

4. An article titled "Early Winter Fashions" in *Harper's Bazar* in November 1909 comments on "the tendency toward queer greens" and notes a particular shade Parisians called *purée de pois* (pea soup). The writer remarks, "While I cannot say I regard it as pretty in all fabrics, yet it is undeniably artistic in satin weaves." The green sash and button covers on Ethel Page's gown are satin and perhaps of this "queer green" about which the fashion editor commented.

5. "Social Affairs," *Cincinnati Enquirer,* January 13, 1910.

6. Ibid.; U.S. Federal Census, 1910 and 1920; Charles Frederic Goss, ed., *Cincinnati, The Queen City, 1788–1912* (Cincinnati: S. J. Clarke Publishing Company, 1912), vol. 4, 715–16; "Death Calls Merchant; Two Concerns Headed By William L. Doepke," *Cincinnati Enquirer,* December 10, 1934.

7. "Doepke Estate Left to Widow: Will of Former Head of Department Store Filed," *Cincinnati Times-Star,* December 14, 1934. The equivalent of $12,000 in today's currency equals over $193,000, according to Historical Currency Conversions: http://futureboy.homeip.net/fsp/dollar.fsp?quantity=12000&currency=dollars&fromYear=1934.

United States
Wedding Dress, 1915
Silk, beads, faux
pearls
Gift of Mr. and Mrs.
Robert W. Wenning
2000.220

26 / WEDDING DRESS

1915
UNITED STATES

The changes in fashion between 1910 and 1915 were dictated by necessity and by women's continuing desire for independence. During the war years, beginning in Europe in 1914, women moved into the workforce in large numbers and required clothing that fit their new lifestyle. Lighter fabrics, fewer layers, and shorter skirts provided women with freedom of movement.[1] The independent woman of the early twentieth century was often attired in a suit consisting of a separate blouse, skirt, and jacket. Although corsets were still worn, the bodices of dresses were no longer boned. The only structure in many gowns was a wide inner belt that hooked around the waist.

The looser fit of women's clothing precipitated the decline of dressmakers whose trade depended on a custom fit. By 1910, ready-to-wear fashions were commonplace in department stores. Although Hilda Korb (b. abt. 1891) could have found an acceptable ready-made wedding gown, it is evident by the style and construction of this dress that she had it made specifically for her marriage to Henry F. Wenning (b. abt. 1887) in 1915.

Korb's multi-layered gown features a kimono-style bodice characterized by a lapped front that forms a V neck and deep armseyes. The bodice consists of layers of sheer fabrics bordered by a high waist—a style that was widely accepted by 1910. The skirt is draped to create the much-desired lampshade effect of the period. The sheer lace overlay on the lower skirt is pulled up asymmetrically and fastened with a pearl and bead ornament like the one securing the bow at the center front waistline. The back of the dress is equally if not more interesting than the front (fig. 1). The fan-shaped bow that emerges from the draped skirt is as alluring as the gathered fabric at the back of the wedding gown worn by Ida Peltz Rost in the early 1880s (see cat. 16).

Little is known about the Wennings. It is believed Hilda and Henry were married in Chattanooga, Tennessee. In 1920 they were living in Covington, Kentucky, where they raised their five children.[2]

1. Note that the dress was originally longer, as evidenced in the couple's wedding photo (fig. 2). The dress was altered at some point and could not be restored to its original length. In 1915 everyday dresses and suits tended to be short, while special occasion gowns would have retained the longer, more formal hemline.

2. Donor information; U.S. Federal Census, 1920 and 1930.

Figure 1
Back view.

Figure 2
Wedding photo of Hilda Korb and Henry Wenning, 1915.

Probably France
Wedding Dress and Slip, 1921
Silk, faux pearls, beads
Gift of Christine Tailer in memory of Winifred Tailer
2005.643a,b

27 / WEDDING DRESS AND SLIP

1921
PROBABLY FRANCE

Catharine Harding (1900–90) wed Lorillard Suffern Tailer (1897–1979) at four o'clock in the afternoon on April 6, 1921, at St. Bartholomew's Church on Park Avenue in midtown Manhattan. Harding's elegant yet simple gown of silk net over satin with pearl embellishment originally had a satin court train covered with a length of heirloom point lace.[1]

Catharine was the daughter of Horace J. (1863–1929) and Dorothea Barney Harding (1871–1935). Horace Harding was a banker, chairman of the board of the American Express Company, and a trustee of the Frick Art Collection. In 1908 Harding purchased the town house of Mrs. Charlotte M. Tytus at 10 East 77th Street in Manhattan. He later moved his family to 955 Fifth Avenue. The Hardings presented Catharine, their eldest daughter, to society at a ball at the Ritz-Carlton Hotel.[2]

Lorillard Suffern Tailer was the son of T. Suffern Tailer (d. 1928), a banker and social leader who owned homes in New York City and Newport, Rhode Island. The *New York Times* society pages reported on the bridegroom's bachelor party two days before the wedding. Guests included Cornelius Vanderbilt, Jr. and Cornelius V. Whitney—both sons of New York millionaires.[3]

Unfortunately, the Harding-Tailer marriage was an unhappy one. Passenger lists indicate that Catharine traveled frequently to Europe, both with and without her husband. Family history holds that she kept apartments in Paris and Dublin and associated with F. Scott Fitzgerald and other expatriate writers in Europe. In 1934 Catharine divorced Lorillard, citing "extreme cruelty."[4]

Given her wealth, social standing, independent nature, and association with the most avant-garde writers of the period, it is hardly surprising that Harding would wear a very chic wedding gown. Her dress, however, is more than chic; it is ahead of its time. Dress designs varied widely in the 1920s, but the spare design of this gown was more likely to have been seen later in the decade. Although there is no label in the dress, construction details of this and an evening gown in the Cincinnati Art Museum's collection worn by Catharine Harding indicate that it was probably made in France.

1. "Miss Harding Weds L. Suffern Tailer," *New York Times*, April 7, 1921.

2. Horace J. Harding biographical information, http://www.nycago.org/ Organs/NYC/html/ResTytusCM.html; "Miss Harding Debutante," *New York Times*, November 30, 1919.

3. "T. S. Tailer's Estate Is Set At $1,588,886," *New York Times*, October 10, 1934; "L. S. Tailer Gives Bachelor Dinner," *New York Times*, April 2, 1921.

4. Several passenger lists dated between 1921 and 1934 indicate travel to and from France. Mrs. Tailer continued to travel frequently to Europe after her divorce. New York Passenger Lists, 1820–1957, http://www.ancestry.com/; "Divorces L. S. Tailer: Former Catherine Harding Makes Charge of Cruelty in Reno," *New York Times,* April 24, 1934.

28 / WEDDING DRESS

1924
UNITED STATES

Falling just below the knee, this dark blue and brown sheath dress was fashionable in the mid-1920s, when androgynous styles were popular. The overdress is constructed of sheer blue silk woven with large amorphous shapes in a brown textured pile weave. It is trimmed at the hem with brown ostrich feathers. Although it is characteristic of its time, it is not a typical choice for a wedding dress.

In fact, Winifred Miller (1898–1987) purchased this dress on her wedding day, October 25, 1924. In the summer of that year, Miller's younger sister, Louise Frances Miller, had died of polio. Shortly after this, Winifred and Paul Gustav Bez (1900–40) decided to marry. A graduate of Wellesley College, Miller was employed as an administrative assistant to the president of Roberts Brass Works in Detroit. She managed the office, supervised the other assistants, was responsible for international correspondence, and prepared the Roberts family's income tax.

On her wedding day, Miller left work at noon and purchased everything she needed. The death of her sister had affected her deeply. She did not want to wear a white gown or have a traditional large wedding, so she chose this dark dress. The couple was married quietly at St. Luke's Evangelical Lutheran Church in Detroit. They lived in Detroit and, later, in Columbus, Ohio, remaining happily married until the untimely death of Paul Bez in 1940.[1]

1. Information from the curatorial files of the Ohio State University Historic Costume and Textiles Collection; Janet Winifred Bez Ebert, Ph.D., interview with author, January 5, 2010.

Figure 1
Winifred Miller in her wedding dress, 1924.

United States
Wedding Dress, 1924
Silk, feathers
On loan from
The Ohio State
University Historic
Costume and
Textiles Collection

United States
Hat, 1920s
Silk
Gift of Mrs. Fred J.
Wrampelmeier
1964.633

29 / WEDDING DRESS AND PANIERS

1928
UNITED STATES

Jeanne Lanvin (1867–1946) was one of the most influential designers of the twentieth century. Although she was known for her matching mother/daughter designs, Lanvin's signature was the *robe de style*, which she introduced in the early 1920s. This style featured a full skirt, often supported by hoops set on the hips. The design referenced eighteenth-century gowns with *paniers*—hoops that held the skirt out to the sides in an exaggerated manner.

Most styles of the 1920s emphasized a straight, androgynous look, but the House of Lanvin insisted on creating an alternative. Lanvin held firm to her belief that "modern clothes need some sort of romantic quality." Her designs were feminine, pretty yet sophisticated, and the antithesis of the *garçon* mode that was so popular in the period.[1]

Dorothy Conway's wedding gown does not bear a Lanvin label, but the *robe de style* was such a popular design that it was copied by Parisian couturiers and American dressmakers alike. Conway could easily have chosen a dress with a slimmer silhouette, but undoubtedly found the fuller skirt more appealing. The gown is embellished with rhinestones, steel and glass beads, and triangular paillettes. The daringly low V neckline is moderated with a set-in piece of fabric. The deep back scoop neckline and sleeveless bodice are characteristic of the progressively revealing fashions of the period, as is the uneven hemline.

Dorothy Conway married John C. Rush on the morning of December 1, 1928. The local newspaper described the bride's gown as ivory chiffon velvet.[2] Reportedly, the wedding was followed by a breakfast for approximately one hundred guests at the Hyde Park Country Club in Cincinnati. The couple enjoyed a honeymoon in the East, then a southern tour to the Pacific coast that lasted a year or more.[3]

1. Valerie Steele, *Women of Fashion: Twentieth Century Designers* (New York: Rizzoli, 1991), 36–37.

2. The couple was married in the Roman Catholic Church of the Assumption. "Nuptials of the Week," *Cincinnati Enquirer*, December 2, 1928.

3. Ibid.

United States
*Wedding Dress and
Paniers,* 1928
Silk, rhinestones,
cut steel and glass
beads, paillettes
Gift of Mrs. Dorothy
Conway Rush
1973.533a–c

Jeanne Lanvin
(1867–1946)
France
*Wedding Dress and
Headpiece,* 1931
Silk, linen
Gift of Mrs. Edgar J.
Mack, Jr.
1999.229a,b

30 / WEDDING DRESS AND HEADPIECE

1931
JEANNE LANVIN (1867–1946)
FRANCE

The stately elegance of this wedding gown speaks to the creative and technical expertise of its designer, Jeanne Lanvin. Like many Cincinnati women before her, Elaine Joseph traveled to France to have her dress made by a Parisian couturier. By the early 1930s, fashions had become less androgynous and designers were interested in emphasizing the curvaceous female form.

Each piece of this elegant gown is cut on the bias, a concept pioneered by Madeleine Vionnet (1876–1975). This method of cutting fabric on an angle across the grain allowed garments to cling to the body. Vionnet's sleek gowns revolutionized women's clothing design.[1] Soon other couturiers were using this innovative technique. In this gown, it is most easily seen in the expansive train, which is constructed of three large squares set on the bias angle. This concept of squares set on point is carried throughout the entire dress, allowing the garment to drape perfectly on the figure. A lace peplum is the one bit of embellishment on this otherwise spare gown. It modestly covers the hips and is lined with stiff net to make it stand away from the body. The bodice back also consists of squares set on the bias, forming a soft cowl neckline and an inverted point that echoes the V neckline in front (fig. 1). The bias cut of the waist sash allows it to gather softly and embrace the waist.

Probably at the request of her client, Lanvin cleverly created long sleeves that were detachable from the dress. Cut with a point that covered the hand and an upper section that fell in a V almost to the elbow, the fabric tucks up into the short sleeve and is held in place with elastic. With a wedding date in late June 1931, Elaine Joseph wanted an appropriately modest gown for the ceremony but knew the humid Cincinnati weather would make long sleeves uncomfortable during the reception.

Elaine Joseph (1910–2003) and Edgar J. Mack, Jr. (1909–98) were married for sixty-eight years. After graduating from Princeton University, Edgar Mack joined the securities and investment firm Seasongood and Mayer and became a partner. During World War II, he served five years in Europe and the United States, reaching the rank of lieutenant colonel. Assigned to intelligence work in the European theater, he earned a Bronze Star. Both Elaine and Edgar Mack were active in the community the greater part of their lives.[2]

1. For an exhaustive look at the work of designer Madeleine Vionnet, see Betty Kirke, *Madeleine Vionnet* (San Francisco: Chronicle Books, 1998).

2. Laura Pulfer, "Taking Note of a Good Life," *Cincinnati Enquirer*, December 1, 1998; *Princeton Alumni Weekly*, April 7, 1999; Laura Pulfer, "A Lady's Gift: Culture and Good Works," *Cincinnati Enquirer*, November 3, 1996.

Figure 2

Mr. and Mrs. Edgar Mack in 1986 on their fifty-fifth wedding anniversary. Mrs. Mack wore her wedding gown for significant anniversaries throughout her life.

United States
Wedding Dress, 1933
Silk, linen
Gift of Melody
Sawyer Richardson
2006.135

31 / WEDDING DRESS

1933
UNITED STATES

"She came upon the arm of her father, with measured step
and her customary poise. . . . Tall and slim, with the grace of
a flower stalk swaying in the wind, she was a vision of youthful
charm in her white satin gown."[1] Rosemary Sawyer (1908–95)
was the only child of Besse Genevra Gratigny (d. 1958) and
George Amzi Sawyer (d. 1948). On June 10, 1933, Rosemary
Sawyer married John Moore Richardson (1908–88).

The newspaper writer who commented so floridly on Sawyer's
deportment also described her wedding gown. The "princess
line was broken at the back of the bodice, which was built
entirely of superb Alençon lace, that, following the shoulder
line, formed a shallow yoke on the front of the bodice, this
effect being distractingly becoming. . . . The long sleeves that
came almost to the knuckles of the hand in a deep V, were
picturesquely puffed at the elbow, a fashion that matched her
exquisite cap of Alençon lace."[2] Like Elaine Joseph's gown,
Sawyer's dress was bias-cut to hug her tall slender frame. The
sleeve puffs at the elbow are an attractive variation on the
typical 1930s sleeve, which was most often long and tight to the
arm from shoulder to wrist.

Following long-held tradition, Rosemary Sawyer Richardson's
daughter, Melody Sawyer Richardson, wore this same gown
when she married David Brockwell Kidd in 1964. The gown
was unaltered in design, although Richardson updated the veil.

1. "In Society," *Cincinnati Enquirer,* June 11, 1933.

2. Ibid.

Figure 1
Detail of the lace
bodice back.

Figure 2
Rosemary Sawyer's bridal photo, 1933.

Figure 3
Melody Sawyer Richardson wore her mother's wedding gown when she married in 1964. The dress was not altered, but she updated the veil. "Married Last Evening," *Cincinnati Enquirer*, June 27, 1964.
Photo by Harry Carlson.

32 / WEDDING DRESS

1934
GERMAINE MONTEIL (ACTIVE 20TH C.)
FRANCE

Mary Elizabeth Williams (1907–2006) married Lawrence
H. Kyte (1899–1986) in a morning ceremony October 10,
1934, at St. Xavier Church. She was "a vision of loveliness in
her slender, clinging gown of cream velvet."[1] Her dress was
designed with a square neckline, long sleeves, and a twelve-foot
attached train that in the wedding photos seems to dwarf the
bride's petite frame. The dress had no embellishment except for
small self-fabric bows at the neckline corners. Williams carried
a large muff that matched her dress and wore a rosepoint veil
created in Belgium—a family heirloom. Her attendants were
dressed in turquoise velvet. Like the wedding gown, their
costumes were bereft of trimmings, but they wore mink scarves
and carried matching muffs adorned with bronze-tinted
orchids. The accessories were gifts of the bride.

In the midst of the Great Depression, this lavish wedding
joined two of Cincinnati's most prominent families. The
couple departed that day for Quebec. From there they sailed
for Europe and spent a month traveling in France and the
British Isles.

Williams's gown bears two labels—that of Germaine Monteil
and Mrs. Eugene Gray. Monteil was a popular American
designer whose work was sold without attribution in major
department stores including Henri Bendel, Bergdorf
Goodman, and Saks. She was called "the American Vionnet."
In the mid-1930s, however, Monteil became interested in
cosmetics and seems to have largely abandoned fashion design.
Mrs. Eugene Gray was a specialty retailer in Columbus, Ohio,
who opened her shop in 1917 and continued in business until
1953. She offered imported Parisian and New York designs.
This gown of creamy velvet seems to have been a Monteil
design that Mrs. Gray sold in her establishment, probably
providing a custom fit for the bride.[2]

Germaine Monteil
(active 20th c.)
France
Wedding Dress, 1934
Silk
Gift of Elizabeth
Williams Kyte
2004.188a

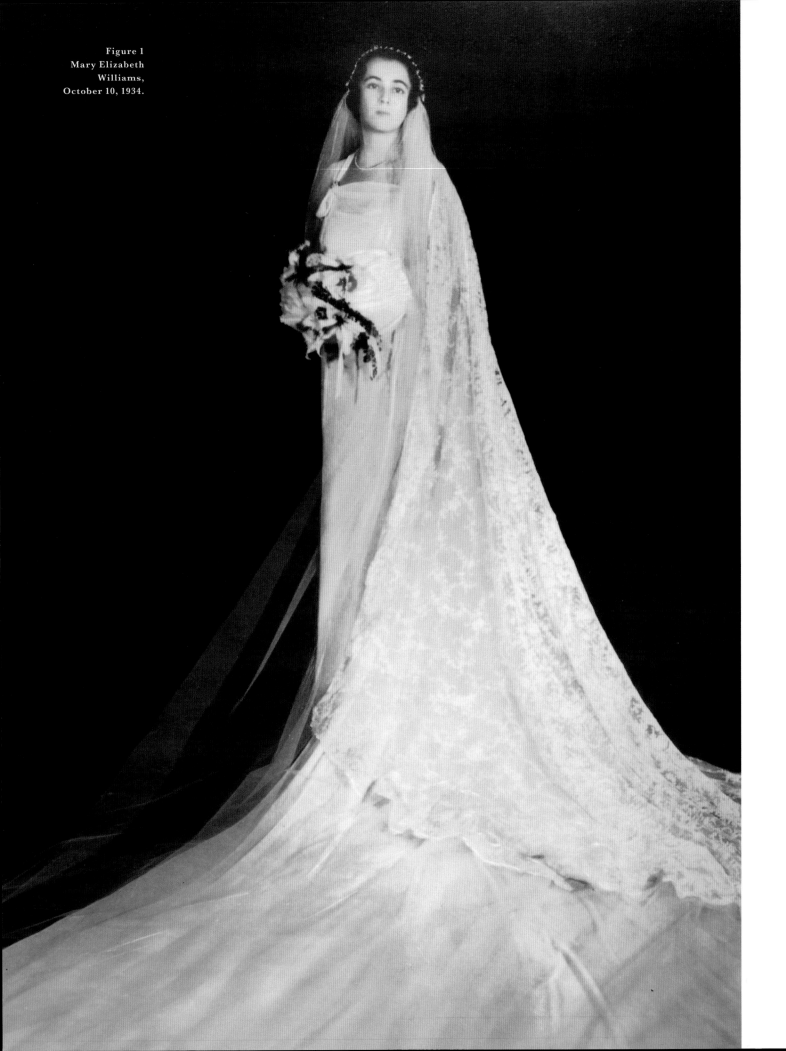

1. "Papal Benediction at St. Xavier Church," *Cincinnati Enquirer,* October 10, 1934.

2. Caroline Rennolds Milbank, *New York Fashion: The Evolution of American Style* (New York: Harry N. Abrams, 1989), 125. Madeleine Vionnet (1876–1975) was known for pioneering the bias cut, which allowed her clothes to cling to the body. Information regarding Mrs. Eugene Gray was provided by Gayle Strege, curator of the Ohio State University Historic Costume and Textiles Collection in Columbus, Ohio. See *Capital Fashion: 1851–1965*, exh. cat. (Columbus: Ohio State University Historic Costume and Textiles Collection, 2003), 7.

33 / WEDDING DRESS, BELT, AND HEADPIECE

1935
MARY WIDMEYER MATTOX (1878–1958)
UNITED STATES

The United States was in the midst of the Great Depression when Evelyn Marie Wright (1913–2009) married James Benton Mattox (1912–2001) in August 1935. Short of funds to purchase a dress, Wright was fortunate that her future mother-in-law offered to make her wedding gown. Mary Mattox, a fine seamstress, crafted a sleek, form-fitting, and very fashionable dress of machine-made lace. The bride chose blue because it was her favorite color. Although today this may seem an unusual choice, wedding dresses in pastels including blue, pink, beige, and yellow were suggested in the earliest issues of the first bridal magazine, *So You're Going to Be Married*, initially published in 1934. Called "heavenly blue" or "bridal blue," the color was associated with happiness, love, and the Virgin Mary.[1]

Wright's gown was constructed with a modest neckline. The dolman sleeves are wide at the armseye and taper to a tight fit at the wrist, where they end in a point over the back of the hand—a characteristic 1930s design. The slim skirt widens and drapes gracefully around the ankles. The original headdress is a matching blue lace cap with an unusual brim of netting that extends over the forehead and around the crown of the head.

Despite the economic hardships of the Depression and her middle-class status, Evelyn Wright was wed in a very fashionable gown. Although she probably only wore the dress once, on her wedding day, its color would have enabled her to wear it again for other formal occasions, as nineteenth-century brides did. It was suggested that a clever 1930s bride might extend the life of her wedding dress by trimming off the train and wearing it as an evening gown.[2]

Wright and Mattox were married in the United Church of Christ in Carthage, Ohio, where Wright had grown up. James Mattox's family settled in Cincinnati after World War I. Mattox studied radio engineering at the University of Cincinnati and worked as a control engineer for WCKY, a local radio station, in the 1940s. The couple had five daughters and were married for sixty-six years.[3]

1. References to pastel-colored wedding gowns can be found in the Autumn/Winter 1935 and the Spring/Summer 1936 issues of *So You're Going to Be Married*.

2. *So You're Going to Be Married*, Autumn 1935, 33.

3. Rebecca Billman, "Jim Mattox led IBEW union, managed firm," *Cincinnati Enquirer*, September 7, 2001.

Figure 1
Evelyn Marie Wright in her blue lace wedding gown, 1935.

Mary Widmeyer
Mattox (1878–1958),
United States
*Wedding Dress, Belt,
and Headpiece,* 1935
Synthetic, wool
Gift of the Mattox
Family
2006.105a–d

935
GIDDING & CO. (ESTABLISHED 1907)
UNITED STATES

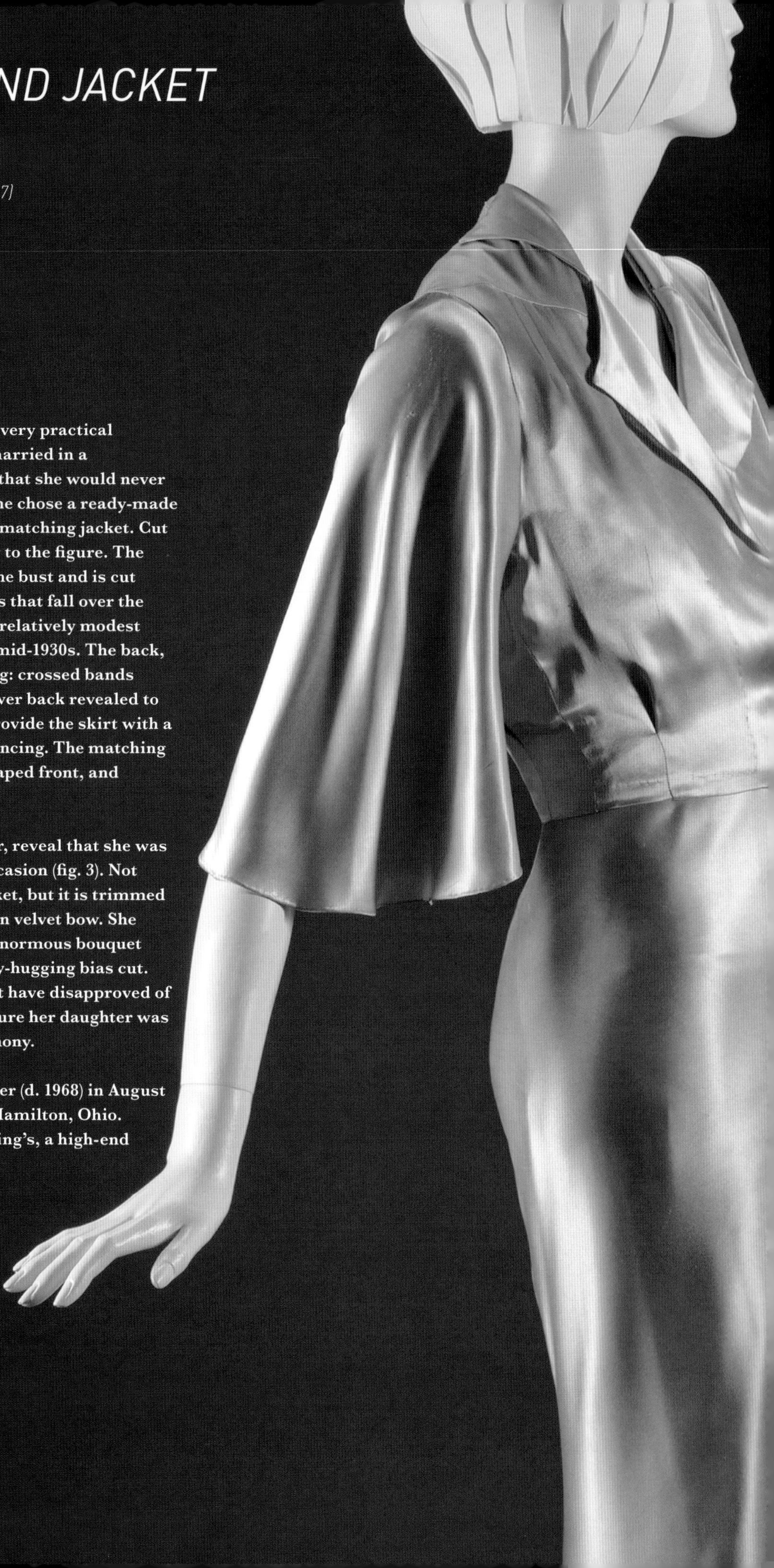

Ann Isabel Eaton (1911–98) was a very practical woman. She did not want to be married in a traditional white wedding gown that she would never be able to wear again. Instead, she chose a ready-made dress of bold yellow satin with a matching jacket. Cut on the bias, it clings suggestively to the figure. The bodice is softly gathered under the bust and is cut to form what appear to be sleeves that fall over the shoulders. From the front, it is a relatively modest and characteristic design of the mid-1930s. The back, however, reveals sensuous styling: crossed bands leave the shoulder blades and lower back revealed to the waist. Knife-pleated gores provide the skirt with a bit more fullness—perfect for dancing. The matching jacket has butterfly sleeves, a draped front, and turned-down collar.

Eaton's wedding photos, however, reveal that she was completely covered up for the occasion (fig. 3). Not only is the bride wearing the jacket, but it is trimmed at the neckline with a large brown velvet bow. She wears a velvet hat and holds an enormous bouquet that conceals any hint of the body-hugging bias cut. One wonders if her mother might have disapproved of Eaton's choice and wanted to insure her daughter was sufficiently modest for the ceremony.

Ann Eaton married John F. Schuler (d. 1968) in August 935, at St. Stephen's Church in Hamilton, Ohio. She purchased her dress at Gidding's, a high-end Cincinnati retailer.

Figure 1
Dress with Jacket.

Gidding & Co.
(established 1907)
United States
Dress and Jacket,
1935
Silk
Gift of Sue Ann
Schuler Painter
and Karen Schuler
Lybrook in memory
of their mother, Ann
Eaton Schuler
2008.106a–c

Figure 2
Back view.

Figure 3
The bride and groom and their wedding party, 1935.

35 / WEDDING DRESS AND CAPE

1946
KIVIETTE (ACTIVE MID-20TH C.)
UNITED STATES

The Summer 1946 issue of the *Bride's Magazine* reflected the optimism of a nation that had just emerged from war. An article titled "Designed for Brides" in that same year begins, "A toast . . . to you, the beautiful American Bride, with your clear-eyed smile and your head in wedding clouds . . . you'll dream your wedding first, then make it come true. Your Imagination is the priceless, precious philosopher's stone that can turn . . . you to a fairy princess for this most precious day."[1] In the post-World War II era, the American Dream seemed within reach of every young couple. This flowery rhetoric reflects the prodding of the emerging bridal industry that promoted the idealization of the white wedding and the consumerism that accompanied it.

Although the Association of Bridal Manufacturers had persuaded Congress to ease restrictions specifically for wedding gowns during World War II, particular fabrics were still scarce in the post-war years.[2] A frequent suggestion in the *Bride's Magazine* was to choose a versatile design that enabled a bride to transform her wedding dress into an evening gown. For the Summer 1946 issue, the editors had chosen five American designers to present "their unique approach to wedding dresses." Three of these created gowns were "convertible with a click of the snaps, a toss of the veil, a dropping of the cape."[3]

The design by Kiviette was described as "a breath-taking costume that will make your wedding among the most imaginative of the year." Although historically influenced modes were not uncommon in the pages of the *Bride's Magazine* in this period, this draped medieval-style dress with a hooded cape was probably not a frequent choice among brides. The writer emphasized the adaptability of the gown. "Without the cape, the dress stands revealed as a beautifully molded column of white. . . . Notice how easily it moves, how well it will dance long after the rose-petals and rice have fluttered from its folds."[4]

Constructed of sheer white rayon, the fitted bodice is draped across the bust. Substantial padding widens the shoulder line, retaining the military look popular during the war. Rows of gold and white beading outline the low V waistline. The multi-layered full skirt drapes softly over the hips and would, indeed, serve as a wonderful dress for dancing.

Cincinnatian Mary Helen Luhrman saw this issue of the magazine and, much like Minnie Crosby in 1892 (see cat. 21), chose to be an unconventional bride. She purchased this medieval-esque design by Kiviette. The dress was priced at $295, the cape at $150.[5] Luhrman had just enough time to order the dress for her August 22 wedding to Allan G. Bohmer.

1. *Bride's Magazine*, Summer 1946, 74.

2. Katherine Jellison, *It's Our Day: America's Love Affair with the White Wedding, 1945–2005* (Lawrence: University Press of Kansas, 2008), 67.

3. *Bride's Magazine*, Summer 1946, 74, 112, 117.

4. Ibid., 78, 112.

5. Ibid., 78.

Kiviette (active mid-
20th c.)
United States
*Wedding Dress and
Cape,* 1946
Nylon, rayon
Gift of Mrs. Allan G.
Bohmer
1972.372a,b

United States
Wedding Dress, 1947
Synthetic
On loan from
Timothy and
Leslie Maloney

36 / WEDDING DRESS

1947
UNITED STATES

In the fall of 1947, when Carol Ann Homan (1924–2004) was about to be married, she was faced with the dilemma of many brides of the period. Although World War II was over, materials that had been rationed for war purposes were still in short supply. This included most fabrics, particularly silk. While many wartime brides wore a best day dress or suit, the fledgling bridal industry had successfully lobbied Congress, even during wartime, to ease restrictions on some fabrics, specifically those used for wedding dresses. A white wedding, they argued, was what the boys were fighting for—it was part of the American Dream.

After the war, it took a significant amount of time for factories to retool for domestic production and for supply routes for overseas goods to be reestablished. The fabrics available in late 1947 were inferior. Despite Homan's affluence, she and many other brides-to-be found it difficult to obtain a white wedding dress made of quality fabric. Homan was finally successful finding appropriate fabric and had her gown custom-made by a local dressmaker for her October wedding.

Homan's friend Mary Louise Hackstedde planned to be married in January of 1948 and Carol Homan Haile, remembering the difficulty she had experienced, offered to lend Hackstedde her wedding gown. Gratefully, Hackstedde wore the dress. No alterations were necessary, as the two women were similar in size. This practice of sharing wedding gowns, both during and shortly after the war, was not uncommon.[1]

The dress continued to be worn by succeeding generations. Tucks and seam alterations are evident in the bodice of the gown but, surprisingly, there is little evidence of major renovations and the dress retains its 1940s styling. Fashioned of optical white synthetic fabric, the gown is indicative of its time. Synthetic fabrics such as rayon and nylon were becoming increasingly popular due to the scarcity of silk. These fabrics were less expensive, easier to clean, had a bright silk-like sheen, and a brighter white coloration.

The most recent bride to wear the gown was Leslie Pugh, who married Timothy J. Maloney in 1982. The couple were close acquaintances of the Hailes.

1. Mary Louise Hackstedde Krehbiel, interview with author, March 20, 2010. Carol Ann Homan married Ralph Virden Haile, Jr. (1922–2006) on October 18, 1947. Mary Louise Hackstedde married Robert C. Krehbiel on January 15, 1948.

Figure 1
Carol Ann Homan, October 1947.
Photo by Carl Carlson.

Figure 2
Mary Louise Hackstedde in the same wedding gown worn by Carol Ann Homan
Haile in 1947.
Photo by Carl Carlson.

37 / SUIT: JACKET, SKIRT, AND ASCOT

1948
IRENE LENTZ GIBBONS (1907-62)
UNITED STATES

Irene Lentz Gibbons (1907–62), better known simply as Irene, is renowned for her work as a Hollywood costume designer. A music major at the University of Southern California, she began designing her own clothes and, at the urging of friends, soon opened a small shop on campus. Dolores Del Rio was the first actress to purchase a dress from Irene's shop, and soon other stars were buying her designs. Irene was offered a position with Bullocks Wilshire department store, where she worked for eight years as the designer for their exclusive couture salon. Her clientele were actresses and, as she became increasingly involved with their personal clothing, she was subsequently consulted about their screen wardrobes. Irene designed costumes for films at most of the major Hollywood studios, including RKO, Columbia, and United Artists, before succeeding Gilbert Adrian as chief designer at MGM in 1942. She also ran her own highly successful clothing design business. Irene is especially known for suits with fine detailing that made them both sophisticated and distinctive.[1]

The suit that Marilyn Maxwell (1927–95) wore for her wedding to Dr. Harry Fox (d. 1995) on August 29, 1948, was designed by Irene and is indicative of her style. Long darts, extending from the bust down over the hips, fit the jacket to the body. The center front placket of the jacket conceals the button closure and serves as a decorative device. By discontinuing the placket just below the natural waistline, the designer created a rectangular cutout. The placket construction is echoed by the same shape on the center front of the skirt, continuing a visual line from the neckline to the hem. This is the type of sensible suit that Irene encouraged women to plan their wardrobes around, rather than buying an elaborate garment for one particular occasion.

Marilyn Maxwell probably chose to be married in a suit because this was her second marriage. However, during the war years the *Bride's Magazine* had frequently suggested "bridesy" suits that were both flattering and practical.[2] Maxwell was a woman of sophisticated tastes, as she had been a photo model for *Vogue* and *Harper's Bazaar* wearing designs by Christian Dior, Traina-Norell, Jean Dessès, and hats by Lilly Daché. She accessorized her brown wool Irene suit with a bright red velvet ascot.

1. Colin McDowell, *McDowell's Directory of Twentieth Century Fashion* (Englewood Cliffs, NJ: Prentice-Hall, 1935), 158.

2. For references to "bridesy suits" see the *Bride's Magazine*, Autumn 1943, 98; Spring 1942, 42; Autumn 1943, 2; Summer 1942, 51.

Figure 1
Marilyn Maxwell and Dr. Harry Fox on their wedding day, 1948.

H. & S. Pogue Co.
(established 1863)
United States
Wedding Ensemble:
Dress, Mitts, and
Headpiece, 1952
Linen, silk, nylon
Gift of Edith Krohn
Magrish in memory
of Kate Magrish
Foreman
2001.33a–c

38 / WEDDING ENSEMBLE: DRESS, MITTS, AND HEADPIECE

1952
H.& S. POGUE CO. (ESTABLISHED 1863)
UNITED STATES

The romanticism associated with history seems to lend itself to weddings, and historical fashions are often reinterpreted in bridal gown designs. This was true even in the nineteenth century. For instance, Ada Davis's 1874 gown laces down the center back when the predominant style was a more practical hook and eye closure at the center front (see cat. 10). The Watteau pleats of the eighteenth century are incorporated into the aesthetic dress worn in 1892 by Minnie Crosby (see cat. 21).

Similarly, several elements in Kate Magrish's 1952 wedding gown design are derived from vintage dress. It features an open skirt at the center front—a typical eighteenth-century style that revealed a decorative petticoat. Here, a pleated underskirt is exposed. The round shape of the skirt is supported by a hoop or crinoline much like those worn in the mid-nineteenth century. Hoop skirts were popular in the 1950s and 1960s for traditional gowns. Magrish's fitted bodice is shaped with a V that falls below the waistline—also a familiar construction of the previous century. This confluence of reinvented design devices drew on the model of the fairy-tale princess, like Cinderella in her ball gown.[1]

Kate Magrish (1931–82) married Richard E. Foreman (b. 1926) in June 1952. Not only is her gown a compilation of historical styles, but it exhibits an interesting dichotomy between formality and simplicity. While it references fashionable eighteenth-century aristocratic dress, it is constructed of eyelet fabric—a material generally made of cotton and used for girls' dresses or women's informal summer frocks. The choice of eyelet is perhaps an allusion to innocence and purity. Like Elaine Joseph's wedding gown (cat. 30), Magrish's dress has short sleeves that are extended, perhaps for the sake of modesty during the ceremony, by mitts that give the appearance of long sleeves.

1. Walt Disney's animated feature film *Cinderella* premiered in 1950.

Figure 1
Kate Magrish Foreman's wedding photo, taken in the garden of her parents' home in Cincinnati, Ohio, 1952.

39 / WEDDING ENSEMBLE: DRESS, CRINOLINE, AND HEADPIECE

1954
CHRISTIAN DIOR (1905-57)
FRANCE

Christian Dior was one of the most important couturiers of the twentieth century. His first collection, shown in Paris in 1947, was dubbed the New Look. It restored femininity to women's fashions, which had languished during World War II. Dior's pinched waists and full skirts emphasizing the female form were distinctive after years of practical suits produced under severe wartime fabric restrictions. Dior continued to present a different style or look with every collection until his death in 1957.[1]

This couture wedding dress designed by Dior was worn by Sheila Mackintosh (b. 1931), who married Count Jean de Rochambeau in 1954. The Countess is the great-niece of Mary Emery, whose wedding gown is illustrated in this publication (see cat. 3). The Countess de Rochambeau worked as a contributing editor for *Vogue* in Paris for more than twenty years and had close relationships with many of the most important couturiers of the 1950s and 1960s. She knew Christian Dior personally, and he designed this dress for her.[2]

Constructed of off-white silk organza, the gown is both elegant and sophisticated while retaining a sense of informality. The center front button closure, the turned-down collar, the cuffs on the three-quarter-length sleeves, and the smooth shape of the skirt over the hips suggest the simplicity of a shirtwaist-style dress. The soft V of the back neckline suggestively reveals the nape of the neck and is echoed in the shape of the low, round back waistline. In contrast to the fitted front, the deep box pleats at the center back create an expansive skirt that widens into a sprawling train (fig. 1).

Like Charles Frederick Worth in his 1874 design for Katherine Phillips (see cat. 12), Dior rejected the use of lace as embellishment on this gown. Instead, he chose an allover embroidery pattern worked in ivory and pure white silk contrasting not only the shades but the sheen of the fibers. The cloverleaf design reflects the bride's Scottish heritage. The simple crescent-shaped headpiece is decorated with traditional wax orange blossoms, and the double-layered cathedral-length veil that flows from the bandeau settles around the bride like rising mist.

1. See Diana De Marly, *Worth, Father of Haute Couture* (New York: Holmes & Meier, 1990), for complete information on the life and career of Christian Dior.

2. *Foremost Women in Communications: A Biographical Reference Work on Accomplished Women in Broadcasting, Publishing, Advertising, Public Relations, and Allied Professions* (New York: Foremost Americans Publishing Corporation, 1970), 536; Countess de Rochambeau, interview with the author, May 2007.

Christian Dior
(1905–57)
France
*Wedding Ensemble:
Dress, Crinoline, and
Headpiece*, 1954
Linen, silk
Gift of Countess de
Rochambeau
2008.49a–c

Figure 1
Detail of bodice
back.

Figure 2
The Countess de Rochambeau in her bridal gown at her mother's home, the Pavillon Colombe in Saint-Brice-sous-Forêt, north of Paris, where she was married. American author Edith Wharton lived in the Pavillon Colombe after World War I.
Photo by Studio Peeters.

40 / WEDDING ENSEMBLE: DRESS, BELT, AND HAT

1955
MOLLY PARNIS (1905-92)
UNITED STATES

Although most brides of the 1950s were wearing formal white wedding gowns, Bernice Newman (b. 1929) chose this stylish satin day dress. Her choice was dictated in part by the groom, who did not wish to wear a tuxedo. Consequently, Newman did not feel it was appropriate for her to wear a formal gown. Her dress was purchased at Lum's Department Store in Philadelphia—the bride's hometown and the site of the intimate wedding. She accessorized the dress with matching pumps and a small brown velvet hat embellished with sequins, beads, and veiling.

Like Ellen Curtis and Ann Eaton (see cats. 15 and 34, respectively) before her, Newman was a practical bride who chose an informal dress that could be worn again rather than a single-use white wedding gown. Unlike many 1950s brides, she continued to work after her marriage. Almost immediately after the wedding, the couple moved to Long Island, where Newman worked as a chemist for Brookhaven National Laboratory. Her husband, Joel Weisman (b. 1928), was a nuclear engineer.[1]

1. Mrs. Joel Weisman, interview with the author, April 2005.

Molly Parnis
(1905–92)
United States
*Wedding Ensemble:
Dress, Belt, and Hat,*
1955
Silk, faux jewels,
sequins, beads,
veiling
Gift of Bernice
Weisman
2005.661a–c

41 / WEDDING DRESS

1967
CHRISTO (B. 1935)
BULGARIA, WORKS IN UNITED STATES

Christo is an international artist best known for his monumental projects such as *Valley Curtain* (1972) in Rifle Gap, Colorado, and *Running Fence* (1976) in Marin and Sonoma counties, California. In 1995 Christo wrapped the Berlin Reichstag in metallic silver fabric. His most recent project, *The Gates, Central Park, New York City, 1979–2005* (2005), featured 7,503 steel gates stretched across twenty-three miles of Central Park walkways. The gates were decorated with saffron-colored cloth panels. Although Christo's displays, which are temporary and involve hundreds of workers, are controversial among environmentalists, they have been critically acclaimed. Since 1961, most have been collaborative efforts with Christo's wife, Jeanne-Claude (1935–2009).[1]

Wedding Dress, one of Christo's lesser-known pieces, was part of *The Museum of Merchandise*. This exhibition of Pop and Op art and artist-designed furnishings and fashions was held in 1967, at the Young Men's/Young Women's Hebrew Association in Philadelphia. Attendees entered the exhibition through the door of Christo's *Store Front*, a twenty-four-by-ten-foot wood and Plexiglas structure. Beyond was a staging of flashing lights, pulsing rock music, and brightly colored chairs, lamps, dinnerware, and window treatments—all one-of-a-kind objects designed by contemporary artists. The evening ended with a fashion show, the finale of which was a barefoot model wearing Christo's "wedding dress"—a white satin top and shorts. Her "train" was an enormous bundle of fabric bound in ropes and pulled by the bride like a beast of burden.

This performance piece communicated the unrest felt by many women in the 1960s, the early years of the "second-wave" feminist movement. Author Betty Friedan wrote in the late 1950s about what she called "the problem that has no name." She received passionate responses from women who felt isolated and dissatisfied with their lives as homemakers and experienced marriage as a trap. The consciousness-raising that occurred among women in the mid-1960s led to wide acceptance of feminism and the passage of the Equal Rights Amendment in 1972.

Although Christo's *Wedding Dress* might seem to be a piece that speaks purely to its own time, the fact remains that inequalities between the sexes persist. Not only does the "glass ceiling" of the workplace still exist, but disparities remain within the institution of marriage. While most modern brides enter marriage with the assumption that the workload will be equally shared with their partners, research continues to demonstrate that women bear the greater burden of housework and childcare—even though most are employed full-time.

1. For a full discussion of Christo's work, see *Christo*, exh. cat. (Sydney: Art Gallery of New South Wales, 1990).

Christo (b. 1935)
Bulgaria, works in
United States
Wedding Dress, 1967
Rope, silk
On loan from the
artists Christo and
Jeanne-Claude

Photo by Ferdinand
Boesch. Copyright:
Christo, 1967.

Paco Rabanne
(b. 1934)
Spain, works in
France
Wedding Dress,
1967–68
Leather, aluminum
Museum Purchase:
Lawrence Archer
Wachs Fund
2008.107

42 / WEDDING DRESS

1967–68
PACO RABANNE (B. 1934)
SPAIN, WORKS IN FRANCE

While many brides err on the side of tradition and choose a gown that is conservative in design, the bride who wore this dress was exceptionally avant-garde, even for the 1960s. This garment was commissioned from Paris designer Paco Rabanne for a late 1960s wedding. It is constructed of white leather rectangles linked together with small metal rings; alternate segments are embellished with beaten aluminum strips riveted to the leather. The engineered structure of this dress is indicative of the designer's work.

Rabanne studied architecture at the École Nationale des Beaux-Arts in the 1950s, but he was also interested in fashion. His mother had been the chief seamstress for couturier Cristóbal Balenciaga. Rabanne began his fashion career as a freelance accessories designer, but his architectural background led him to begin designing soft sculptures. His first couture collection, titled 12 Experimental Dresses, was presented in Paris in 1964. The collection featured a series of futuristic garments made of incongruous materials resembling space-age prototypes rather than high-fashion garments. Like other emerging designers of the 1960s, Rabanne rejected traditional couture methods. He believed that the only avenue for advancing fashion was the utilization of new materials and techniques. Rabanne experimented with plastics, aluminum, and leather to create some of the most avant-garde garments of the 1960s.[1]

Rabanne's work with unusual materials was a product of his time. Technological advances that had originated during the war years resulted in the production of new plastics that flooded middle-class homes in the 1950s. In addition, the 1960s space race revolutionized ideas about life, art—and clothing. Garments became spare, geometric, and futuristic. Clothing began to reflect the social and cultural changes in attitudes toward women and their bodies. Colors were bold. Skirts were short. Dresses were one shape, one size fits all, unisex, and strategically transparent.

The bride who wore this gown was, like designers and artists of the period, a product of the time. Her choice of gown communicated her sense of self-assurance, even in such a ritualistic setting as the wedding ceremony. This was her opportunity to present herself, her ideas, and identity to a chosen audience of friends and family.

1. Richard Martin, ed., *The St. James Fashion Encyclopedia: A Survey of Style from 1945 to the Present* (New York: Visible Ink Press, 1997), 331–32; Colin McDowell, *McDowell's Directory of Twentieth Century Fashion* (Englewood Cliffs, NJ: Prentice-Hall, Inc., 1985), 226.

43 / WEDDING DRESS, TRAIN, BOW, AND HEADPIECE

1969
PRISCILLA OF BOSTON (ESTABLISHED 1945)
UNITED STATES

The wedding dress worn by Nancy Ann Stillpass in 1969 was created by Priscilla of Boston, one of the best-known bridal gown manufacturers of the twentieth century. In 1945, Priscilla Kidder opened the Bride's Shop on Newbury Street in Boston, offering unique handmade gowns. Before long, high-end department stores began carrying Priscilla designs. Kidder rose to international fame when she designed the bridesmaid dresses for Grace Kelly's 1956 wedding to Prince Rainier of Monaco. Priscilla gowns also were chosen by two presidential daughters: the wedding dresses worn by Luci Baines Johnson, who married in 1965, and Julie Nixon in 1968 were seen by millions of television viewers and readers of popular magazines. *Newsweek* dubbed Priscilla Kidder the "Queen of the Aisle" in 1968; a year later, *McCall's* magazine called her "The Lady Who Marries the Best People." Needless to say, if one had the means to purchase a Priscilla of Boston gown in the late 1960s, one did so.[1]

While brides of the 1960s might opt for anything from a mini to a peasant dress, Stillpass chose a formal gown. These more conventional designs were featured as frequently in bridal magazines as avant-garde styles. Here, a lace-covered bodice is complemented by an Empire waistline—an early-nineteenth-century style that reappeared in the mid-1960s. The gown is constructed of a weighty synthetic fabric that maintains a columnar shape. Like the 1948 Kiviette design worn by Mary Helen Luhrman (see cat. 35), Nancy Ann Stillpass's Priscilla dress was "convertible." The design featured a detachable train that snapped to the back waistline. It would have been worn for the ceremony but removed for the reception, where it would have proved too cumbersome to negotiate the greeting of guests and dancing.

The headdress is the most striking element of this ensemble. Its design resembles the lace mantilla that became popular in Spain in the seventeenth and eighteenth centuries. The mantilla was draped over and supported by a large hair comb that lifted the veil off the head and allowed it to fall over the shoulders. Stillpass's veil cascades over a peaked hat that replaces the traditional comb. The floral lace appliqué that embellishes the edges of the net veiling falls decorously across the bride's forehead. Like gown designs, bridal headpieces in

the 1960s varied widely. A bride might wear a simple wreath of flowers, a lace scarf tied under the chin, an oversized bow from which a veil fell down the back, or a structured hat or crown. Tall headdresses draped with lace veiling are seen in both the 1967 and 1968 issues of the *Bride's Magazine*. In the August/September 1968 issue, descriptions of two gowns mention lace mantillas, one of which was a Priscilla of Boston design.[2]

1. Priscilla of Boston website, http://www.priscillaofboston.com/about_history.jsp

2. *Bride's Magazine*, October/November 1967, 117; December/January 1967–68, 118; August/September 1968, 145, 165.

Figure 1
Bridal photo of Nancy Ann Stillpass, 1969.
Photo by C. Jos. Malott.

Priscilla of Boston
(established 1945)
United States
*Wedding Dress,
Train, Bow, and
Headpiece,* 1969
Synthetic
Gift of Mr. and Mrs.
Joseph Stillpass
1990.1298a–d

Molly Parnis
(1905–92)
United States
Wedding Dress, 1969
Synthetic, lamé
Gift of Mrs. Alvin A.
Gould
1986.702a,b

44 / WEDDING DRESS

1969
MOLLY PARNIS (1905-92)
UNITED STATES

In 1969, Norma Lee Bledsoe Osterman (1930–2010) was getting married for the second time. She was a young widow who had met Alvin Arthur Gould (1903–93) in April. Gould took little time deciding he wanted to marry Osterman; he proposed in June and they were married in August.

Tall and slim, Osterman had been a model. After the death of her first husband, she worked as a fashion consultant at Gidding Jenny, a high-end Cincinnati retailer. The store carried designer garments and many of the city's fashionable women shopped there. Marrying for the second time, Osterman felt a cocktail dress was most appropriate. She purchased this Molly Parnis design at Gidding Jenny. Parnis was an American designer known for conservative interpretations of current trends cut from extraordinary fabrics.[1]

Osterman made a choice similar to that of many brides in the 1960s. Mini-dresses cut in a simple A-line shape were "in." They were illustrated in the *Bride's Magazine* alongside peasant styles and traditional gowns like the dress Nancy Ann Stillpass wore the same year (see cat. 43). The dress was flattering and, characteristic of the designer, the fabric exceptional: a complex weave with a repeat design of white baroque scrollwork. Fringed edges that surround sheer hexagons lend texture and stand in sharp contrast to the sheen of the gold lamé incorporated into the motifs. Osterman had her bridesmaids' dresses custom-made in off-white crepe with gold detailing at the neckline and sleeve ends to coordinate with her dress.

1. Norma Lee Osterman, interviewed by her granddaughter, Amanda Newman, August 2009.

Figure 1
Norma Lee Bledsoe Osterman and Alvin Arthur Gould at their wedding, 1969.

45 / RUSSIAN FANTASY BRIDE ENSEMBLE

1986
BOB MACKIE (B.1940)
UNITED STATES

In the search for "the perfect dress"—what the owners of Kleinfeld's bridal salon in New York describe as "the dress of your dreams" and "a fairy-tale thing"—brides-to-be are often encouraged by saleswomen to think back to girlhood fantasies about their wedding day.[1] What did they imagine themselves wearing—a gown admired in a shop window, seen in a movie, or perhaps lovingly fitted on a Barbie doll? Choosing a wedding gown, whether traditional or avant-garde, is often about tapping into long-held fantasies, and there is no designer who can rival Bob Mackie when it comes to fantasy.

Mackie's illustrious career includes designing for television, film, and stage. He has dressed some of the most famous celebrities of the twentieth century, including Rita Hayworth and Diana Ross, Liza Minnelli and Madonna. Mackie is perhaps best known for the astounding costumes he has created for singer and actress Cher.[2]

In this ensemble, Mackie has pulled design concepts from the grandeur of Imperial Russia and created an opulent sheath gown studded with beading and rhinestones. The lavish coat is embellished with embroidery recalling the gold and silver ornamentation of the dress of the tsars and tsarinas, with fur trimming that evokes the bitter cold of Russian winters. It is more a costume than a dress, and, in creating it, Mackie touches on the element of theatricality that the wedding ritual conjures.

1. Ronald Rothstein and Mara Urshel, *How to Buy Your Perfect Wedding Dress* (New York: Fireside, 2001), 8, 147; Kamy Wicoff, *I Do But I Don't: Walking Down the Aisle Without Losing Your Mind* (Cambridge, MA: Da Capo Press, 2006), 137–38.

2. Frank DeCaro, *Unmistakably Mackie: The Fashion and Fantasy of Bob Mackie* (New York: Universe Publishing, 1999).

Bob Mackie (b. 1940)
United States
*Russian Fantasy
Bride Ensemble*, 1986
Silk, leather, fur,
beads, rhinestones
On loan from
Bob Mackie

Image: Courtesy
of Kent State
University Museum

46 / GOTHIC WEDDING DRESS: BODICE, SKIRT, OVERSKIRT, AND WINGS

2000
KRISTINA M. MANNING (B.1951), MAKER
SANDRA LANDEROS THOMAS (B.1976), DESIGNER
UNITED STATES

Contemporary brides are increasingly choosing alternative clothing that expresses uniqueness and individuality. They see their wedding as an opportunity to make an aesthetic and personal statement before an audience of their own choosing. Sandra Landeros did just that with her distinctive Gothic gown. She decided to depart from traditional styles altogether to create a dress that expressed her personality and vision.

Designed by the bride and constructed by her mother, the dress is highly symbolic. Landeros says, "My wedding gown was inspired by love and pieced together with symbolic values. . . . The design of the dress was inspired by the starry night sky." Landeros was careful in choosing materials that reflected her ideas. The black velvet embellished with streams of gold paillettes signifies the starlit sky. The moon is suggested in the silvery green satin fabric ornamented with tiny pearls. The black feather wings are a particularly unique element and reference an angelic state the couple felt they had reached in their connection with each other.

Landeros and her husband, Shane Thomas (b. 1973), represent the Goth subculture that developed in the late 1970s. "Goths" were originally associated with punk music and wore primarily black clothing that drew from diverse historical styles. The Goth look evolved to incorporate cyber elements and reinventions of historical modes during its revivals in the mid-1980s and late 1990s.[1] As bright colors began to appear in fashionable twentieth-century wedding attire and brides experimented with individualistic expressions, Goth brides became more common. Many, however, bought or rented a Goth costume or assembled attire from purchased pieces. Landeros is unusual in designing and creating a singular gown imbued with personalized symbolism.

While the Goth subculture is popularly associated with death, deviance, subversion, and evil, many contemporary Goth enthusiasts associate their interest in the movement with a nouveau spiritualism that does not relate to organized religion. Sandra Landeros describes the design of her dress and her wedding as "symbolizing the dark ages of being apart, and the angels we had become, and the romance we had finally found."

Figure 1
Sandra Landeros and Shane Thomas strike a dramatic pose in their wedding clothes in front of a wrought-iron cemetery fence.
www.rosenthalphotography.com

1. Valerie Steele and Jennifer Park, *Gothic: Dark Glamour* (New York: Yale University Press, 2008), 3–10.

Kristina M. Manning (b. 1951),
maker
Sandra Landeros Thomas (b. 1976),
designer
United States
*Gothic Wedding Dress: Bodice, Skirt,
Overskirt, and Wings,* 2000
Synthetics, beads, paillettes,
feathers
On loan from Sandra
Marie Landeros Thomas and
Shane Clinton Thomas

www.rosenthalphotography.com

47 / WEDDING DRESS

SPRING/SUMMER 2000
YOHJI YAMAMOTO (B. 1943)
JAPAN

Most women choose to wed in clothing that conforms to the accepted image of a bride within their culture and generation. Bridal gowns are easily identified by their opulence, formality, distinctive fabrics and embellishments, and careful craftsmanship. Traditionally, the bride is costumed to reflect the attributes she is expected to embody: purity, modesty, and docility. This dramatic example of bridal dress was designed by Yohji Yamamoto. One of the most influential designers of the twentieth century, Yamamoto has combined both formality and familiarity in this design.

The dress is executed in cotton muslin—a simple fabric that does not correspond to the exalted position of a bride. Muslin is commonly used to create the working pattern that serves as a guide when the finished garment is cut from exceptional fabrics. The choice of materials and construction are emblematic of Yamamoto's deconstructive eye. The piece evokes the sense of a work in progress. The large basting stitches left in place connote a transitional, unfinished aesthetic. Yamamoto fuses hasty finishing with couture detail—a signature of his design aesthetic. Like many contemporary bridal gowns, this piece fuses dichotomous ideas: purity versus sexuality, modesty versus narcissism, docility versus assertiveness. The result is a sculptural gown that conforms in its imposing nature to the concept of bridal elegance, yet its unfinished state refers, perhaps, to the boudoir or to a bride *en chemisette*.

2000
CLAUDY JONGSTRA, MAKER (B. 1963)
ARLETTE MUSCHTER, DESIGNER (B. 1970)
THE NETHERLANDS

In the past twenty years, like other aspects of Western culture, the allure of the white single-use wedding dress has spread across the globe. In particular, Asian brides have adopted this mode—sometimes wearing traditional clothing for the ceremony and changing into a Western-style white gown for the reception. This elegant design was created for a Japanese bride by Dutch artist Claudy Jongstra.

Appearing to be a somewhat traditional white gown from the front, the back view reveals a colorful phoenix in flight. The phoenix is a mythological bird embraced by many cultures. It is generally illustrated, as it is here, with long tail feathers. The bird was believed to live for centuries. At the end of its life cycle, it built a nest that spontaneously ignited, and both the bird and the nest were reduced to ashes from which a new phoenix arose to begin life again. Symbolizing rebirth and renewal, this dramatic life cycle corresponds to the transformational rite of passage the bride and groom participate in when they are wed.

Trained as a fashion designer, Claudy Jongstra graduated in 1989 from the Hoogeschool voor de Kunsten, Utrecht, and soon established her own design studio. In 1994 she was inspired by an exhibition of feltmaking that transformed her work. Intrigued by the process, Jongstra refined this age-old technique, resulting in a new approach to the traditional concept of felted fabric. For Jongstra, felting offers the exciting possibility of aggregating several different materials such as silk, linen, or acetate together with wool, producing surprisingly lightweight fabrics that retain an earthy, organic quality.[1]

This design combines Merino wool, raw silk, cotton gauze, silk organza, raw cashmere, and raw linen hand-felted to produce a soft fabric with various textures and sheens across the surface. The image of the phoenix is felted directly into the cloth by arranging fibers naturally colored with vegetable dyes in place before the process begins. Because the gown was made for a Japanese bride, the design incorporates a wide belt resembling an obi. The phoenix's tail feathers snake around the waist. The notched, thick felt forms the traditional bow at the center back.

This gown is the second of three comparable pieces. The first was produced for the bride and presented in an exhibition at the Salone del Mobile, Milan, in 2000. The piece seen here was commissioned by Murray Moss of Moss Gallery, New York, and subsequently purchased by the Cincinnati Art Museum. A third dress of similar design is now in the collection of the Fries Museum, Leeuwarden, the Netherlands. Each piece is related, but unique, as the felting process is not an exact science.

1. Artist Claudy Jongstra's website, http://www.claudyjongstra. com/node/19

Claudy Jongstra (b.
1963), maker
Arlette Muschter (b.
1970), designer
The Netherlands
*Wedding Dress
Japonesque,* 2000
Wool, silk, cotton,
cashmere, linen
Museum Purchase:
Lawrence Archer
Wachs Fund
2009.165a–c

Figure 1
Detail of felted phoenix on train.

Figure 2
The obi of the dress
is embellished with
felted phoenix tail
feathers.

49 / WEDDING DRESS

SPRING 2002
GEOFFREY BEENE (1927-2004)
AMERICAN

American designer Geoffrey Beene's work has been described as cerebral and modern. These characteristics are clearly exhibited in this wedding gown design from his Spring 2002 collection. Beene has captured the essence of solemnity with a monastic form in white satin. There is nothing about this dress that reflects the exaggerated concept of the fairy princess, a driving force for many bridal choices. He has moved the wedding gown out of the realm of fantasy and placed it squarely in the realm of modernity, formality, and elegance.

Beene's design references the expansive, unembellished 1860s skirts and the spare satin gowns of the 1930s (see cats. 7 and 31, respectively). This garment is not designed to reveal the female form in an overly emphatic way as do most contemporary wedding dresses. There is nothing sexual about this garment. It speaks more deeply to the momentous nature of the ritual about to be enacted. The only allusion to femininity is the ruffle at the back of the neck that is held by a band of satin. The pleats created by the band fall down the back of the gown, referencing the eighteenth-century *robe à la française*.[1]

Regarded as both a superb craftsman and an artist by his colleagues, Beene was known for creating clothes that were pared down to the essentials. The Beene look is strong and individual. His collections often offered a view of how fashion would develop into the next century. Above all, he created fashions that were easy to wear, comfortable, and beautiful.

1. The *robe à la française* was a style of eighteenth-century dress characterized by pleats that fell from the neckline to the hem. Called Watteau pleats, they were named for the French painter Antoine Watteau (1684–1721), who often portrayed women in this style of dress.

50 / WEDDING DRESS

FALL 2003
VERA WANG (B. 1949)
UNITED STATES

When a twenty-first-century woman begins the search for her wedding gown, the first name that comes to mind is Vera Wang. Wang's bridal gowns are known internationally for their modern styling, luxurious fabrics, and couture quality. Her market is the high-end customer.

Vera Wang began her fashion career as an editor for *Vogue* and became design director of women's accessories for Ralph Lauren. It was Wang's personal search for a wedding gown, however, that prompted her to establish her own business. In 1989, as she prepared to marry Arthur Becker, Wang discovered that her dream dress was simply not in the marketplace, so she designed her own gown—a simple slip-like sheath far different from prevailing styles. In 1990, Wang opened a luxury bridal salon at the elegant Carlyle Hotel on Madison Avenue. Her modern designs were hailed as fresh and innovative.

The impact of Vera Wang's bridal gown designs cannot be underestimated. Although the full-skirted, lacy styles that Wang rejected for herself continue to be popular, her trademark look—sleek, body-hugging slip dresses with minimal embellishment—continue to define the modern bride.

Evoking classic Greek or Roman dress, this example epitomizes the Wang look—a simple sheath of lightweight silk that requires a slim, toned body. The bodice, in both front and back, is seductively cut to the top of the waist yoke. Narrow lace insertions crisscross the yoke and create subtle interest on the skirt. Gathered self-fabric flutters at the shoulders. This dress is designed to focus attention, not on itself, but on the body of the bride.

Figure 1
This design from the 2001 Collection is strapless—a popular choice for many contemporary brides. The fit of this gown is unforgiving and requires a svelte figure. Both long tassels and feathers serve as stunning embellishments on the skirt.

Vera Wang (b. 1949)
United States
Wedding Dress, Fall
2003
Silk
On loan from Vera
Wang

Zac Posen (b. 1980)
United States
*Wedding Dress:
Bodice, Skirt, and
Train*, 2004
Silk
On loan from
Alexandra Posen

Photo by
Christian Oth

51 / WEDDING DRESS: BODICE, SKIRT, AND TRAIN

2004
ZAC POSEN (B. 1980)
UNITED STATES

Red wedding dresses have become increasingly popular in Western cultures in the past decade. As the virginal symbolism of white has lost much of its meaning for the modern bride, colorful gowns have gained renewed popularity. Red has always been a bridal color in some cultures. In China, red symbolizes happiness, love, and prosperity and is thus a traditional color for wedding attire. Red is also common in Indian, Japanese, and African weddings. For Alexandra Posen, however, the color was more about poppies.

Fashion designer Zac Posen designed his sister's poppy-laden gown as an homáge to their childhood and to Alexandra's gutsy sense of style. He knew she could pull off a dress of such intense color and immense proportions. The gown's six-foot train is covered with oversized organza poppies in red and fuchsia, inspired by the field of poppies in the movie *The Wizard of Oz*.

Alexandra Posen and artist Nils Folke Anderson were married in a meadow on a Pennsylvania farm. Together, the couple walked down a freshly mowed aisle amidst fields of tall grass. The gown with a bustier bodice and trailing skirt held a surprise for the guests and the groom: At the reception, the bride suddenly removed her long skirt to reveal a short version underneath in which she could dance freely.[1]

1. Diane Meier Delaney, *The New American Wedding* (New York: Viking Studio, 2005), 106; Rebecca Paley, "Weddings/Celebrations; Vows; Alexandra Posen and Nils Anderson," *New York Times*, July 4, 2004; Sarah Haight, "For Many a Modern Bride It's a Non-White Wedding," *W* magazine, June 2008.

Susie MacMurray (b. 1959)
England
Mixture of Frailties, 2004
Inside-out latex gloves, cotton calico, mounted on dress form
Collection of the artist

Photo courtesy of the artist.

52 / MIXTURE OF FRAILTIES

2004
SUSIE MᴬᶜMURRAY (B. 1959)
ENGLAND

First trained as a musician, London-based artist Susie MacMurray creates sculptural pieces, often in situ in historical spaces. Her piece *Mixture of Frailties* offers obvious domestic references. Traditionally, women have been sequestered as managers of the domestic space. This piece, fashioned of the latex gloves used for household cleaning, was inspired in part by the artist's continuing interest in fairy tales, perhaps alluding to Cinderella or other female characters in conventional roles. For MacMurray, the process of making the piece resonates with the repetitive actions of many human activities—in this case, cleaning.

MacMurray is attracted to materials that generate a sense of ambivalence and therefore provide insight into incongruent juxtapositions such as power and fragility or seduction and repulsion.[1] Here she has merged the stately beauty and singularity of a wedding gown with the mundane nature of the latex glove. Used for the dirtiest of jobs, the multiplicity of the glove forms nevertheless creates a decorative surface that is reminiscent of a frothily tiered wedding gown. The pristine state of the gloves confirms that they have never been used. Perhaps they would never be utilized by a woman who could afford to wear such a confection. Or do they represent the many pairs of gloves this woman will use once she has entered into the marital bond?

Like the performance piece *Wedding Dress* created by Christo (see cat. 41), MacMurray examines traditional roles and raises the continuing issue of women's equality. The span of time between the creation of the two works, approximately thirty-five years, reminds us that the issue is still relevant.

1. Artist Susie MacMurray's website, http://www.susiemacmurray.co.uk/.

53 / DRESS AND UNDERSKIRT

2005
LILIANA CASABAL
FOR MORGAN LE FAYE (ACTIVE 20TH C.)
ARGENTINA, WORKS IN UNITED STATES

Visual artist Anne Elizabeth Thompson (b. 1963) knew she did not want a conventional white wedding gown. Instead, she chose a green silk blouse and pleated knee-length skirt designed by Miu Miu, which she paired with a colorful floral brocade coat. Thompson's intention was to purchase two high-quality garments that she would wear many times after her wedding.

Thompson was forty-one when she and Nathan Boyer (b. 1974), also a visual artist, became engaged. They decided not to wait to try to start a family and, to their surprise, Anne became pregnant in March 2005. The wedding was planned for June. Although Thompson was not very far along in her pregnancy, the Miu Miu ensemble no longer fit her properly. Together, Thompson and her fiancé purchased the gown she ultimately wore—a Liliana Casabal design of olive green and black. Its looser styling was a better fit. Despite its unusual color, the dress was, in the bride's eyes, more traditional with its long full skirt and tulle petticoat.

Although conceiving prior to getting married was not in this modern couple's plans, in the sixteenth century it was not uncommon for a bride to be pregnant when wed. Many couples of the rural and lower classes consummated their relationship soon, if not immediately, after their betrothal, sometimes as a rebuff against parental opposition, but more often as a fulfillment of their promise to each other. Although Church officials condemned intercourse before marriage, research suggests that as late as the 1790s as many as thirty percent of brides were not virgins and were possibly pregnant when wed.[1]

In general, the strict morality of the nineteenth century made premarital relations a thing of the past until the 1960s. Although many twentieth-century brides were not virgins, the pregnant bride has become more common in the past decade. Celebrities Jennifer Garner and Amanda Peet were both pregnant when they married. Tom Cruise and Katie Holmes had their child before they were wed. But this trend is not just for celebrities any longer. A recent survey of bridal shop owners conducted by maternitybride.com reveals as many as one in six brides is pregnant.[2] Wedding gown designers are catering to these new needs with specialty lines and high-waisted gowns that are often in traditional white.

1. David Cressy, *Birth, Marriage, and Death: Ritual, Religion, and the Life-Cycle in Tudor and Stuart England* (Oxford: Oxford University Press, 1997), 277–81; John R. Gillis, *For Better, For Worse: British Marriages, 1600 to the Present* (New York: Oxford University Press, 1985), 30–31; Lawrence Stone, *The Family, Sex and Marriage in England, 1500–1800* (New York: Harper & Row, 1977), 607–15, 628–29; Marilyn Yalom, *A History of the Wife* (New York: HarperCollins, 2002), 113–14; Jack Larkin, *The Reshaping of Everyday Life 1790–1840* (New York: Harper & Row, 1988), 193; Nancy F. Cott, *A Heritage of Her Own: Toward a New Social History of American Women* (New York: Simon and Schuster, 1979), 170.

2. Brian Dakss, "Wedding Gowns for Pregnant Brides," April 11, 2007, *cbsnews.com,* http://www.cbsnews.com/stories/2007/04/11/earlyshow/living/beauty/main2671386.shtml.

Liliana Casabal
for Morgan Le Faye
(active 20th c.)
Argentina, works in
United States
*Dress and
Underskirt*, 2005
Cotton, nylon
On loan from Anne
Thompson

David R. Zyla
(b. 1966)
United States
Wedding Dress:
Bustier and Skirt,
2008
Silk
On loan from
All My Children

54 / WEDDING DRESS: BUSTIER AND SKIRT

2008
DAVID R. ZYLA (B.1966)
UNITED STATES

Like the wedding dress worn by Kate Magrish in 1952 (see cat. 38), this contemporary gown draws on historical design devices while maintaining a twenty-first-century sensibility. Constructed with a separate bodice and skirt, it evokes the romanticism associated with nineteenth-century bridal attire. The wide neckline, complex construction, stiff boning, narrow piped trim, center front point, and pleated detailing across the bust are remarkably reminiscent of Mary Muhlenberg's 1838 wedding dress (see cat. 3). This nineteenth-century styling is paired with a skirt that incorporates decidedly eighteenth-century elements. Both Ellen Curtis and Katherine Burton Pease (see cats. 15 and 17, respectively) wore gowns with a similar divided skirt. Here, the bifurcation reveals a petticoat composed of tiers of pleated fabric and delicate lace. The skirt panels are pulled back and draped asymmetrically, forming an updated version of the *panier*. Despite these historical allusions, the silhouette of the gown is decidedly contemporary. The slim, fluted skirt, in particular, suggests a Vera Wang influence. The self-fabric flowers on the proper left shoulder dot the skirt, tying the design together and eliminating the need for garish trims.

Actress Debbi Morgan wore this dress as Angie Baxter for her wedding to Jesse Hubbard, played by Darnell Williams, in the soap opera *All My Children*. Daytime television's first African American supercouple, the two were married for the second time, in February 2008, after a twist of plot in which the Hubbard character died and reappeared. The gown was designed by David R. Zyla, who has been head costume designer for the soap opera since 2001; he has earned three Daytime Emmy Award®

nominations for Outstanding Achievement in Costume Design. Zyla has also designed for Broadway and regional theater productions, film, and commercials. He created the wardrobe for First Lady Hilary Rodham Clinton's trip to Asia, and headed his own design label.

Figure 1
Debbi Morgan as Angie Baxter and Darnell Williams as Jesse Hubbard on *All My Children*, February 2008.
© Steve Fenn/ American Broadcasting Companies, Inc.

55 / WEDDING DRESS

2009
MONIQUE LHUILLIER (B. 1971)
PHILIPPINES, WORKS IN UNITED STATES

WEDDING DRESS

2009
ANDREW GN (B. 1966)
SINGAPORE, WORKS IN FRANCE

On February 13, 2009, the soap opera *All My Children* broadcast the first lesbian wedding on daytime television. Bianca Montgomery, played by Eden Riegel, wore a Monique Lhuillier one-shouldered, Grecian-style gown embellished with gold sequins. The bridal gown designed by Andrew Gn and worn by Montgomery's partner Reese Williams, played by actress Tamara Braun, was appropriately more streamlined to correspond with her character's profession as an architect.

Whether brides are heterosexual or lesbian, their choice of wedding attire generally reflects the accepted image of a bride. A wave of lesbian weddings took place in California during a brief period in 2008 when same-sex marriages were deemed legal. Sanctioned by law or not, when lesbian couples marry some choose gender-neutral or masculine forms of attire, but many opt for traditional gowns. No matter their sexual orientation, most women from an early age have envisioned their wedding day and what they might wear.

Although much controversy surrounds this issue, same-sex marriage is currently legal in the United States in New Hampshire, Massachusetts, Connecticut, Iowa, and Vermont. In Europe, gay couples can marry in Sweden, Norway, the Netherlands, Belgium, and Spain. The inclusion of a lesbian wedding in a mainstream soap opera suggests a broader acceptance of the concept and perhaps forecasts the eventual widespread legalization of same-sex marriage.

Reese Williams (Tamara Braun), left, and Bianca Montgomery (Eden Riegel), right, were the first lesbian couple to be wed on a soap opera.
© Lou Rocco/ American Broadcasting Companies, Inc.

Monique Lhuillier
(b. 1971)
Philippines, works
in United States
Wedding Dress, 2009
Silk
On loan from
All My Children

Andrew Gn (b. 1966)
Singapore, works in
France
Wedding Dress, 2009
Silk
On loan from
All My Children

SELECT BIBLIOGRAPHY

American Life Histories: Manuscripts from the Federal Writers' Project, 1936–1940. Interview with Mrs. H. C. Gates. http://memory.loc.gov.

Ames, Blanche Butler. *Chronicles from the Nineteenth Century: Family Letters of Blanche Butler and Adelbert Ames.* Clinton, MA: Colonial Press, 1957.

Amnéus, Cynthia. *A Separate Sphere: Dressmakers in Cincinnati's Golden Age 1877–1922.* Lubbock: Texas Tech University Press, 2003.

Amt, Emilie, ed. *Women's Lives in Medieval Europe: A Sourcebook.* New York: Routledge, Chapman, and Hall, 1993.

Arch, Nigel, and Joanna Marschner. *Splendor at Court: Dressing for Royal Occasions Since 1700.* London: Unwin Hyman, 1987.

Astell, Mary. *Some Reflections Upon Marriage.* London: Printed for John Nutt, 1700.

Bailey, Beth L. *From Front Porch to Back Seat: Courtship in Twentieth-Century America.* Baltimore: Johns Hopkins University Press, 1988.

Baritz, Loren. *The Good Life: The Meaning of Success for the American Middle Class.* New York: Harper & Row Publishers, 1990.

Beale, Harriet S. Blaine, ed. *Letters of Mrs. James G. Blaine.* 2 vols. New York: Duffield & Co., 1908.

Bell, Catherine M. *Ritual Theory, Ritual Practice.* Oxford: Oxford University Press, 1992.

Berriot-Salvadore, Evelyne. "The Discourse of Medicine and Science." In Davis and Farge, *Renaissance and Enlightenment Paradoxes.*

Bissonnette, Anne. *Fashion on the Ohio Frontier: 1790–1840.* Kent, OH: Kent State University Press, 2003.

———. "The 1870s Transformation of the *Robe de Chambre*." In Amnéus, *A Separate Sphere.*

Blackstone, Sir William. *Commentaries on the Laws of England.* Vol. 1, *Of the Rights of Persons.* 1765. A facsimile edition with an introduction by Stanley N. Katz. Chicago: University of Chicago Press, 1979.

Blum, Stella, ed. *Victorian Fashions and Costumes from Harper's Bazar, 1867–1898.* New York: Dover Publications, 1974.

Boorstin, Daniel. *The Americans: The Democratic Experience.* New York: Random House, 1974.

Bowne, Eliza Southgate. *A Girl's Life Eighty Years Ago: Letters of Eliza Southgate Bowne.* Edited by Clarence Cook. New York: Charles Scribner's Sons, 1887.

Bradfield, Nancy. *Costume in Detail, 1730–1930.* Boston: Plays, Inc., 1968.

Bradshaw, Paul F. "Weddings." In *Encyclopedia of Early Christianity*, edited by Everett Ferguson. 2nd ed. New York: Garland Publishing, 1997.

Breines, Wini. *Young, White, and Miserable: Growing Up Female in the Fifties.* Boston: Beacon, 1992.

Brooke, Christopher. *The Medieval Idea of Marriage.* Oxford: Oxford University Press, 1989.

Brown, C. M., and C. L. Gates. *Scissors and Yardstick; or, All about Dry Goods.* Hartford, CT: C. M. Brown and R. W. Jacqua, 1872.

Brumberg, Joan Jacobs. *The Body Project: An Intimate History of American Girls.* New York: Vintage Books, 1998.

Calder, Jenni. *Women and Marriage in Victorian Fiction.* New York: Oxford University Press, 1976.

Cathey, Cornelius O., ed. *A Woman Rice Planter.* Cambridge, MA: Macmillan & Co., 1922.

Chambers, John Whiteclay II. *The Tyranny of Change: America in the Progressive Era, 1890–1920.* 2nd ed. New Brunswick, NJ: Rutgers University Press, 2000.

Christo. An exhibition catalogue for the John Kaldor Art Project. Sydney: Art Gallery of New South Wales, 1990.

The Cincinnati Directory, for the Year 1834. Cincinnati, OH: E. Deming, 1834.

Cincinnati Society Blue Book and Family Directory. Cincinnati, OH: Peter G. Thomson, 1879.

Cist, Charles, ed. *The Cincinnati Directory for the Year 1842*. Cincinnati, OH: E. Morgan and Company, 1842.

The City of Cincinnati and Its Resources. Cincinnati, OH: Cincinnati Times Star Co., 1891.

Clark, Clifford Edward, Jr. *The American Family Home, 1800–1960*. Chapel Hill: University of North Carolina Press, 1986.

Cleaver, Robert. *A Godly Forme of Houshold Gouernment*. London: Eliot's Court Press for the assignes of Thomas Man, 1630.

Cohen, Lizabeth. *A Consumers' Republic: The Politics of Mass Consumption in Postwar America*. New York: Vintage Books, 2004.

Cole, George S. *A Complete Dictionary of Dry Goods and History of Silk, Cotton, Linen, Wool and other Fibrous Substances*. Chicago: W. B. Conkey Company, 1892.

Coleman, Elizabeth A. *The Opulent Era: Worth, Doucet, and Pingat*. New York: Thames and Hudson, 1989.

Coontz, Stephanie. *Marriage, a History: From Obedience to Intimacy or, How Love Conquered Marriage*. New York: Viking Penguin, 2005.

Cott, Nancy F. *The Bonds of Womanhood: "Woman's Sphere" in New England, 1780–1835*. London: Yale University Press, 1977.

———. "Divorce and the Changing Status of Women in Eighteenth Century Massachusetts." In Gordon, *The American Family in Social-Historical Perspective*.

———. *A Heritage of Her Own: Toward a New Social History of American Women*. New York: Simon and Schuster, 1979.

———. *No Small Courage: A History of Women in the United States*. Oxford: Oxford University Press, 2000.

———. "Passionlessness: An Interpretation of Victorian Sexual Ideology, 1790–1850." *Signs* 4:2 (1978): 219–36.

———. *Public Vows: A History of Marriage and the Nation*. Cambridge, MA: Harvard University Press, 2000.

———. *Root of Bitterness: Documents of the Social History of American Women*. Boston: Northeastern University Press, 1986.

Crampe-Casnabet, Michèle. "A Sampling of Eighteenth-Century Philosophy." In Davis and Farge, *Renaissance and Enlightenment Paradoxes*.

Cressy, David. *Birth, Marriage, and Death: Ritual, Religion, and the Life-Cycle in Tudor and Stuart England*. Oxford: Oxford University Press, 1997.

Crofts, Robert. *The Lover: or, Nuptiall Love*. London: B. Alsop and T. F[awcet] for Rich: Meighen, 1638.

Cunningham, Patricia A. "Healthful, Artistic, and Correct Dress." In Thieme, *With Grace and Favour*.

———. *Reforming Women's Fashion, 1850–1920: Politics, Health, and Art*. Kent, OH: Kent State University Press, 2003.

Cunnington, Phillis, and Catherine Lucas. *Costume for Birth, Marriages and Death*. London: Adam & Charles Black, 1972.

Dale, Tim. *Harrods: A Palace in Knightsbridge*. London: Harrods Publishing, 1995.

Dauphin, Cécile. "Single Women." In Fraisse and Perrot, *Emerging Feminism from Revolution to World War*.

Daves, Jessica. *Ready-made Miracle: The American Story of Fashion for Millions*. New York: G. P. Putnam, 1967.

Davidoff, Leonore, and Catherine Hall. *Family Fortunes: Men and Women of the English Middle Class, 1780–1850*. Chicago: University of Chicago Press, 1987.

Davis, Ada M. Personal journal, 1874. Collection of the Cincinnati Art Museum.

Davis, Natalie Zemon, and Arlette Farge, eds. *Renaissance and Enlightenment Paradoxes*. Vol. 3 of *A History of Women in the West*, edited by Georges Duby and Michelle Perrot, translated by Arthur Goldhammer. Cambridge, MA: Belknap Press of Harvard University Press, 1993.

DeCaro, Frank. *Unmistakably Mackie: The Fashion and Fantasy of Bob Mackie*. New York: Universe Publishing, 1999.

D'Emilio, John, and Estelle B. Freedman. *Intimate Matters: A History of Sexuality in America*. 2nd ed. Chicago: University of Chicago Press, 1997.

Decorum: A Practical Treatise on Etiquette and Dress of the Best American Society. New York: Union Publishing House, 1880.

Degler, Carl N. *At Odds: Women and the Family in America from the Revolution to the Present*. New York: Oxford University Press, 1980.

Delaney, Diane Meier. *The New American Wedding: Ritual and Style in a Changing Culture*. New York: Viking Studio, 2005.

Deloney, Thomas. *The Pleasant History of John Winchcomb*. London: E. Crowch for Thomas Passenger, 1672.

De Marly, Diana. *Worth, Father of Haute Couture*. New York: Holmes & Meier, 1990.

Denning, Michael. *Mechanic Accents: Dime Novels and Working-Class Culture in America*. London: Verso, 1987.

Derks, Scott. *The Value of a Dollar: Prices and Incomes in the U.S. 1860–2009*. 4th ed. Amenia, NY: Grey House Publishing, 2009.

Duby, Georges. *The Knight, The Lady, and The Priest: The Making of Modern Marriage in Medieval France*. Translated by Barbara Bray. New York: Pantheon Books, 1983.

———. *Love and Marriage in the Middle Ages*. Translated by Jane Dunnett. Chicago: University of Chicago Press, 1994.

Eck, Lois. "I Thought My Life Was Over." *Ladies' Home Journal*, April 1945.

Ehrenreich, Barbara. *Fear of Falling: The Inner Life of the Middle Class*. New York: Pantheon Books, 1989.

Estes, David Foster. *The History of Holden Massachusetts, 1684–1894*. Worcester, MA: Press of C. F. Lawrence & Co., 1894.

Farge, Arlette. "Protesters Plain to See." In Davis and Farge, *Renaissance and Enlightenment Paradoxes*.

Ferrell, Lori Anne. "An Imperfect Diary of a Life: The 1662 Diary of Samuel Woodforde." *The Yale University Library Gazette* 63 (1989): 137–44.

Flanagan, J. F. *Spitalfields Silks of the 18th and 19th Centuries*. Leigh-on-Sea, England: F. Lewis, Publisher, 1954.

Foster, Shirley. *Victorian Women's Fiction: Marriage, Freedom and the Individual*. Towata, NJ: Barnes & Noble Books, 1986.

Fowler, Marian. *In a Gilded Cage: From Heiress to Duchess*. New York: St. Martin's Press, 1993.

Fox, Richard Wightman, and T. J. Jackson Lears, eds. *The Culture of Consumption: Critical Essays in American History, 1880–1980*. New York: Pantheon, 1983.

Fraisse, Geneviève, and Michelle Perrot, eds. *Emerging Feminism from Revolution to World War*. Vol. 4 of *A History of Women in the West*, edited by Georges Duby and Michelle Perrot, translated by Arthur Goldhammer. Cambridge, MA: Belknap Press of Harvard University Press, 1993.

Frank, Stephen M. *Life with Father: Parenthood and Masculinity in the Nineteenth-Century American North*. Baltimore: Johns Hopkins University Press, 1998.

Frick, Carole Collier. *Dressing Renaissance Florence: Families, Fortunes, and Fine Clothing*. Baltimore: Johns Hopkins University Press, 2002.

Friedan, Betty. *The Feminine Mystique*. New York: W. W. Norton & Company, 1997.

Frost, S. A. *The Art of Dressing Well: A Complete Guide to Economy, Style, and Propriety of Costume*. New York: Dick & Fitzgerald, Publishers, 1870.

Fukai, Akiko. "Rococo and Neoclassical Clothing." In Starobinski et al., *Revolution in Fashion: European Clothing, 1715–1815*.

Funderburk, Joan Arta Uhrig. "The Development of Women's Ready-to-Wear, 1865 to 1914: Based on New York Times Advertisements." PhD diss., University of Maryland, 1994.

Gamber, Wendy. *The Female Economy: The Millinery and Dressmaking Trades 1860–1930*. Urbana: University of Illinois Press, 1997.

Gant, Liz. "The Lowdown on Costs." *Essence*, June 1978.

Geller, Jaclyn. *Here Comes the Bride: Women, Weddings, and the Marriage Mystique*. New York: Four Walls Eight Windows, 2001.

Gennep, Arnold van. *The Rites of Passage.* Translated by Monika B. Vizedom and Gabrielle L. Caffee. Introduction by Solon T. Kimball. Chicago: University of Chicago Press, 1960.

Gies, Frances, and Joseph Gies. *Marriage and Family in the Middle Ages.* New York: Harper & Row Publishers, 1987.

Gillian, Gill. *We Two: Victoria and Albert: Rulers, Partners, Rivals.* New York: Ballantine Books, 2009.

Gillis, John R. *For Better, For Worse: British Marriages, 1600 to the Present.* New York: Oxford University Press, 1985.

Gilman, Charlotte Perkins. [As Charlotte Perkins Stetson] *Women and Economics: A Study of the Economic Relation Between Men and Women as a Factor in Social Evolution.* 3rd ed. Boston: Small, Maynard & Company, 1900.

Godineau, Dominique. "Daughters of Liberty and Revolutionary Citizens." In Fraisse and Perrot, *Emerging Feminism from Revolution to World War.*

Glendale Heritage Preservation. *Glendale's Heritage: Glendale, Ohio.* Cincinnati, OH: Young & Klein, 1976.

Gordon, Michael, ed. *The American Family in Social-Historical Perspective.* 2nd ed. New York: St. Martin's Press, 1978.

Goss, Charles Frederic. *Cincinnati, The Queen City, 1788–1912.* Cincinnati, OH: S. J. Clarke Publishing Company, 1912.
Gouge, William. *Of domesticall duties eight treatises.* London: John Haviland for William Bladen, 1622.

Greater Hamilton: A Review of Its Manufacturing, Merchantile [sic] *Commercial Industries and Enterprises.* 1909.

Greve, Charles Theodore. *Centennial History of Cincinnati and Representative Citizens.* 2 vols. Chicago: Biographical Pub. Co., 1904.

Guy, Ali, Eileen Green, and Maura Banim, eds. *Through the Wardrobe: Women's Relationships with Their Clothes.* Oxford: Berg, 2001.

The Habits of Good Society: A Handbook for Ladies and Gentlemen. New York: Carleton, Publisher, 1864.

Hackstaff, Karla B. *Marriage in a Culture of Divorce.* Philadelphia: Temple University Press, 1999.

Hall, Edwin. *The Arnolfini Betrothal: Medieval Marriage and the Enigma of Van Eyck's Double Portrait.* Berkeley: University of California Press, 1994.

Hall, Peter Dobkin. "Marital Selection and Business in Massachusetts Merchant Families, 1700–1900." In Gordon, *The American Family in Social-Historical Perspective.*

Halttunen, Karen. *Confidence Men and Painted Women: A Study of Middle-Class Culture in America, 1830–1870.* London: Yale University Press, 1982.

Hammerton, A. James. *Cruelty and Companionship: Conflict in Nineteenth-Century Married Life.* London: Routledge, 1992.

Hanson, Kitty. *For Richer, For Poorer.* New York: Abelard-Schuman, 1967.

Hartley, Cecil B. *The Gentlemen's Book of Etiquette and Manual of Politeness: Being a Complete Guide for a Gentleman's Conduct in All His Relations Towards Society.* Boston: J. S. Locke & Company, 1874.

Hartmann, Susan M. *The Home Front and Beyond: American Women in the 1940s.* Boston: Twayne Publishers, 1982.

Haynes, Henrietta. *Henrietta Maria.* New York: G. P. Putnam's Sons, 1912.

Hellerstein, Erna Olafson, Leslie Parker Hume, and Karen M. Offen, eds. *Victorian Women: A Documentary Account of Women's Lives in Nineteenth-Century England, France, and the United States.* Stanford, CA: Stanford University Press, 1981.

Herbert, Jeffrey G., ed. *Restored Hamilton County Marriages, 1870–1884.* Cincinnati, OH: Hamilton County Chapter of the Ohio Genealogical Society, 1994.

Hertz, Rosanna. *More Equal Than Others: Women and Men in Dual-Career Marriages.* Berkeley: University of California Press, 1986.

High on a Hill: The Story of Christ Church, Glendale 1865–1964. Cincinnati, OH: T. H. Carruthers, 1965.

History of Cincinnati and Hamilton County, Ohio: Their Past and Present. Cincinnati, OH: S. B. Nelson & Co., Publisher, 1894.

Hobsbawm, Eric. "Introduction: Inventing Traditions." In *The Invention of Tradition*, edited by Eric Hobsbawm and Terence Ranger. New York: Cambridge University Press, 1995.

Houghton, Walter E. *The Victorian Frame of Mind 1830–1870*. New Haven, CT: Yale University Press, 1957.

Howard, Vicki Jo. "American Weddings: Gender, Consumption, and the Business of Brides." PhD. diss., University of Texas at Austin, 2000.

Howard, Vicki. *Brides, Inc.: American Weddings and the Business of Tradition*. Philadelphia: University of Pennsylvania Press, 2006.

Hufton, Olwen H. *The Prospect Before Her: A History of Women in Western Europe, 1500–1800*. New York: Alfred A. Knopf, 1996.

Hunt, Morton. *The Natural History of Love*. Revised and updated. New York: Anchor Books, 1994.

Illustrated Business Directory and Picturesque Cincinnati. Cincinnati, OH: Spencer and Craig Printing Works, 1894.

Ingraham, Chrys. *White Weddings: Romancing Heterosexuality in Popular Culture*. New York: Routledge, 1999.

Isidore of Seville. *Isidore of Seville: The Medical Writings*. Philadelphia: American Philosophical Society, 1964.

James, E. O. *Marriage and Society*. London: Hutchinson's University Library, 1952.

Jellison, Katherine. "From the Farmhouse Parlor to the Pink Barn: The Commercialization of Weddings in the Rural Midwest." *Iowa Heritage Illustrated* 77 (Summer 1996).

———. *It's Our Day: America's Love Affair with the White Wedding 1945–2005*. Lawrence: University Press of Kansas, 2008.

Jones, Jacqueline. *Labor of Love, Labor of Sorrow: Black Women, Work, and the Family from Slavery to the Present*. New York: Basic Books, 1985.

Joselit, Jenna Weissman. *The Perfect Fit: Clothes, Character, and the Promise of America*. New York: Henry Holt, 2001.

Kasson, John F. *Rudeness and Civility: Manners in Nineteenth-Century Urban America*. New York: Hill and Wang, 1990.

Kerber, Linda K. "Separate Spheres, Female Worlds, Woman's Place: The Rhetoric of Women's History." *Journal of American History* 75 (1988): 9–39.

Kidwell, Claudia B., and Margaret C. Christman. *Suiting Everyone*. Washington, DC: Smithsonian Institution Press, 1974.

Kissam, Edward. *The Kissam Family in America from 1644 to 1825*. New York: Dempsey and Carroll's Art Press, 1892.

Klapisch-Zuber, Christiane, ed. *Silences of the Middle Ages*. Vol. 2 of *A History of Women in the West*, edited by Georges Duby and Michelle Perrot, translated by Arthur Goldhammer. Cambridge, MA: Belknap Press of Harvard University Press, 1992.

Knibiehler, Yvonne. "Bodies and Hearts." In Fraisse and Perrot, *Emerging Feminism from Revolution to World War*.

Laas, Virginia Jeans. *Love and Power in the Nineteenth Century: The Marriage of Violet Blair*. Fayetteville: University of Arkansas Press, 1998.

Lacey, Peter. *The Wedding*. New York: Ridge Press, 1969.

Langland, Elizabeth. *Nobody's Angels: Middle-Class Women and Domestic Ideology in Victorian Culture*. Ithaca, NY: Cornell University Press, 1995.

Larkin, Jack. *The Reshaping of Everyday Life, 1790–1840*. New York: Harper & Row Publishers, 1988.

Lasch, Christopher. *Women and the Common Life: Love, Marriage, and Feminism*. New York: W. W. Norton & Company, 1997.

Leach, William. *Land of Desire: Merchants, Power, and the Rise of a New American Culture*. New York: Pantheon Books, 1993.

———. "Transformation in a Culture of Consumption: Women and Department Stores, 1890–1925." *Journal of American History* 71 (September 1984): 319–42.

Leonard, John William. *The Centennial Review of Cincinnati: One Hundred Years of Progress in Commerce, Manufactures, the Professions, and in Social and Municipal Life*. Cincinnati, OH: J. M. Elstner, 1888.

Levine, George Lewis, ed. *Constructions of the Self.* New Brunswick, NJ: Rutgers University Press, 1992.

Lewis, Jan. "Motherhood and the Construction of the Male Citizen in the United States, 1750–1850." In Levine, *Constructions of the Self.*

Lewis, Jane E. *Women in England, 1870–1960: Sexual Divisions and Social Change.* Brighton, England: Wheatsheaf Books, 1984.

Ley, Sandra. *Fashions for Everyone: The Story of Ready-to-wear.* New York: Charles Scribner's Sons, 1975.

Linden-Ward, Blanche, and Carol Hurd Green. *Changing the Future: American Women in the 1960s.* New York: Twayne Publishers, 1993.

Marling, Karal Ann. *As Seen on TV: The Visual Culture of Everyday Life in the 1950s.* Cambridge, MA: Harvard University Press, 1994.

Marsh, Margaret. *Suburban Lives.* New Brunswick, NJ: Rutgers University Press, 1990.

Matelski, Marilyn J. *Soap Operas Worldwide: Cultural and Serial Realities.* Jefferson, NC: McFarland & Co., 1999.

May, Elaine Tyler. *Homeward Bound: American Families in the Cold War Era.* New York: Basic Books, 1988.

McBride-Mellinger, Maria. *The Wedding Dress.* New York: Random House, 1993.

Mead, Rebecca. *One Perfect Day: The Selling of the American Wedding.* New York: Penguin Press, 2007.

Memorial Record of Butler County, Ohio. Chicago: Record Publishing Company, 1894.

Michaud, Stéphane. "Artistic and Literary Idolatries." In Fraisse and Perrot, *Emerging Feminism from Revolution to World War.*

Miller, Zane L., and Bruce Tucker. *Changing Plans for America's Inner Cities: Cincinnati's Over-the-Rhine and Twentieth-Century Urbanism.* Columbus: Ohio State University Press, 1998.

Montgomery, Maureen E. *Gilded Prostitution: Status, Money, and Transatlantic Marriages, 1870–1914.* London: Routledge, 1989.

Moore, Gerald E. *Make An Idea Succeed: The Western-Southern Story.* Cincinnati, OH: Western and Southern Life Insurance Company, 1988.

The National Cyclopaedia of American Biography. New York: James T. White & Company, 1935.

Nearing, Scott. *Financing the Wage-Earner's Family.* New York: B. W. Huebsch, 1913.

"No More Miss America." In Alexander Bloom and Wini Breines, eds. *"Takin' It to the Streets": A Sixties Reader.* 2nd ed. New York: Oxford University Press, 2003.

Norton, Mary Beth. *Liberty's Daughters: The Revolutionary Experience of American Women, 1750–1800.* Ithaca, NY: Cornell University Press, 1996.

Nutt, Charles. *History of Worcester and its People.* New York: Lewis Historical Publishing Company, 1919.

O'Day, Rosemary. *The Family and Family Relationships, 1500–1900: England, France and the United States of America.* London: The Macmillan Press, 1994.

Opitz, Claudia. "Life in the Late Middle Ages." In Klapisch-Zuber, *Silences of the Middle Ages.*

Otnes, Cele C., and Elizabeth H. Pleck. *Cinderella Dreams: The Allure of the Lavish Wedding.* Berkeley: University of California Press, 2003.

Patmore, Coventry. *The Angel in the House.* London: John W. Parker and Son, 1868.

Penner, Barbara. "'A Vision of Love and Luxury': The Commercialization of Nineteenth-Century American Weddings." *Winterthur Portfolio* 39 (Spring 2004): 1–20.

Perkin, Joan. *Women and Marriage in Nineteenth-Century England.* Chicago: Lyceum Books, 1989.

Plato, and R. D. Archer-Hind. *The Timaeus of Plato.* London: Macmillan, 1888.

Pleck, Elizabeth H. *Celebrating the Family: Ethnicity, Consumer Culture, and Family Rituals.* Cambridge, MA: Harvard University Press, 2000.

Porter, Rev. James. *The Operative's Friend, and Defence: Or, Hints to Young Ladies, Who Are Dependent on Their Own Exertions.* Boston: Charles H. Peirce, 1850.

Riley, Glenda. *Divorce: An American Tradition.* New York: Oxford University Press, 1991.

Rogers, Daniel. *Matrimoniall honovr.* London: Th. Harper for Philip Nevel, 1642.

Rogers, Millard F., Jr. *Rich in Good Works: Mary M. Emery of Cincinnati.* Akron, OH: University of Akron Press, 2001.

Rothman, Ellen K. *Hands and Hearts: A History of Courtship in America.* New York: Basic Books, 1984.

Rothstein, Ronald, and Mara Urshel. *How to Buy Your Perfect Wedding Dress.* New York: Fireside, 2001.

Rugh, Susan Sessions. *Are We There Yet?: The Golden Age of American Family Vacations.* Lawrence: University Press of Kansas, 2008.

Ryan, Mary P. *Cradle of the Middle Class: The Family in Oneida County, New York, 1790–1865.* Cambridge: Cambridge University Press, 1981.

Sanford, Mollie Dorsey. *Mollie: The Journal of Mollie Dorsey Sanford in Nebraska and Colorado Territories, 1857–1866.* Lincoln: University of Nebraska Press, 1959.

Schneider, Susan Weidman. "Isn't It Ironic . . . Retro Weddings in a Feminist Age." *Lilith*, Spring 2000.

Schoonover, David E., ed. *The Ladies' Etiquette Handbook: The Importance of Being Refined in the 1880s.* Iowa City: University of Iowa Press, 2001.

Seaton, Oren Andrew, ed. *The Seaton Family, with Genealogy and Biographies.* Topeka, KS: Crane & Company, 1906.

Sebesta, Judith Lynn, and Larissa Bontante, eds. *The World of Roman Costume.* Madison: University of Wisconsin Press, 1994.

Seligson, Marcia. *The Eternal Bliss Machine: America's Way of Wedding.* New York: William Morrow & Company, 1973.

Severa, Joan. *Dressed for the Photographer: Ordinary Americans and Fashion.* Kent, OH: Kent State University Press, 1995.

Sigourney, L. H. *Whisper to a Bride.* Hartford, CT: H. S. Parsons & Co., 1850.

Sivulka, Juliann. *Soap, Sex, and Cigarettes: A Cultural History of American Advertising.* Belmont, CA: Wadsworth Publishing Company, 1998.

Sledziewski, Elisabeth G. "The French Revolution as the Turning Point." In Fraisse and Perrot, *Emerging Feminism from Revolution to World War.*

Staniland, Kay, and Santina M. Levy. "Queen Victoria's Wedding Dress and Lace." *Costume: The Journal of the Costume Society* 17 (1983): 1–32.

Starobinski, Jean, et al. *Revolution in Fashion: European Clothing, 1715–1815.* Published in conjunction with an exhibition held at the Kyoto National Museum of Modern Art. New York: Abbeville Press, 1990.

Steele, Valerie. *Women of Fashion: Twentieth Century Designers.* New York: Rizzoli, 1991.

Steele, Valerie, and Jennifer Park. *Gothic: Dark Glamour.* New York: Yale University Press, 2008.

Stevenson, Kenneth. *Nuptial Blessing: A Study of Christian Marriage Rites.* New York: Oxford University Press, 1983.

Stone, Lawrence. *The Family, Sex and Marriage in England, 1500–1800.* New York: Harper & Row Publishers, 1977.

Swinburne, Henry. *A Treatise of Spousals or Matrimonial Contracts.* London: S. Roycroft for Robert Clavell, 1686.

Thackeray, William Makepeace. *Vanity Fair: A Novel without a Hero.* New York: Random House, 1999.

Thieme, Otto Charles. *With Grace and Favour: Victorian and Edwardian Fashion in America.* Cincinnati, OH: Cincinnati Art Museum, 1993.

Thomasset, Claude. "The Nature of Women." In Klapisch-Zuber, *Silences of the Middle Ages.*

Thompson, Dorothy. *Queen Victoria: The Woman, the Monarchy, and the People.* New York: Pantheon Books, 1990.

Thoresby, Ralph. *The Diary of Ralph Thoresby.* Edited by Joseph Hunter. London: Coburn and Richard Bentley, 1830.

Thornton, Alice Wandesford. *The Autobiography of Mrs. Alice Thornton, of East Newton, Co. York.* Durham, England: Andrews and Co., 1875.

Tocqueville, Alexis de. *Democracy in America*. New York: Alfred A. Knopf, 1945.

Totora, Phyllis G., and Robert S. Merkel. *Fairchild's Dictionary of Textiles*. New York: Fairchild Publications, 2000.

Traer, James F. *Marriage and the Family in Eighteenth-Century France*. Ithaca, NY: Cornell University Press, 1980.

U.S. Bureau of the Census. *Sixteenth Census of the United States: 1940, Characteristics of Persons Not in the Labor Force 14 Years Old and Over*. Prepared under the supervision of Leon E. Truesdell. Washington, DC: U.S. Government Printing Office, 1943.

The Village of Glendale, 1855–2005. Cincinnati, OH: Glendale Heritage Preservation, 2004.

Vital Records of Holden, Massachusetts to the end of the year 1849. Worcester, MA: Franklin P. Rice, 1904.

Walker, Nancy A. *Shaping Our Mothers' World: American Women's Magazines*. Jackson: University Press of Mississippi, 2000.

Walters, Lexi. "The Buff Bride's Handbook: Get in Shape for Your Wedding Day." *FitnessMagazine.com*, April 2009. http://www.fitnessmagazine.com/weight-loss/plans/get-in-shape-for-your-wedding-day/.

———. "Legs, Thighs, and Butt: Workouts for Buff Brides." *FitnessMagazine*.com, April 2009. http://www.fitnessmagazine.com/weight-loss/plans/legs-thighs-butt-workouts-for-buff-brides/.

Wang, Vera. *Vera Wang on Weddings*. New York: HarperCollins, 2001.

Ward, W. Peter. *Courtship, Love, and Marriage in Nineteenth-Century English Canada*. Montreal: McGill-Queen's University Press, 1990.

Weiss, Jessica. *To Have and To Hold: Marriage, the Baby Boom, and Social Change*. Chicago: University of Chicago Press, 2000.

Welter, Barbara. "The Cult of True Womanhood: 1820–1860." *American Quarterly* 18 (1966): 151–74.

Wemple, Suzanne Fonay. "Women from the Fifth to the Tenth Century." In Klapisch-Zuber, *Silences of the Middle Ages*.

Westenhouser, Kitturah B. *The Story of Barbie Doll*. Paducah, KY: Collector Books, 1999.

White, Annie Randall. *Twentieth Century Etiquette: A Ready Manual for All Occasions*, 1900.

Wicoff, Kamy. *I Do But I Don't: Walking Down the Aisle without Losing Your Mind*. Cambridge, MA: Da Capo Press, 2006.

Wilcox, Claire. *Vivienne Westwood*. London: Victoria and Albert Museum, 2004.

Williams' Cincinnati Directory. Cincinnati, OH: Williams Directory Co., 1850–1945.

Williams' Hamilton Directory. Cincinnati, OH: Williams & Co., 1892–93, 1906.

Woodham-Smith, Cecil. *Queen Victoria: From Her Birth to the Death of the Prince Consort*. New York: Alfred A. Knopf, 1972.

The Worcester Directory. Worcester, MA: Drew, Allis & Co. 1876.

Wyke, Maria, ed. *Gender and the Body in the Ancient Mediterranean*. Oxford: Blackwell Publishers, 1998.

Xan, Erna Oleson, ed. *Wisconsin, My Home*. Madison: University of Wisconsin Press, 1950.

Yalom, Marilyn. *A History of the Wife*. New York: HarperCollins Publishers, 2002.

Yester-Morn to Yester-Eve: In and Out of Fashion in the 19th Century. An exhibition catalogue. Boston: National Society of the Colonial Dames of America in the Commonwealth of Massachusetts, 1991.

Yolen, Jane. "America's Cinderella." In *Cinderella: A Casebook*, edited by Alan Dundes. Madison: University of Wisconsin Press, 1988.

Zola, Émile. *The Ladies' Paradise*. Los Angeles: University of California Press, 1992.

Zook, Nicholas. *Holden: The Evolution of a Town*. Holden, MA: Holden Bicentennial Commission, 1976.

Zuckerman, Mary Ellen. *A History of Popular Magazines in the United States, 1792–1995*. Westport, CT: Greenwood Press, 1998.

INDEX

Page numbers in *italics* refer to illustrations. Page numbers followed by 'n' refer to notes.